Cultural Curiosity

Cultural Curiosity

THIRTEEN STORIES ABOUT
THE SEARCH FOR CHINESE ROOTS

Edited by Josephine M. T. Khu

UNIVERSITY OF CALIFORNIA PRESS
BERKELEY   LOS ANGELES   LONDON

University of California Press
Berkeley and Los Angeles, California

University of California Press, Ltd.
London, England

Library of Congress Cataloging-in-Publication Data

Cultural curiosity : thirteen stories about the search for
    Chinese roots / edited by Josephine M. T. Khu.
        p.   cm.
    Includes bibliographical references.
    ISBN 0-520-22340-3 (cloth : alk. paper)—
  ISBN 0-520-22341-1 (pbk. : alk. paper)
  1. Chinese—Foreign countries.   2. Ethnicity—China.
  3. National characteristics, Chinese.   I. Khu,
  Josephine M. T., 1964– .
    DS732 .C9   2001
    305.895'1—dc21   00-067224

Manufactured in the United States of America
10   09   08   07   06   05   04   03   02   01
10   9   8   7   6   5   4   3   2   1

The paper used in this publication is both acid-free and
totally chlorine-free (TCF). It meets the minimum
requirements of ANSI/NISO Z39.48–1992 (R 1997)
(Permanence of Paper). ♾

For my parents,
José Bun Kee Khu and
Josette Tiampo Khu,
with love

CONTENTS

Preface

JOSEPHINE M. T. KHU

ONE AFTERNOON IN 1996, THREE ACQUAINTANCES WHO HAD studied in Beijing at least ten years earlier happened to meet in Hong Kong: Nancy Work, whose story opens this book; Lily Wu, whose story concludes it; and myself. We were somewhat astonished to find ourselves all still—or again—living in this general part of the world, and the conversation wandered to the stories of what had brought us all to China in the first place and what had happened to the people we'd known back then. Many of them were, like ourselves, ethnic Chinese (at least in part) who had been born and raised outside of mainland China, Hong Kong, or Taiwan and had established lives and careers in the country of our ancestors.

The stories were engrossing, and in that afternoon the idea for this project was born: to collect stories written by ethnic Chinese who had encountered China for virtually the first time. The accounts were to include explanations of why they'd made the trip, their experiences in China, what impact the encounter had had on their lives, and whether it had led them to assess or reassess their ethnic identity. In order to

Josephine M. T. Khu is a visiting scholar at the Centre of Asian Studies at Hong Kong University.

explain the motivations behind their trips to China, the writers also would be asked to relate the stories of their families' emigration abroad and something of their own lives in the countries in which they were born or raised. Thus, in describing the significance of their experiences in China, each writer would tell a larger story.

The collection of accounts was not to be limited to people of our personal acquaintance, or news of it spread simply by word of mouth. This being the age of the Internet, I publicized the project online and received a fair response. From approximately fifty submissions, thirteen were chosen for inclusion in this book. The use of the Internet undoubtedly gave the book a certain geographic diversity it would not have had otherwise. Collectively, we were acquainted with people from nearly all of the places represented in this book. However, not all of our acquaintances were willing to write, or felt able to write, about their experiences. Thus, the Internet not only enabled news of the project to reach far larger numbers of people with the required backgrounds than we could ever know personally; it also enabled us to find, within that general group, a much smaller but still diverse group of people who were interested in writing about it.

Although I stipulated that the submissions could be in any of a variety of languages, the only essays submitted were, in fact, written in English. A key reason for this was undoubtedly the fact that the language in which the project was publicized was English. Equally important, however, the outcome reflected the limitations of Internet use and accessibility at the time—the Internet was overwhelmingly dominated by Americans, a fact that is easy to forget given the pace at which Internet use has spread in the past five or so years. In the end, the people who submitted their stories were not very different from the people with whom we were personally acquainted. Thus, use of the Internet was a broadening factor, but not as much as we might have expected.

Certainly, the way the stories were collected and the stipulation that they be personally written have had a bearing on the sorts of people and the sorts of stories that ultimately found their way into the book. But for all that, every story is completely individual: the backgrounds of the writers vary greatly, and their stories reflect a wide range of experiences that collectively represent many larger trends.

First, it is significant that many people now have been able to make a trip to the ancestral country. Such a trip represents a significant expenditure of money and time. It is worth reflecting on what the ability to travel and live elsewhere says about a world where such things have become possible and even routine—and it is worth reflecting on who, in today's world, finds such things possible.

Second, the reasons that people choose to spend time and money on such a trip are also significant. Of course, the decision may represent nothing more than one person's will and circumstances, but it may also reflect much about the society in which the person was raised. It may say something about the wealth of a society that allows people the opportunity to travel and about the social and political environment in a person's home country that leads one to perceive such an expenditure of resources as worthwhile.

For most of these writers, searching for roots and clarifying ethnic identity were important issues, although they were not always the key motivating factors behind their encounters with China. But they found that ethnicity was something that they could not disregard in China, whatever their reasons for making the trip. This is because they (or those they met in China) often expected that, due to the ancestral link, China would not seem so foreign to them, or they to the Chinese—an expectation that in some cases was fulfilled, but more often was not.

Indeed, it was almost shocking how foreign China seemed to all of us who first visited it in the mid-1980s. It was a country that was still emerging from decades of diplomatic and economic isolation, as well as years of political upheaval. It possessed a political, social, and economic system that seemed oppressive to those of us accustomed to freer societies. Official distinctions were made among foreigners, locals, and "Overseas Chinese" that determined where individuals were able to live, the level of their access to goods, services, and places, the prices they paid for such goods and services, and so forth.

In the past ten years or so, rapid industrialization and massive social changes have taken place in China. Today, it is a far more open place, and a much greater range of economic, social, and even political expression is now permitted. These developments are reflected in the stories in this book. The contributors encountered a China in different phases of development, and this factor alone led to very different individual experiences of the ancestral country.

It was not always easy to disentangle economic, political, and social realities from what was "Chinese." Although not all of the contributors thought to, or tried to, do this, it was vitally important for many of them to make such distinctions—so different were the realities of contemporary China from the ideas they held of what was essentially Chinese. Were, for example, authoritarian and controlling attitudes and practices a product of communist practice or of Chinese cultural values? Or, indeed, did the issues of "Chineseness" and ethnic identity have less to do with events and developments in China itself and much more to do with circumstances in the contributors' home countries that the encounter with China highlighted or revealed? Not all of the contributors address these questions directly in their narratives, but echoes of them underlie all of the stories in this book.

This book is subtitled "Thirteen Stories about the Search for Chinese Roots," and although not every contributor may have begun his or her trip with an active search for roots, the encounter with China ultimately caused each one to pursue the question and each to discover something of significance.

ACKNOWLEDGMENTS

I WOULD LIKE TO EXPRESS MY SINCERE THANKS TO CHRISTOPHER Robyn, former acquisitions editor at the University of California Press, for his support of this project and for his patience and consideration in dealing with a neophyte author.

I am also very grateful to Monica McCormick, editor at the Press, for her careful shepherding of the manuscript through the publication process.

Kevin Scott Wong of Williams College and John Kuo Wei Tchen of New York University read and commented on the manuscript. I thank them both for supporting its publication and for the numerous, very helpful suggestions they gave regarding the epilogue.

My gratitude goes also to Andrea Louie of Michigan State University for drawing my attention to some useful references in the literature on the Chinese diaspora; to Kathleen Wong (Lau) of Arizona State University for her kind help in publicizing the project; and to my friend Daniel Marier, who lent his computer skills to the preparation of the glossary. Contributor Maria Tham graciously allowed me to appropriate the original title of her story for that of the book.

I am indebted to Richard Chu of the University of Southern California for the copious amounts of time he spent providing references for the writing of the epilogue, and for reading and commenting on the draft.

Most of all, I would like to thank my friend Nancy Work. Nancy coconceived the project and demonstrated her personal commitment to it by helping to solicit contributions, assisting in reading and selecting the stories, and contributing her own story to this volume.

This book is the product of the efforts of not only the individuals who contributed their accounts but of all the people mentioned above. Any mistakes in the text, however, are unfortunately mine.

Full Circle

NANCY WORK

IT IS A FAREWELL SCENE THAT IS FOREVER ETCHED IN MY MEMORY. My beautiful mother standing out in the crowd in her yellow fake fur coat, crying and waving to my brother and me as we boarded the plane in the Taiwan airport. Some years back, my father had obtained his doctorate of science from the Massachusetts Institute of Technology. Not long ago, he had received permission for us, his two children, to immigrate to the United States. We were leaving Taiwan now because he wanted us to have a good education and a chance to succeed in the land of opportunity.

I remember wishing desperately that my mother could come with us, but this was impossible, since my parents were divorced. A sudden terrible, piercing sense of loss and fear came over me and I, too, began to cry. I didn't know when I would see my mother again. At the other end of our trip would be the unknown: a father I had never met because he had left for the States before I was born. I was now six years old, and my brother nine. So far, I had only seen pictures of our father.

When I first arrived in the United States, life was very difficult. Our

Nancy Work is a consultant with a human-resource management consultancy firm in Shanghai, China.

home environment wasn't very conducive to our adapting to our new country, since our stepmother didn't like us and treated us miserably. She even refused to cook for my brother and me. I was very homesick and missed my real mother a lot. In addition, because I couldn't speak a word of English, a lot of kids at school thought I was stupid or retarded. Our father wanted us to do well at school, so he was very strict with us when it came to our studies. We did extra homework all the time. I'll never forget him saying, "Education is the most important thing in the world—nobody can ever take that away from you."

Two years after our arrival, my father and stepmother separated, and my father took us to Michigan, where he had accepted a job as professor of mechanical engineering. My father was extremely dedicated to his work; he was a true scholar, but unfortunately he didn't know how to manage his personal life or take care of his health. He had terrible stomachaches from his ulcers, which would often make him cry out in pain. It would scare me, because then he would say that he wanted to die. His favorite activity became taking us for long walks in the local cemetery and looking at the tombstones, noting the dates and reading the inscriptions. Each time he would tell us where he wanted to be buried.

Only six months or so after he started his new job, my father came down with jaundice. His colleagues had to force him to go to the doctor, because he wouldn't go himself—this problem wasn't important enough to stop his work. The problem turned out to be hepatitis. During his hospitalization of a few months, my brother and I were taken care of by several of his colleagues in turn.

My father's condition worsened, and it was clear that he was going to die. Although without him we would be alone in the States, he told my brother that we weren't to go back to Taiwan, since we wouldn't have the same opportunities there. Thus, after he died, we were not reunited with our mother but were put up for adoption. I was nine years old when I went to live with a Caucasian family of one of my father's colleagues, and eleven when I was legally adopted by them. My brother, who was three years older than I, became a foster child of a Chinese colleague. We would see each other once in a while, but our relationship became very strained after we were separated.

Throughout the eight years that I lived in my adoptive family's home, I was forbidden to contact my real mother in Taiwan. My adoptive parents reasoned that I romanticized too much about my past, and that by cutting off this connection, I would be happier in their home. They even took away and hid all my pictures of my real family. It was as if they were trying to strip me of my past and identity. I was infuriated by this, but I was helpless to stop them. It was to be many years later, after I had left my adoptive family, that one of my adoptive sisters found my old photographs in the attic and returned them to me.

I think that if I had been happy with my adoptive parents, I wouldn't have missed my real family so much or pined so much to go back one day. Since going to live with them, I had rarely been allowed to make my own decisions. I even had to ask permission to take a shower. Whenever I did anything wrong, I was severely punished, physically and verbally. I never felt that my adoptive parents ever loved or cared about me—I was just a charity case to them. Any letters I received were first read by my adoptive mother before being handed to me. All the letters I wrote to family or friends were systematically censored, and if there were things I wasn't supposed to write about, I had to rewrite the letter. She bought me a diary and encouraged me to write down my private thoughts, saying that no one would read the diary except me. I believed her and spilled out my guts into it, only to discover three years later that she and my adoptive father were reading it. They confronted me with my diary and read the parts about them out loud in front of me. How could they have deliberately lied and betrayed my trust? They punished me and then forced me to burn my diary to try to wipe out my thoughts and feelings, but I couldn't be brainwashed.

Any time I brought up the subject of my real family, my adoptive mother would say very disparaging things about them and about how we had lived in poverty in Taiwan. Then I would get a long lecture on how fortunate I was and how grateful I should be to have been adopted by them—that otherwise I could have ended up in an orphanage. Or she would tell me that if I had been sent back to Taiwan, I would have been sold as a slave or a prostitute or have ended up begging on the streets. I was often told that if they hadn't adopted me they would have been able to buy new carpeting for the house, to acquire a boat, and so on. They said that I had been adopted because God wanted them to take me in. They were strict Protestants, and my adoptive mother's father was a minister. If I didn't say I was grateful when my adoptive mother told me to do so, I was slapped in the face and pushed down on my hands and knees in a humble position with my head bowed as if in prayer. Often the lecturing session happened in the morning before school; then I wasn't allowed to go to school until I said it. I felt so humiliated, and in the beginning I resisted. I felt that it would be a lie and a betrayal of self to say it, because I didn't feel grateful to them. But when I started to miss whole days of school or was late, I decided it wasn't worth my pride to resist—I just wanted to get away from her craziness.

Not only did I feel unwelcome in my adoptive family, but the small university town that I grew up in was also very redneck. The population was mostly made up of the descendants of Finnish immigrants. There were only two Asian families there, and no black American families. I used to feel like I was being looked at like a funny animal in the zoo by most of the locals, because they so seldom saw Asians. The fact that I was being stared at like that didn't bother me as much as the degrading comments I used to get daily at school, until I graduated from high school. One of the comments I'll never forget was, "Your face looks like it got run over by a truck," followed by cruel laughter. I tried to block out the ugly racist comments I heard. I used to think that if I were back in Taiwan, people wouldn't make fun of me because I was Chinese. To add to my miseries, my adoptive mother made me wear outrageous and outdated clothes that nobody would be caught dead in. They made me stick out even more. Having to keep the suffering and anger inside caused me to keep mostly to myself and not try to make many friends.

One of the happiest days of my life was when I was finally able to leave my adoptive parents in 1975, at the age of seventeen. It had been almost a year since I had run away from home and called Dial Help, a community-service organization that offered help to people in need. I ran away because of a particularly irrational and violent outburst of hysteria and physical and verbal abuse from my adoptive mother, which caused me to snap. I sought help because I knew I was a minor and couldn't legally escape anywhere. At the same time, if I were to go back to my adoptive parents, I needed protection from them, because I knew my adoptive mother would want revenge for the embarrassment I caused her by running away and seeking help. She was well-known by the people in charity organizations, and at first nobody at Dial Help wanted to take on my case. They were all scared of my adoptive mother. After months of counseling between my adoptive parents and me failed, I was given the option of emancipation from them by my counselor. I was seventeen years old, old enough to apply for independence. I decided this was the best option. I found a lawyer through a social-services agency, and he helped me liberate myself from them. I was half a year away from finishing high school. I felt like a person who had just been released from prison. Now I had a chance to live my life the way I wanted to. After so many years of enduring physical abuse and harangues about how awful my real family was and burning up inside with resentment, one of the things I wanted to do was to find out the truth for myself. Above all, I longed to see my real mother again. I wanted and needed to feel as if I belonged somewhere.

I managed to finish high school with the aid of my real father's social security pension and the help of a friend. That summer before university, one of my adoptive sisters found me a job as a maid in a large house for students so I could have free rent, and then I found some waitressing jobs to support myself. Instead of majoring in music, as I had originally wished to do, I became very practical and decided to major in engineering so that I would have a better chance of achieving financial security. I knew that I would have to find a job immediately after graduation because I didn't have a home to go to, and hang out in, until I found one. By selecting engineering, I was able to get engineering co-op jobs that allowed me to work and help pay my way through university. I would work for either three or six months for an engineering firm, and then alternate and go back to university for the same length of time. During the months I attended university full-time, I also had part-time jobs as a waitress or worked at other odd jobs for the university. While working on my co-op assignments, I would enroll in night classes to fulfill elective course credits that could be transferred to my original university. On the weekends, I worked at other part-time jobs, such as plumbing. I also had to take out some student loans to supplement my income.

After graduating in mechanical engineering, I looked for a company that was doing business in the Far East, and I ended up working for IBM. During my time there, I took every opportunity to take on tasks that would make it easier for me to go abroad and work in another branch office or that would allow me to reenter the job market more easily if I were to take a couple of years off. My goal was to save enough money to go to Taiwan to find my mother. However, one of the obstacles I had to overcome if I was to be reunited with her was my inability to speak Chinese. To find her wasn't enough, since I needed to be able to communicate with her, and I didn't want to use a translator for such an emotional meeting. I had tried learning Chinese through some evening classes at a university, but that never worked out because of my hectic traveling schedule at IBM.

I finally decided to take the radical step of quitting my job to study Chinese in Beijing, where the most standard Mandarin was spoken.[1] My friends at IBM thought I was crazy to leave what was then considered a secure job. At that time IBM was not granting leaves of absence except for exceptional cases, but when I left my managers told me that they would rehire me when I finished in China. Meanwhile, I lined up a part-time job as a consultant for IBM's China office so that I would have a source of income. With the professional part of my life organized, I also put my personal life in order. I put all my belongings in storage and then told my boyfriend of many years not to wait for me, because I didn't know what was going to happen. I was about to embark on the biggest adventure of my life, and I couldn't make any commitments. I had a feeling that what I was about to experience in the next few years would change the way I looked at the world.

When my plane landed in Beijing in September 1986, I kept pinching myself. I could hardly believe I was in China. Somehow, despite my almost nonexistent Chinese, I managed to get to the Foreign Languages Institute where I would be studying. The taxi pulled up at the dormitory for foreigners. When I got out with all my suitcases, I found a crowd of Chinese staring at me with blank looks on their faces. I had never seen that kind of empty expression before, and it gave me a creepy feeling. I had read many books about China, but nothing had prepared me for this. I wondered if I had made a mistake in coming. It was raining, and I had an incredible amount of luggage, but not one of the people standing there looking at me offered to help when they saw me struggling with my bags—not even the people responsible for helping the foreign students. "Welcome to the motherland," I thought.

Gradually, I settled in and became acquainted with some local Chinese. Many of them asked me if I had relatives living in China. When I answered yes, that my father's family was still in China, they would always ask me if I had met them. When I said no, they were very surprised. In fact, I was interested in meeting my father's family, because I remembered my father talking about them, but I didn't know much about their whereabouts. My father had left mainland China just before the Communists took over the mainland in 1949 and had never seen his family again. I was too little to remember any details about how to locate them, and whenever I had asked my brother for information, he never wanted to discuss the subject. I think that it was too painful for him to talk about our parents. Finally, however, I did find out from him the name of our father's hometown. At first, I didn't have much hope of finding my relatives, because I thought it would be like finding a needle in a haystack. But these frequent questions about them motivated me to take the idea of finding my father's relatives seriously. I thought that if I succeeded, I would learn more about my father and what had shaped him as person. I often felt a sense of great loss and pity that I had only known my father for two and a half years of my life.

After studying and working part-time for about a year, I met a Chinese professor who told me that he could help me find my father's family. I gave him the little information I had, and he wrote to the officials of the town they lived in, in Gansu province in northwest China. A few months later, he called me back and told me that my relatives had been located. Apparently had been easy to track down because they had been blacklisted during the Cultural Revolution of the late 1960s.[2] I was surprised that finding them had been this simple. I immediately sent a letter to them. I told them I was studying Chinese and working part-time for IBM to financially support my studies.

I received a letter from someone who said that he was my father's elder brother. He said that the family was all so happy to hear from me and to hear that I was doing so well and was so rich (they seemed to assume that I was rich just because I was working for IBM). Since in every letter they emphasized the word *rich,* I sensed that I was to be their goose that laid the golden eggs. I felt uneasy and worried about their expectations of me. I had heard other overseas Chinese stories about people claiming to be relatives but who were actually strangers just hoping to profit from the relationship. I therefore asked my relatives to provide some information about my father and to send me some pictures of him and of themselves, if they had any. I had no knowledge of my father's family, apart from the memories of my father repeatedly saying, his voice filled with regret, that his older brother was "stupid" for not having left China before the Communists came into power. The only thing I had of his family was a picture, showing his mother, brother, and sisters dressed in Chinese silk robes. When a Chinese friend saw this picture, she told me that my father's family must have been really rich, because in those days most people couldn't afford silk robes. This picture was the only clue I had to my father's existing family. And it was this exact picture that they sent to me as proof that we were truly related.

My father's relatives asked me to visit them several times, but I told them that I was too busy with my studies and that I traveled a lot for my work. Sometimes I would be out of town for two weeks at a time. I said that I would let them know when I could visit them, and when they could visit me in Beijing, but that they must not come without advance notice. Deep down, I was not sure if I was ready to meet them, especially after reading one letter from my uncle saying that he was ill because he missed me so much. I thought, I don't even really know them, and if he's getting sick now from missing me so much, what will he do when he does know me—will he die from the excitement? They also refused to believe that my father had died a long time ago. I knew that the first meeting was going to be tough. I wanted to meet them to find out more about my father—but in my own time.

It was two years after my arrival in China, and more than half a year after my initial contact with my relatives when, after class one day, the dormitory service desk told me that I had a relative waiting for me. I was astonished, and a bit nervous—I just hadn't been prepared for this visit. The relative turned out to be my cousin, my father's older brother's first son, who was in his forties. He had been sent as the family's representative to meet me. I had a hard time believing that he was my relative, because he looked more like an escaped convict. He had an open burn wound the size of a dime on his face, which looked as if it had come from a cigarette, and, from time to time, he would use a piece of paper to dab at the pus oozing from it. He had a weird accent and a speech impediment that made it hard to understand what he was saying. He really gave me the creeps with the way he stared at me. I felt like he was devouring me with his eyes. All I wanted to do was to run away from this guy—I couldn't stand to be alone with him. Luckily, I had an excuse to leave him. I really did have to go to work, so I told him to come back the next day and we would talk. This delay also gave me more time to prepare myself and to ask my Chinese teacher to attend the meeting with him, to give me moral support and easy Chinese translation if I couldn't understand my cousin.

During the meeting the next day, he showed me pictures of my father—further confirmation that he was my cousin. He told me that after the Communist takeover, our family had lost everything we owned. During the Cultural Revolution, my uncle had been severely beaten and paraded around town with a hat and signs that labeled him a capitalist landlord. Fortunately for my grandfather, he had died a few years before 1949, and my grandmother had also died of old age shortly after the takeover. The stories of what happened to our family were typical of those of landlord families. Their land, property, and belongings were confiscated or plundered by the new government. My cousin also told me that our family had been further punished and suffered even more because they had been considered spies, since my father was living in the United States.

It was very sad to hear about the beatings and miseries, but I started to feel that my cousin was trying to put the burden of all that they had suffered onto me because of their connection with my father. I didn't want to have to feel guilty and weighed down about that. I tried to explain that my father didn't have a great life—that after studying for so many years, he had had too little time to live to enjoy the rewards of his hard work. My father died a poor man, with only $500 in his possession. I told him a little bit about myself and about my brother, that we had both worked our way through university. I was still paying back student loans. I wanted him to see the reality: I was just an average person, not someone rich who could help them financially.

At the end of the meeting, I let him know I had no more time to see him. I said that I was too busy, but that I would go and visit them in Gansu later, when I was able to. I explained that I was very Americanized and that I needed advance notice and would give them a reply as to whether I would be available and in town for their future visits. I didn't want to seem mean or cruel hearted, but I needed my relatives to respect my wishes and my privacy. I didn't want them to show up whenever they felt like it and to have to drop everything just to attend to them. I had a lot of Chinese IBM customers who did the same thing—show up without appointments and expect me to cater to them when I had other appointments and projects to take care of. Part of the reason the Chinese just showed up was that most people didn't have telephones, and most people didn't travel much, so they assumed that you would just be there. I said to him that, in America, relationships even among relatives are built up and not assumed and that it would take time for me to get to know them. I tried to communicate all this as diplomatically as I could. I had lived in China for only two years, but that was long enough to know the expectations of Chinese relatives. I could tell he was disappointed, but I was not ready to take on all the responsibility of their term, *relative*. Friendship and trust must be earned. Maybe my attitude came from years of being so independent and having to fend for myself.

My uncle's family continued to write to me. I didn't write to them nearly as often, because I am lazy about writing letters in general and because I didn't have a lot to say to them that I thought that they would be able to relate to. I don't know whether they feared that my stay in China would be limited and that I might leave without visiting them. But, in fact, I ended up staying in China much longer than the originally planned two or three years. IBM China asked me to work for them full-time, and then I married a Frenchman who was working in China.

In the spring of 1990, three and a half years after my arrival in China, my aunt and her daughter showed up at the IBM office looking for me. I was surprised to see them, since, once again, my relatives had appeared without prior notice. My aunt told me she had some business in Beijing, so she wanted to meet me. She wanted to try Beijing duck, the specialty of Beijing, so my husband and I took them out to dinner to have some. This visit with my aunt and her daughter went much more smoothly. She didn't dwell on the miseries, beating, and torture after 1949 and during the Cultural Revolution and didn't try to make me feel guilty about the past. She seemed normal and easy to talk to, unlike my cousin, and expressed herself in a self-assured way. She felt so comfortable with us that she was even giving me personal advice—she tried to persuade me for several minutes to have a double eyelid operation to improve my looks! My husband remarked on how alike my aunt and I looked. It was a lot easier to believe that she was really my father's sister than it had been to believe my cousin and I were related.

Since this visit gave me a better impression of my relatives, I started to think more seriously about visiting them. They had been telling me that my uncle was getting old and that his health wasn't good, so I should try to go soon. The most important thing that I wanted to do for my relatives was to try to get back for the family the part of the house that would have belonged to my father. Apparently there was a new regulation in China that overseas Chinese could make a claim on their share of housing if their family's house had been taken away from them after 1949.[3] My relatives assured me that if I went to the local government and applied personally on behalf of my dead father to get my father's share of the house, I would succeed. This would then get back what was rightly my father's for me, but really it was for them. I had no desire to keep a residence in Gansu.

In the fall of 1991, my husband's project in China was coming to an end, and his company was planning to send him back to France. I handed in my notice of resignation to IBM. We decided this would be a good time to visit my uncle and family and to take care of getting back my father's part of the house for my relatives. We didn't realize just how remote a place Gansu province was, although it is true that we took a somewhat roundabout, scenic route to get there. We first went to northern Sichuan province. Then we worked our way north by public bus through the grasslands and the mountains until we reached the city of Lanzhou, the capital of Gansu. It wasn't the easiest way to go, since part of the route we took had not yet been opened to foreigners. We had to stop in at the local government office controlling foreign visitors and beg them to issue us travel permits so that we could go through the various small cities along the way and take the public buses. We were checked many times by bus ticket sellers and police during our trip. Since my husband was Caucasian, we couldn't go very far without being noticed. Sometimes there were so few buses going to the destination we wanted that we had to wait two days to get a place on the bus.

After arriving in Lanzhou, we bought train tickets to my father's home village. Then I called my uncle's neighbor, since my uncle didn't have a telephone, to let my relatives know the exact time of our arrival. When our train got close to my father's hometown, I tried to imagine what it must have been like when my father lived there. The area was mostly farmland. When our train stopped at our destination, we saw my relatives right away. We couldn't miss them. They were the ones dressed in their best, with flowers in their hands, shouting out my Chinese name. All of a sudden, I felt embarrassed. I didn't think that they would make such a public scene of our visit. I could see the excited expectation in their eyes. It was as if I were seeing this whole scene in a movie. My husband and I, foreigners, looking bedraggled, dirty, and tired after traveling in the boondocks of China, and there waiting for us, my dozen or so Chinese relatives, clean and fresh, shouting in joy as they waited for their long-lost relative. What a contrast!

My husband and I looked at each other hesitantly as if to say here goes, then took a deep breath. We were greeted warmly with flowers and happy smiles as we got out of the train. I hardly recognized my cousin, since it had been already quite a few years since I had last seen him. I spotted my aunt and her daughter in the crowd. We were introduced to everyone in a very organized way, then whisked away into one of the cars they had borrowed from their workplace. Later we found out that all the members of the family who had been able to come had gathered together one week before we arrived and had held a family powwow. It was then that they had choreographed the meeting at the train station—who should be there to greet us, which car we were to ride in, what was to be said, what we were supposed to do for the whole of our visit, and so forth.

After a short drive, we arrived at my father's hometown in the early afternoon. We went immediately to my uncle's house, which was also the house where my father had grown up. It was a very run-down, large, traditional Chinese house with a courtyard. Where one family used to live with several generations, there were now about five different families living in very crowded quarters. My uncle and some of his sons were living in part of this house, while the rest of it was now occupied by other families who had been allocated this housing by the government. My uncle was at the door waiting for us. My husband and I were served the special tea of that area, with dried *longans,* raisins, and rock sugar, and hand-fed small snacks. They were trying to make us feel like Chinese emperors, but we felt very uncomfortable and embarrassed not to be able to feed ourselves. My uncle wrote a poem of welcome with brush and ink on white rice paper for us and gave us this calligraphy as a souvenir. We were also given sweaters that my relatives had made. I was shown our family tree and introduced to all the family members present. I had a hard time remembering everyone's name, since there were about twenty people in all. Almost every member of my father's immediate family, and their descendants, was present.

We spent the first afternoon and evening talking about the past. I was told that I had an aunt whose husband had worked as an official in the old government, but that soon after 1949, my aunt's husband had committed suicide, because he wasn't able to endure all the harassment and humiliation that was being inflicted on him. All our family members had suffered in the past. The stories about how my uncle had been persecuted and had taken most of the beatings for the family were told again—this time in even more detail. The stories were told by my uncle's sons and his oldest daughter, and were repeated many times again by his oldest grandson later.

I heard and felt the bitterness and anger in their voices while they were recounting the past. They kept on saying how lucky my father was to be in the States. I told them again that my father had had a very difficult life and that he had worked very hard but unfortunately hadn't lived long enough to enjoy his life. I also told them that, after my father died, my brother and I hadn't had the easiest time either. I had lived through my own "cultural revolution," although I didn't really tell them much about my situation except that I hadn't gotten along with my adoptive mother and that my brother and I had both worked our way through university. It was a bit ironic, but in the end, it was my uncle who was the lucky man. He was almost eighty years old, in relatively good health, and surrounded by all his loved ones who cared so much about him. I could see the feelings in their eyes when they talked about their father. I couldn't help but feel sorry for my own father, who had died young and had never seemed happy.

There was a distinct pecking order in the family. The most important members did most of the talking. The grandson, twenty-one years old, was the chosen one in the family. He was the one they thought had the most potential, and they picked him to be promoted to me. I use the word *promoted* because they were trying to sell him to me as if he were a product. He latched onto my arm for dear life during our entire visit—I could barely go to the bathroom. In this way, he was able to monopolize my attention and to control the situation. He proudly told me that he was very good at Chinese history and literature and that he was going to an evening college. They told me that because my father was in the United States, the authorities had not allowed any of my uncle's children to attend university and that the grandchildren were the first generation that had the chance to go. My uncle wanted me to sponsor his grandson to study in the States.

The biggest problem in fulfilling this wish was that I didn't have the financial qualifications to be a sponsor. To sponsor someone at that time meant getting a letter from one's employer stating that you made $50,000 a year—and I was just about to quit my job and move to France and study French. Another problem was that the grandson couldn't speak any English. After getting to know him and chatting with him about his goals and how he proposed to achieve them, I realized that he would never make it in the States. He didn't have a realistic idea of what it meant to study abroad or what to do with his background in Chinese history and literature. Nor did he appear to have the drive to work hard or the hustle to succeed. But my relatives believed that simply going to the United States was the key to success and fortune. On top of all this, the grandson's personality really irritated me: he was the know-it-all type. He would repeat things like a broken record in a nagging way, as if the more times he said something, the more convinced I would be—especially on the subject of going to the States.

On the second day of our visit, we went with my relatives to several government offices to apply to get back my father's share of the house. My relatives wrote the appropriate letters, and I just signed them. I even had my relatives write extra letters for the future, which I signed, each one pressing the government to move faster in resolving the case. These letters were to be dated when they were needed. This was the easiest way I could think of to ensure that my relatives could get the house the fastest.

After submitting the application, my relatives took my husband and me to visit my grandparents' burial place. It was in the middle of a rice field, with a view of the river. My cousins told me with a lot of emotion that before 1949, this was our family's land, along with the farmland by the river. Altogether, we had owned about two hundred *mu* (around thirteen and a half hectares) of land. Our family had also owned a lot of buildings and material goods. My grandfather had been the second largest landowner in the city, and the most prominent businessman. My relatives described the original burial place, which had had large cypress trees and large tombstones, but now there was nothing to show that it was a grave. They marked off the exact area where my grandparents were buried by the number of footsteps from the road, and then they had me get down on my hands and knees in the middle of the rice field and kowtow three times on the tomb. My cousins told me that my father had sent $5,000 for the maintenance of the graves, but that the government had taken most of the money and given them only a fraction of it. It was sad to hear all the stories, but the important thing to me was that I learned that my father had been a very filial son.

Having completed the most important parts of my mission, my husband and I wanted to do a little sightseeing and visit the Maijishan grottoes, one of China's famous Buddhist temples, dating back to the fifth century A.D. My relatives didn't want us to go, and we couldn't understand why. We thought it was because it was a fairly long drive and that they didn't want us to take a taxi because it would cost a lot, but we kept on telling them that we would pay for it. Maybe the other reason that they didn't want us to go was that it wasn't in their plans for us to do so, and they might lose control of us. Finally, after we insisted, they let us go, but the grandson was to accompany us.

It was on this little detour that I got an earful about my aunt, whom the grandson called "the traitor." She never married, but had adopted one of my uncle's daughters. Apparently, during the Cultural Revolution, when the government was purging all the landlord families, my aunt, who was working for the army at the time, denied that she was part of our family to avoid being beaten and punished. Since that time, my uncle and aunt hadn't had any contact with each other. It was just one week before we arrived that they had had their first reunion and reconciliation.

Many things started to make sense. Since our arrival, it had mostly been my uncle's sons and daughters taking charge, as when we had gone to the city government offices and to the graves. I had noticed, too, that my aunt's attitude toward me wasn't as sharp edged as the others, who acted as if I owed them something for their sufferings. My aunt mostly told me little things about my father, like when he was a student how he used to study without realizing the time of day. Often he would forget to eat. Here were the makings of the ulcers that would torture him later in his life. She also mentioned some of the things he liked to eat, such as noodles. Later, when my aunt had a chance to talk to me alone, she asked me to sponsor her daughter, who already had a college degree, to go the States.

Our visit was intended to be a short one of only three days. The next day, therefore, we were scheduled to take the train back to Lanzhou. To our surprise, my uncle's eldest daughter and first grandson, and my aunt and her daughter, accompanied us. My aunt and her daughter lived in Lanzhou, and I think the relatives from my uncle's side were afraid to leave my aunt alone with us. During the train ride, I felt as if I were being pulled in two directions. It was as if they realized that it was their last chance to get something from me, so that it was time to be less polite and to just get to the bottom line.

In the train our group had to be separated, but the grandson managed to get a seat next to me. He backstabbed my aunt and boasted about his achievements the whole time. At one point, my uncle's daughter and my aunt took me to the back of the train where we could have some privacy, away from my husband, and told me that when I got to France I should get a job. They said that they were worried about me because with my husband's good looks, he didn't appear the type who would stay faithful, and he would possibly leave me for other women. If I had a job, I would have financial security, and this would be reassuring to them. Then, all at once, the two of them started to shed tears. It was as if they had both turned on a faucet at the same time.

I was very surprised. It was great acting, and I was embarrassed by what they had said. I really didn't quite know what to say, so I didn't say much except that I would wait and assess the situation when I got to France. In a flash, I imagined them during the Cultural Revolution, how they must have learned how to cry on demand. I had the impression that they were more concerned about getting some support from me than they were about my welfare. In a Chinese family, when a woman is married, she belongs to her husband's family, and her financial responsibilities and obligations lie there first. So by making my own money in France, I would have more independence in the way I spent it, and I think they hoped that I would spread some of it to them. When I told my husband what they thought about him, we both laughed.

When we got to Lanzhou, my aunt took us to a restaurant. After lunch, we realized we were running late. We had to catch an airport bus to get to the airport. Catching this bus was very important, because the airport was about an hour from the city, and we didn't want to miss it. We had left our luggage at the head office of my cousin's workplace, so we had to go there first. We had been walking for a while, looking for buses. We were about to take a small local bus to get our luggage when my relatives told us to get off—at fifty *fen* (then about ten cents), it cost too much. They wanted us to take another bus that cost less, twenty *fen* per ticket. We told my relatives that we would pay for the fare, but they didn't want to get on the bus. We had to walk another kilometer to catch the cheaper one.

It was at this point that my husband exploded and started shouting. He couldn't believe that we had to waste so much time and walk so far, all to save thirty *fen*. He said he couldn't take it anymore from my relatives. He felt like a prisoner—we were controlled by them the whole time. I kept on reasoning with him, saying that in a few hours the whole visit would be over. This visit had been harder and more stressful for him than I had realized. He couldn't speak Chinese, and I had to translate everything for him. I had patience with my relatives because they were my relatives, and I wanted to understand their situation. Except for my signing the letters and meeting some of the government officials, we had been pretty much spectators throughout the visit. I'm not sure what my relatives thought of this public display of emotion from my husband. In any case, when we finally parted from them, it was a relief. We felt free again.

Afterward, thinking it all over, I felt glad that I had made the visit that I had put off for such a long time. I felt that I had accomplished my objectives and fulfilled my obligation to my uncle. I was thankful that my father had left to go to the United States when he had, and that my destiny wasn't in Gansu. I was also relieved and contented to see that my relatives weren't too badly off now. They all had jobs and housing, and they seemed much better off than the average Chinese. I wished that I had the means to help them more, but it is hard to help one and not the other. Most of all, I had learned something about my father's beginnings, and my curiosity about his family was also satisfied.

Growing up in the United States, I suffered a lot of racial prejudice from Caucasians because of my Asian physical features, and I was constantly reminded of it by the strange stares from people. This negative attention made me feel awkward and uncomfortable. I often wished I didn't stick out, because I felt just as American as everyone else. In China, I thought I would easily blend in with the crowd because I looked Chinese, but I was wrong, because my thinking, attitudes, reactions, body language, and behavior stood out. Living in China showed me how American I was in most of my ideas and principles. My sense of independence, helping oneself, directing my destiny, and making things happen instead of depending on my family to succeed permeated everything I did. These concepts seemed very strange to my relatives in China. But I also realized that the many opportunities available to me in the United States had made it possible for me to develop such an attitude of independence, while my relatives in China, with far fewer options, often had no choice but to depend on one another to succeed in life.

Before my China days, I generally avoided Chinese-looking people, partly because I was embarrassed and ashamed that I couldn't speak Chinese. I've had Chinese come up to me and ask me if I was Chinese and, when I said yes, start talking to me in Chinese. When I looked stupefied, they would be incredulous that someone Chinese couldn't speak her mother tongue. I felt like an impostor, because, on top of the fact that I couldn't speak Chinese, I had grown up in a white family. It was all too difficult to explain. Now I am comfortable and sure of myself. I can hold my head up when I am approached. I understand their expectations, their cultural background, and my roots.

I took my trip to China to prepare myself linguistically to communicate with my mother. I did succeed in finding her, two years after I'd first arrived in China. However, I found that the difficulty wasn't in communicating with her in Chinese after all. Rather, the problems were with having different expectations and ideas, being separated since childhood, and with leading such different lives. The whole purpose of my journey to China was to find my mother, but in the end, that's the part of it I can't write about. It is too painful, complicated, emotional, and personal. I still have a relationship with my mother, and I am still trying to understand her. I feel fulfilled in having attained my lifelong dream of reuniting with her, even though the ending was not the fairy-tale one that I had hoped it would be.

During my first five-year adventure in China, I got to know myself better, and I benefited in other ways. After living in France, I returned to China to live because my husband was sent back to work on a project for his company. Now, after many years of living in China and starting my own family here, my new roots have become intertwined with my old ones, and I feel at home in both countries.

Through a Window

GRAHAM CHAN

I NEVER WANTED TO GO BACK. HONG KONG WAS AN ALIEN PLACE, from which aliens speaking a language I did not understand and sharing none of my interests would occasionally intrude on my ordered, British life. As children, we had suffered the ordeal of Sunday lunch in Chinatown. We would be deposited in hard plastic seats and expected to keep quiet and not fidget while Dad chatted with his friends for hour after weary hour. At least the food was a consolation. The boredom could be endured as the price we had to pay for the most delicious food in the universe—food that only Dad could obtain for us, since only he could speak Cantonese. Occasionally, we would become the subjects of the conversation. At such times, we would stare sheepishly and shamefacedly into space, avoiding the eyes of the people discussing us, forced to remain stupidly silent whenever we were directly addressed—embarrassed beyond measure as Dad had to explain yet again that we could only speak English.

Forty years later, I feel the same way whenever anyone speaks to me

Graham Chan is a librarian in Liverpool, England. He is the editor of Brushstrokes, *a magazine of British Chinese writing and drawing.*

in Cantonese, and it's even worse now that Dad is no longer around to explain why I am so stupid.

They were not unkind, those people in the restaurant—just different, and not only in the language they spoke. We always went to the same restaurant: the Central Cafe in Liverpool. There was a serving hatch through to the kitchen, and sometimes we would slip away from our table and stand at the hatch. It was a window into a different world of heat, noise, and confusion. There unkempt, sinewy little men performed amazing feats with fearsome choppers and knives or stirred impassively at sizzling pans. They seemed oblivious and impervious alike to the flames leaping chest-high and the scalding fat spitting in all directions. Once one of them handed me a whole roasted turkey leg. I looked uncertainly at my parents, not knowing whether I could accept, afraid equally of provoking parental wrath for accepting gifts from strangers and of committing some dreadful Chinese social blunder by refusing such a magnificent offer. In the end, since my parents were otherwise preoccupied, I took it. After all, we had been told, like all our English friends, not to accept sweets from strangers, but no one had ever said anything about turkey legs.

It was hard to think of ourselves as being the same as the restaurant people, even though we knew they were the same as our Dad—which is, in effect, the same thing as saying that it was hard for us to identify with our Dad. We knew he loved us and would do all he could to look after us, but he wasn't like anybody else's dad: he didn't usually come home for meals, he never joined in our games, he didn't play football or golf, and he took forever to read the newspaper (and once he picked it up, none of us dared to ask him for it). In fact, we didn't even see him very often. On most days, when we got up in the morning he would already have gone out to work, and he would not come back until after we had gone to bed at night. Even when he was around, we never talked to him much. This was partly because his English, while good for a Chinese person of his age and class, had definite limitations, and partly because he rarely talked to us. He was a stern and distant figure of authority, to be obeyed without question and respected rather than loved, although eventually, when we began to learn and to understand more about his past, the love would come.

On the rare occasions when he did talk to us, we were fascinated, but even more mystified. He would tell us about tigers lurking in the forest and about hunting for wild boar in the mountains. He would also talk about villages surrounded by walls, with the houses built into the walls, and about voyages on coal-burning ships to places where people lived along rivers in wooden houses built on poles over the water. It would be many years before I even managed to work out where he came from, since sometimes his stories were about China, sometimes Hong Kong, sometimes Singapore or Indonesia or Borneo.

Whenever I asked him where he was born, he would talk about a village somewhere near Weihjau or Doongwoon; the names meant nothing to me, though I guessed they might be the nearest major towns. Sometimes he would tell me how he used to get there from Hong Kong: take the main-line Kowloon-to-Canton train, but get off at Sekloong and take a local train to the nearest station at a place called something like Tintong-weih.[1] That line and that station probably weren't there anymore, because he had read in his monthly magazine, *China Reconstructs*,[2] that now they had built a road that went past the village. In his day, there was no road, just a path from the station. When he had some money, he could hire a kind of sedan chair and be carried the rest of the way; otherwise he would walk. But what was he doing in Hong Kong? How long did he live there, and where? And how did he come to be on those coal-burning ships? The questions and the mystery persist to this day, since my father never gave anything more than vague replies to my questions.

The story did not begin to take a more solid shape until it reached the point when, working on a ship of the Blue Funnel line, he arrived in Liverpool. That we could understand, knowing the status of Liverpool as one of the major ports for trade between Britain and the Far East, and the Blue Funnel line as one of the major companies carrying that trade.[3] As late as the 1960s, when I was at school, their ships with their mainly Chinese crews were an everyday sight in the river Mersey, although by then the seamen's hostels and gambling clubs and restaurants that Dad sometimes talked about no longer existed. Those places belonged to a Chinatown we had never known. Along with much else in Liverpool, the original Liverpool Chinatown had been obliterated by German bombs in the Second World War, but we could see the logical progression from ship to shore job, to fish-and-chip shop or restaurant, followed by thousands of young men from Hong Kong and southern Guangdong province, especially in the years just before, during, and after the war.[4]

It was those men who created the great Chinese restaurant boom of the late 1950s and 1960s, when a newly prosperous British public, free at last from the privations and shortages of wartime and with appetites whetted by foreign travel, fell eagerly on this exciting, tasty, and cheap addition to their diet.[5] The dwindling number of those involved who are still alive remain reticent about what went on behind the scenes. They do not want to reveal too much about the black-market deals, the double-crossing partners, the holes in tills, or the schemes for bribing, evading, or otherwise outwitting police and health inspectors as well as immigration, customs, and tax officers, and all the vast apparatus of local and national officialdom, even sometimes down to the level of driving test examiners. As a child I was mostly unaware of the skullduggery, though from time to time I would overhear and worry about furious arguments between Mum and Dad over some doubtful practice or individual. It touched me more closely when I was a teenager, when Dad would sometimes tell me to reply to letters he had received threatening dire consequences if he did not immediately do this, that, or the other. As in many Chinese families in Britain, dealing with official correspondence was normally a job for the English-educated children. Nevertheless, most of what I know about those days I learned in recent years. Occasionally I would be with Dad in a Chinese shop or restaurant, and we would encounter some elderly Chinese man who greeted Dad as if he were a long-lost friend. Afterward, when I asked who it was, Dad would mention a restaurant where the man had worked and add a comment such as, "He's a rascal," with withering disdain. I would have to press him for any further explanation, and he warned me once not to ask too many questions.

There are some things, however, of which I was always fully and acutely aware, even as a young child. They are things many of us try not to think about, or try to dismiss as unimportant or atypical, even though they are still happening, things that do not happen to white businesses: the smashed windows and racist graffiti, the verbal and physical assaults, the customers who think it hilariously funny to mimic what they assume to be our accents or to try to leave without paying the bill. I remember my heart sinking whenever the phone rang late at night. It would invariably be the police summoning Dad to deal with the latest incident. Children look to their parents for security and protection, and I was afraid of those dark forces from which my father could manifestly not protect himself, let alone me. I sometimes wonder whether it was this extra burden, over and above the normal cut and thrust of business, that forced Dad to devote almost his entire attention to the restaurant, so that he became a virtual stranger to us and we increasingly turned instead to our mother.

She represented an even earlier phase of the Chinese diaspora, and one that was even harder than Dad's to fathom. She had been born in Britain and had lived here all her life, but she could tell us very little about how her family had come to be here. Partly because of language barriers between her and her mother, and partly because life for them had been such a relentless, exhausting struggle, there had been little time or leisure for reminiscing about the past. Finally, our grandmother herself became too old to remember.

Ironically, much of what we knew we learned from Dad, who was able to speak to our grandmother in Mandarin. This in itself was significant. Although Dad had been born in China, he had moved to Hong Kong at an early age and always seemed to regard Hong Kong as his home. This impression was reinforced by the fact that in those days, apart from a few relatives on our mother's side, every Chinese person we met also seemed to come from Hong Kong. Even now it is unusual to hear Chinese people in Britain speaking anything other than Cantonese, the version of Chinese spoken in Hong Kong. We children therefore tended to equate being Chinese in Britain with coming from Hong Kong.[6] For our grandmother to be speaking Mandarin, not Cantonese, was decidedly odd. It meant that she came from somewhere nowhere near Hong Kong. But where? Dad, in his usual maddeningly vague way, described this place simply as "the North."

Years later, by piecing together snippets gleaned from the collective memories of various relatives and elderly family friends, my siblings and I have deduced that Mum's parents came from Hubei province, in central China. However, the mystery remained of just what impelled a group from their village to begin walking toward the west and to carry on walking across Russia, Poland, and Germany, settling in France for a while, before moving to Britain to escape the First World War.[7] We presume they did not actually walk every inch of the way. There is mention at some point of a lake that they crossed by boat, and from time to time, they may have taken trains. However, we have no details of that earliest Long March, apart from a single, cryptic comment of our grandmother: "It's terribly cold in Russia." Our grandparents' journey, however, ended at a laundry in Liverpool, and that is where our mother's story began.

It is a story that for many years was a nightmare of poverty, humiliation, and unending toil. To be endured were the fog of heat and steam, the itching pain of chapped hands, the nauseating stink of dirty clothes in which lice or maggots would sometimes be found, and the mind-numbing drudgery of ironing and folding shirts, hour after hour. Every night my mother would struggle to keep her eyes open while her legs ached and her head drooped. She would feel desperate for sleep, but getting to bed meant first having to grope her way in the darkness to the bare, drafty room she shared with her sister at the top of the stairs. Sometimes she would be so exhausted she would simply crawl into a cupboard under the counter and fall asleep, surrounded by dirty laundry. Her father had abandoned his children early, fleeing the country after a run-in with the police over something rumored to involve opium, leaving my grandmother penniless with five children.

Of course, they were not the only poor people in Liverpool. But Mum recalls proudly that, no matter how desperate they were, they never had to go to school in police boots, as some other children did. These were the big, clumsy, black boots that the police gave free of charge to the poorest children, who would otherwise have gone barefoot. Nor did anyone in Mum's family ever have to join the line outside the pawn-shop on Monday morning. This was when many white women would pawn their husbands' suits to borrow the money they needed to feed their families until the next Friday—when they would extract the money from their husbands' pay packets to redeem the suits so that they could pawn them again the following Monday.

Mum especially needed that meager ration of pride, because, apart from being poor, her family had the additional burden of being Chinese. Somehow, every celebration of the glories of the British Empire seemed designed to emphasize that she was one of the lesser breeds. At school, teachers made pointed references to the backwardness of China and the dedication of the Christian missionaries in trying to bring civilization to that benighted country. In her own small ways, she rebelled: she never joined in singing the national anthem, and even now she refuses to contribute to charities involved with Christian missionaries.

It is ironic that Mum should be provoked into asserting her Chineseness when her upbringing, her interests, and her attitudes are all thoroughly British. She has never been to China and speaks only English. She loves gardening, reading, and listening to Western classical music. Unlike the typical Chinese wife, she never worked with Dad in the family business. For a while, she did the tax returns for him, but eventually it became too much, and she insisted that he get a proper accountant. We have never been the typical Chinese family: we have never lived above the shop, and it was only on rare occasions, when Dad was absolutely desperate, that we children were summoned to help out in the chip shop or the restaurant. I am not sure if Dad spared us because he knew we did not want to do it or whether, like many other immigrants, he wanted us to concentrate on getting a good education so we could enter the professions and do better than he had. Whatever the reason, home and business were largely separate worlds.

Friends who had to work in their parents' businesses almost since they were infants, at the same time as studying and being expected always to be top of the class, are envious of my easier experience, and I know I should be grateful. But it guaranteed that we would see little of our father, that we would never learn to speak Cantonese, and that we would never fully belong in either world, Chinese or British. Apart from the odd occasion such as Sunday lunch, our lives were overwhelmingly English and became ever more so as we grew older and even Sunday lunch ceased to be a regular event. Like Mum, I loved reading and listening to music, and the books I brought home from the library were English: stories about the Secret Seven or the Swallows and Amazons.[8] I was nearly forty before I learned about the Monkey King, and the only Chinese music I had ever heard was the Chinese opera that Dad sometimes used to listen to, a dreadful cacophony of clashing cymbals and high-pitched squawking.[9] It was rare for us even to see any other Chinese people. In the middle-class suburb where we lived, the entire Chinese community was us.

On the few occasions when we met Chinese people at our home or at the homes of our relatives, we children would feel acutely embarrassed. Such encounters usually happened at Christmas, whenever we visited my aunt (Mum's sister) and her family. Our families were very close, and we looked forward to the visit. Unfortunately, there would always be at least one day when my uncle, who was a surgeon at one of the major teaching hospitals, would bring home some medical students from Hong Kong. My uncle came from a wealthy Hong Kong family and felt a responsibility to welcome these students and show them some hospitality—but they were such dolts! They would be ushered into the room where we children were merrily chatting and would sit there like dummies, saying not a single word, except perhaps to ask how many Chinese students there were in Liverpool. This seemed to be the only question any of them were capable of asking. I took to replying rudely that I hadn't the faintest idea and couldn't care less, both of which were true. I remember once when my aunt put her head round the door, saw us all sitting in glum silence, and grimaced sympathetically before withdrawing again.

It was the same on the few occasions when relatives of Dad's turned up at our house, always without warning. If we wanted them to say anything, we had to virtually lever it out of them. To my shame, I once closed the door on someone who turned out to be my cousin. Well, he was a complete stranger who immediately began speaking in Cantonese, forcing me to tell him I could only speak English. He made no attempt to explain who he was. He asked for my father, and, on being told Dad was out, stood there like the inevitable silent dummy. What was I supposed to do? Of course the reason they were silent was that their English was not good enough for them to join in the conversation. I realized this many years later when I was in Hong Kong and the tables were turned with a vengeance. Then it was I who was sitting like a silent dummy while everyone else chatted in Cantonese.

During the first forty years of my life, I can recall only once meeting anyone else like me, aside from my brother, sister, and cousins on my mother's side: British-born, English-speaking. British in outlook, a "banana": yellow on the outside, white on the inside. That solitary occasion was also at my aunt's house, where a youth of my own age turned up one day. For a few momentous and exhilarating hours, we talked nonstop before he departed again. I do not know who he was, and I cannot remember what we talked about, but I think for both of us it was a revelation to discover we were not unique. The term *banana* had not even been coined then; we were so few there was no need for a word to describe us.

None of this would have mattered if I had been able to shrug off my Chineseness and get on with being British, but I doubt that any banana will ever fully succeed in that endeavor. I have always found that no matter how anglicized we may seem, you only have to scratch gently at the surface, even of those with white partners, to release a whole range of feelings to the contrary: resentment of the perennial, mocking jokes and stereotypes about Chinese people; primeval, involuntary feelings of pride whenever China thumbs its nose at the rest of the world by doing things like exploding a nuclear bomb, or damming the Yangzi River, or booting the British out of Hong Kong; and anger at hearing white people lecturing the Chinese on democracy and human rights as though these were still the days of gunboats and extraterritoriality and foreign concessions.[10]

One of my cousins spent a year studying in Taiwan, where some of her fellow students were Chinese from America. She told me how impressed and envious she was that they had no hesitation in describing themselves as Americans. They had been encouraged to think that way from birth, whereas we were never sure what to say when asked about our nationality. Our passports say we are British, but the message we have received throughout our lives from all sections and levels of British society, ranging from politicians of both right and left to the semi-literate thugs shouting abuse at us on the streets, is that to be British, you must be white. Even our passports are no guarantee: there are various kinds of British passports, some of which do not give the holder any right to live in Britain.[11]

People do not even have to be hostile to get their message across. At school, there was one teacher who kept us all in constant dread simply with his unpredictability: one moment he would be calm and kind, the next he would go into a boiling fury, raging at us, cuffing us with the flat of his hand, shriveling us with sarcasm. I still occasionally have nightmares about him, but actually he seemed to have a soft spot for me. He had served in the army overseas, and he had some knowledge of Chinese history and culture. He would allude to ancient Chinese legends and quote Chinese proverbs and invite me to confirm the truth of what he had said. I would do so meekly, and afterward, when my schoolmates questioned me further, I would have to admit that I had had no idea what he was talking about. I was glad to be exempt from the effects of his temper, but I was embarrassed at being singled out and treated as different from the rest of the class.

All this eventually led to the inescapable conclusion that I would have to learn Cantonese. It was the key to joining the fold, without which I could never hope to belong, as well as the only way to obtain the most delicious food in the universe without relying on Dad. I carried this vague intention around with me for years without doing anything about it. This was partly through laziness, but also partly because I could never find any means of putting it into practice. If you want to learn Mandarin, it's easy: there are lots of evening classes, you can go into any bookshop and buy a self-study book complete with audio tapes. But, at least until recently, for Cantonese there was nothing. There is the traditional Chinese Sunday school run by one or another of the Chinese community associations, but that is for learning to write Chinese and caters to people who already know how to speak Cantonese. I know this because at one point I tried to attend their classes.

I remembered as a child being taken to a Chinese school once, not for the purpose of learning anything but simply because Dad needed to speak to someone after Sunday lunch and had brought me along. It was on a run-down street near Chinatown, on the upper floors of what seemed to be an old warehouse. A musty lobby on the ground floor with ancient photographs of Chinese people on the walls led to a rickety, wooden staircase. At the top of this staircase was a large open area, subdivided into sections used for various purposes. A performance area with a stage lay at one end. There was also a games area with some pool tables. I saw what seemed to have once been a small shop with a counter and some display cases behind it, although it was clear from its dilapidated state that nothing had been sold there for many years, as well as an office and several large classroom areas with old wooden tables and chairs. Another staircase led up to the next floor, where there were more classrooms.

After he had completed his business, Dad spoke briefly in Cantonese to two youths who were sitting on a settee near the pool tables looking at Chinese magazines. I could not understand what he was saying, but it was obvious from his tone that he was displeased about something. When we were outside I asked him what it had been about. He replied that he had asked the youths what they were doing and had told them to stop wasting their time. "They just come to play games and chase girls," he snorted derisively.

I didn't say anything, but I secretly sympathized with the youths. There had been a performance of some kind in progress on the stage—mercifully not opera, but one of those traditional, graceful dances by enchanting Chinese girls in flowing, pastel-colored costumes. I had never seen anything so pretty before, and I felt a pang of regret that I could not be one of those youths.

It was more than twenty years before I went looking for that place again, and to my astonishment it was still there, exactly the same as I remembered it. I arrived just as classes were about to begin and was nearly trampled underfoot by hordes of Chinese children charging up the stairs. I managed to find the office and spoke to one of the teachers, who listened in evident disbelief as I tried to explain what I wanted. "You mean, you can't speak any Cantonese at all?" he asked incredulously.

He handed me over to a boy of about sixteen who had been sitting outside the office, who explained in English that all the classes were for learning to write Chinese. Even then, you would normally start in the beginners' class when you were five or six years old. He himself had been a late starter, so he was in a class with mainly ten- to twelve-year-olds. Nevertheless, I was welcome to sit in on the class to see if it could help me. When I sat down in the classroom, one of the children asked me something in Cantonese. My companion emitted a raucous laugh. "He wants to know if you are the new teacher!" he guffawed.

Once the class started, it was obvious that it was useless: I couldn't understand a single word, and I slunk away after a few minutes.

I eventually found a class I could attend at a Chinese community center. Apparently, this class had been running for a few years before I stumbled across it, but unfortunately the teacher had left to return to Hong Kong. To replace her, they had drafted a young woman with no previous experience in teaching anything. She clearly hadn't a clue what to do, and she wasted most of the time reading words and phrases from a book and writing them on a blackboard in Chinese. I sat through it in a fog of dismay. I couldn't see myself learning much this way, but I could see that Cantonese was a far more difficult proposition than French or German, which I had mastered somewhat easily at school. Until then I had not been aware of the subtleties of tone and pitch that determine meaning, so that every word can mean six or seven completely different things, depending on how you say it. To my untrained, Western ear, every one of them sounded exactly the same.

I was not the only one to be disheartened. One of the other new beginners was a teenage girl who attended with her English boyfriend. Her boyfriend seemed keener than she was; at one point I heard her whisper to him: "I don't think I can do this." She and I were the only Chinese people in the class apart from the teacher. The others were all friends or wives or girlfriends of Chinese people, or kung fu enthusiasts wanting to learn more about the underlying culture, or people who had lived in Hong Kong. It was bad enough to be trying to learn my own language, but it was almost unbearable to have to do so in the company of white people, most of whom could already speak it better than I could.

I did not return to that class, but I did buy the book, and afterward, when I was leafing through it, I realized that if I worked through it systematically and got Dad to tell me how to pronounce the words, I might pick up at least a smattering. So for nearly seven years I had a weekly lesson with Dad. We went through that book three times, as well as other books that I bought in Hong Kong. After a few years, I also went back to the community center, which by then had acquired a more experienced teacher, and this time I was able to cope. But to become proficient in any language you have to study and practice every day, and I either did not have the time or did not force myself to make the time. Besides, Dad was the only person available for me to practice with, and I usually only saw him once a week. He taught me to say: "I was born in England and only speak a little Cantonese." He emphasized that I must say this as soon as I met anyone Chinese. They would then appreciate my difficulty and be patient, but it did not work out that way. I practiced it so often that my pronunciation was absolutely perfect, so whenever I said it, everyone thought I spoke excellent Cantonese and were totally nonplussed when I could not understand anything they said.

So despite all this effort, my Cantonese remains only a smattering, and by the time he died, I think even Dad had got fed up. Nevertheless, he was pleased that I had made even this feeble effort. He never tried to push Chineseness onto me. He realized it made me uncomfortable and that it was more important that I succeed in the white, British world. But when the invitation arrived for me to go to Hong Kong to work as a consultant on a short-term computing assignment, I knew that both he and Mum would be deeply disappointed if I turned it down. Even though we no longer had any friends or relatives there, even though I had been there only once before, when I was an infant too young to remember anything about it, even though Mum and Dad had never been back since then either—in some indefinable way Hong Kong was still home, and I felt that to say no would be to slam the door forever on my Chinese identity. No matter what my fears were, I could not bring myself to do that. Besides, there was my professional pride: the people in Hong Kong had invited me because they thought I could help them. To refuse would be tantamount to admitting that I couldn't.

Everyone except my parents, who knew better, said that my inability to speak Cantonese would not matter: Hong Kong was a British colony, everyone there spoke English. But I knew that was not true, because of all those non-English-speaking dolts I had met when I was younger. However, my fears went beyond the language difficulty. Everything I had ever heard or read about Hong Kong led me to believe that it was a nation of workaholic geniuses. For more than a year, my contacts there had been sending me questions by electronic mail about their new computer system, having discovered somehow that I was responsible for maintaining a similar system where I worked, but I had not come to the logical conclusion that this must mean that I knew more than they did. Instead, all I could see was that they had an awful lot of problems, and I was unsure of my ability to fix them.

After arriving in Hong Kong, I quickly discovered that I could fix them, and I was soon fixing them by the handful, though I was having to work the same kind of hours as everyone else—and those were indeed fearsome, far longer than anyone in Britain would tolerate. In that respect I proved I was as Chinese as anyone: I, too, was a workaholic. However, that was the least of my worries. What my employers had not told me was that their computer system was a complete shambles, full of bugs, that it could never be made to do the things they wanted, and that most of the staff was fighting tooth and nail to stop it from being brought into use. They had bought a system that was probably the worst on the market and totally unsuited to their needs, and they seemed to expect me to wave some kind of magic wand and make everything right. I did my best, and they were generous in their praise and gratitude, but not even a genius could have made it right. That I eventually realized this and ceased to feel any guilt about it was due to one of my fellow workers. When we were working late one Saturday, she took me to lunch, one of those lunches that verge on becoming something more, as confidences are exchanged and heads lean closer together. When I mentioned my self-doubts and my regret that I was not doing more to help, she reacted vehemently. "But you've already done so much! You've fixed every problem for us! You shouldn't feel guilty; it's not your fault the system is no good. You only feel that way because you are such a nice guy. You are not like most people: you are warm."

Well, she was young and pretty, and I had certainly felt warm toward her, but I felt the same about most of my immediate colleagues.

I stayed in Hong Kong for six months, and I never expected in such a short time to become so fond of so many people. They took me to lunch most days. They also included me in their group outings to movies, flower shows, indoor amusement arcades, bars, and lots of restaurants. They introduced me to the simple pleasures of table tennis, badminton, and walking in the mountains. All the girls were so slim and well-groomed that they were a delight to the eye, even when their faces were not particularly attractive. When one of them came in wearing a traditional high-necked, long dress because she was going to visit her fiancé's parents, she looked so pretty I insisted that she wait while I ran back to my residence for my camera. I once put my arm around that same girl's shoulders in a reflex action to comfort her when she'd been having a particularly bad day on the computer. When I thought about it afterward, I was appalled at the possible consequences, but she had evinced not the slightest hint of displeasure, not a trace of that flinching or freezing that tells you immediately if a woman does not want you to touch her. I suppose I could do that kind of thing without giving offense, because they all knew I was warm, but I had to keep a tight hold of my emotions to stop myself falling hopelessly in love with some of them. There was no such danger with the men, but for all of them, men and women, I felt a deep admiration, a pride almost. They all worked so incredibly hard, yet they all had time for sports or other outdoor activities, and they were all doing some kind of part-time studying for further qualifications, or else they were building complex computer networks in their living rooms just for the experience. They all spoke at least three languages: Cantonese, English, and Mandarin. They never seemed to sleep.

The standard complaint about Hong Kong is that the people there never think of anything but money. They are superficial, have no culture, and have somehow ceased to be Chinese without acquiring any of the nobler features of Western civilization. This attitude is one aspect of the snobby view of mainland China as the only true repository of Chineseness, or at least those parts of it that have not yet inconveniently turned themselves into replicas of Hong Kong. It is the same complaint that is leveled against us, the overseas Chinese everywhere— the attitude that would have us all learning Mandarin and tai chi. Certainly there were times when I was infuriated by the buffeting of the indifferent, rushing crowds, ill at ease in the company of high society at formal occasions, frustrated by authoritarian bureaucracy, but perhaps this had as much to do with my own limitations as with the failings of people who repeatedly demonstrated personal kindness, generosity, and hospitality toward me. Even on the subway, it was common to see men give up their seats for elderly people or pregnant women. It began to dawn on me that they had achieved what I had been looking for all my life: a culture somewhere in between East and West, ancient and modern. It was not without its tensions: the girl who wore that traditional long dress did not want to dress like that, but it was a compromise she was willing to make to show proper respect for her elders, and unlike me she knew exactly how to do it. Unlike me, everyone I met was familiar with both Shakespeare and the Monkey King.

My Hong Kong colleagues wanted me to stay permanently. One of them asked me, "Why do you want to go back to Britain? You should stay with your own people. This is where you belong." How fervently I wished that were true! It was such a relief not to be different, to be able to blend anonymously into the crowd, not to be immediately marked out for special treatment or abuse. One evening after work, my colleagues took me to Lan Kwai Fong, the hot nightspot area where young people crowded into Western-style bars and clubs looking for excitement. It was a favorite haunt of white expatriates, and at first I was a bit dubious about going there. But I was reassured by the incongruous sight, even there, of a group of middle-aged Chinese men wearing white cotton vests and khaki trousers, sitting at a table in the open under a single, naked light bulb, playing mahjong.

We ended up in a bar, drinking beer and nibbling on potato chips and peanuts. I could not see why my friends regarded this as such an adventure, but I was quite happy because, for the only time in the whole six months, I could do the ordering. We were the only Chinese people in the bar, all the staff were British, and the menus were in English. I knew about this kind of scene, so I did all the talking—in English. It was, moreover, the only time in my life that I had been able to walk into a bar without worrying about the reception I would get, without wondering if I was going to be stared at like some kind of freak, or worse, if I was really unlucky and it turned out to be full of working-class lager louts. It made me almost giddy to realize that here I had a perfect right to go anywhere I liked—it was the whites who were the strangers. This was my country, not theirs.

But those feelings lasted only as long as I did not have to speak to anyone. I simply could not cope with the crippling effects of being unable to speak Cantonese. Even for some of my colleagues at work speaking English was an effort, and I was hesitant about forcing them to speak it just for my benefit unless it was essential. At lunch, I would hear other foreigners speaking English to their Chinese colleagues with complete self-confidence, but then no one expected anything different from them. Except when it was an intimate one-on-one, I felt too ashamed to follow suit, hence the silent dummy routine. Outside work, the minutiae of daily life were a constant struggle. At the hostel where I lived, the maids came in to clean every day, but they would replace the toilet rolls only when they had run out, creating the potential for extreme embarrassment. I wanted to ask them to leave a spare toilet roll at all times, but they spoke no English, so I had to ask the receptionist, who had been born and raised in Britain, to pass the message on, which she did with considerable amusement.

Everyone naturally assumed that I could speak Cantonese. I suspect that sometimes they were so shocked when they discovered I could not that they would respond in petty ways. There was a cashier in the canteen who, I am sure, was deliberately nasty. Just as with any other Cantonese word, the word for rice can mean lots of other things, depending on how you say it, but even if I were pronouncing it wrong, surely in a canteen there could not have been much doubt about what I wanted. Nevertheless, she consistently affected not to understand anything I said. Once I am certain that she tried to swindle me out of a large amount of change, giving in only when I refused to be browbeaten. On the other hand, another cashier in the same canteen was kindness itself.

One of the things that dismayed me most in Hong Kong was that, unlike anywhere else I have ever been, you cannot go into a canteen or a fast-food outlet and point to what you want. In Hong Kong you always have to order and pay for what you want first at the cashier, then go and collect it from the counter. The only thing that saved me from starving in the first few weeks was that some places have an English version of the menu, but this is never as comprehensive as the Chinese menu, and you miss out on the specials. This other cashier went out of her way to guide me through the menu and teach me the names of some of the dishes, struggling sometimes to use her own broken English and reacting with delight whenever I managed to say something intelligible in Cantonese. Once I asked her for a ham and egg sandwich. She nodded encouragingly as I slowly and painfully pronounced each word, then clapped her hands, beaming radiantly, when I finished. She, too, told me I should stay in Hong Kong.

Perhaps I was too timid, perhaps I should have stuck it out, perhaps in time I could have become fluent. But in the end, I could take it no longer. As I flew out of Kai Tak airport and looked down at the place where my heart will remain forever more, I felt once again, just as I had in the Central Cafe when I stood at the serving hatch all those years before—that I had been given a glimpse through a window into another world, where I could have belonged if fate had been different. But the window had closed, leaving me still outside.

It took me three years to recover. When I returned to Britain, I was physically exhausted and mentally destroyed. I had lost interest in everything I used to do. The sound of Western music made me feel sick, and even seeing my closest friends, some of whom I had known from childhood, became a chore. I played Cantopop incessantly, having discovered that Sally Yip was the loveliest thing I had ever seen or heard.[12] I searched frantically for somewhere to play table tennis. I became, frankly, a bore.

I owe my rehabilitation largely to a young woman I met when I went to a creative writing class she was offering for Chinese people who wanted to write in English. I could not imagine why Chinese people would want to do anything so outlandish, but in my search for some kind of salve I was willing to try anything. I was right to suspect that Chinese people would have no interest in the course. No one except me turned up, so it folded that night. However, in addition to encouraging me to write, the teacher introduced me to other British Chinese and got me involved in a succession of workshops and discussion groups. She is long gone now, gone back East like so many of us, but, at least as far as I am concerned, her work is done. I was slowly brought back to life by the cathartic sharing of experiences with others like me, the agonized arguments about our identity, and the slap-up meals in Chinese restaurants afterward.

I no longer need to define myself, to choose between Chinese or British. I see now that we can have our own culture combining both, as valid and valuable as anyone else's. Given the choice, I would still prefer to be someone else. But now, at last, I can stand at that window and look with equanimity at what I might have been, without regretting what I am.

Travels Afar

MARIA THAM

FOR CENTURIES, THE CHINESE HAVE EMIGRATED TO ALL CORNERS of the world. A few adventurous souls went to Pakistan, where I was born and raised. I am not precisely sure how my family came to be in that part of the world. My family's origins lie in the See Yip area of the southern Chinese province of Guangdong, which is famous for producing the pioneers of Chinese emigration to North America in the nineteenth and first half of the twentieth centuries. Many Guangdong people also emigrated to the countries of Southeast Asia. But all I know is that my paternal grandfather and his brothers instead chose to set out for India to seek their fortune.

My grandfather and his siblings died long before I was born, and my father, being a person of very few words, has never communicated his personal thoughts or feelings to his children. From the bits and pieces I gathered from my mother over the years, I have a vague idea as to why they left China, but I do not have precise information or a definite time line. I believe that my grandfather and his siblings had some contacts in India who promised them jobs in a dockyard in Calcutta. My

Maria Tham is a product-marketing manager with a Silicon Valley–based corporation. She resides in Santa Clara, California.

father, who was an only child, followed in their footsteps when he was in his late teens or early twenties.

I do not know much about my father's life in India.[1] But I do know that he never intended to stay abroad for so long. Like numerous immigrants, he hoped to make a fortune and return to China. He did go back to get married, in 1947, when he was twenty-seven. It was an arranged marriage, brokered by a matchmaker. But only a few months after the wedding, my father returned to India to work, leaving my pregnant mother behind. After the turmoil between India and Pakistan after independence in 1947, the dockyard closed down. When my father returned to India, he could not find a job. After a few years of futile searching, he decided to explore other options.

Fortunately, my father heard of a position in a restaurant in Pakistan and was able to relocate to Karachi. It took my father eleven lonely years, first in India, and then in that restaurant in Pakistan, to save enough money to bring my mother and my brother, who had been born in his absence, to Pakistan. But finally he succeeded. My three other siblings were all born in Karachi—as was I, the youngest, in 1968.

Pakistan was no United States in terms of financial and employment opportunities, and my parents were never able to make enough money to achieve their goal of a comfortable retirement in China. When civil war broke out in 1971, my family wanted to leave Pakistan, but we did not have the financial means to return to China or to go anywhere else. I remember vaguely when I was younger that my father once heard of a potentially lucrative employment opportunity in Bangladesh, but that did not work out. Life was very hard, but my parents tried to make the best of the situation. Besides, life in China was also hard. I think that even if we had had the money to return, if one weighed the advantages and disadvantages of living in rural China versus living in urban Pakistan, the latter was probably better.

In Karachi—and perhaps in all of Pakistan—there were just three See Yip Cantonese families, including our own. The few other Chinese who live in Karachi primarily originate from Hubei province in central China or are Hakkas, who also come from a different part of China and whose dialect is different from ours. Hence, when I was growing up, I often wondered about my Chinese heritage, specifically about my See Yip heritage. One may wonder why I put so much emphasis on See Yip heritage as opposed to just my Chinese heritage. It is because whenever I asked about my heritage, my mother always told me that I was See Yip Chinese, not Hubei or Hakka Chinese.

Being a member of one of the only three See Yip families, I was aware that we were near outsiders in the small Chinese community in Karachi. Only two other families understood our dialect. When growing up, I wondered how one could possibly come from a place so remote that no one of your own kind would follow you. How come there were so many more Hakkas and Hubeis than See Yip people? To me it was an absolute mystery. Question after question flowed through my mind, but I pushed them to the back of my mind, because I was young and did not have the time or facilities to find the answers.

What little I learned about the See Yip people was from my mother, who tried her best to tell me what she knew. Being illiterate, and speaking only the See Yip village dialect, she could only relate to me the stories of her life and of See Yip life in general. She also has no idea how to read a map. Thus, while I learned to understand and speak the dialect to communicate with her, I never knew the geographical location of the places she mentioned. To me, the names of places, villages, traditions, my relatives, and so on were just sounds that became very familiar with each passing year, but they were still a blank in my mind since I did not know how to read and write Chinese to ask other Chinese. No matter how many times my mother talked about the See Yip people, it was hard for me to grasp or picture what she was referring to. Before I actually went to China at the age of twenty-seven, I never got any further information about what being See Yip meant or where See Yip people came from in China. There was no framework to get more information. The Chinese community in Karachi was too small to have a Chinatown or any Chinese schools or cultural institutions offering instruction.

At the same time, none of us actively sought to discover our roots, because, like most people, we were more concerned with simply trying to make ends meet and bettering our lives whenever possible through education and employment. Life in Pakistan—a poor, developing country, full of religious and ethnic divisions—is tough, and most people did not have the luxury of diverting their energy to exploring personal questions. People tried to get employment or make money as soon as possible. In Pakistan, nobody I knew researched his or her roots beyond the superficial level. I never questioned any Hubei or Hakka about their background, because when I was in Pakistan it was a nonsubject. One just did not do something like that. Generally speaking, people in Pakistan are brought up to accept everything and not question things, which is different from an upbringing in the United States, where children question everything from a very young age.

Hence, most of us Chinese simply accepted the fact that we were all Chinese and that we were See Yip, Hubei, and Hakka respectively. People tended to stick to their own group: Hubeis with Hubeis, Hakkas with Hakkas. My family tended to be left out. Each group settled into its own profession: Hubeis in dentistry and Hakkas in restaurant management. The members of each group also tended to live close together in certain parts of town. Most of them also were related through marriage or blood. In general, even though the Chinese have lived in Pakistan for generations, most still preferred to marry their own kind. Ideally, one married someone from one's own group. The next best was to marry someone Chinese from another group. Marrying a non-Chinese Pakistani was considered taboo, although it did occasionally happen. In some instances, those who married non-Chinese Pakistanis were ostracized or cut off by their families. But then sticking to one's own community was nothing unusual in Pakistan, and such practices were in keeping with local norms.

My family and I interacted with the other Chinese primarily on social occasions. The children met in school or at church; the parents played mahjong. They did not speak our dialect, and we communicated with them in English (primarily among the younger generation, since we were all taught English in school), Urdu (the local language), Cantonese (of which See Yip is a subset and which some people understood), or plain sign language, using our hands and facial expressions.

Because of the closeness of the individual groups, the Chinese in Karachi retained their language at least to some extent, despite having lived in Pakistan for several generations. Most Chinese seemed at least to understand their local dialect but tended to speak Urdu, since they very often interacted daily with the local people, especially with their employees. My family was more Chinese in that while almost all the other Chinese families have been in Karachi for generations (although some Hubeis and Hakkas did later bring over some of their relatives), my parents were first-generation immigrants. Certainly we were the only first-generation See Yip Chinese in Pakistan, and the only members of the Tham clan who settled here. My parents only learned to speak a smattering of Urdu and still speak only See Yip. My siblings and I spoke See Yip and English, which we learned in school. We picked up slang Urdu from the neighborhood children.

In part, my parents' lack of prowess in Urdu might have been due to the fact that they never expected to stay in Pakistan for so long. Culturally, it must have been difficult for them to live there. Even though my parents may have wanted to continue a Chinese lifestyle, they could not do so, because in Pakistan there was almost nothing Chinese available. Most of the standard things you see in Chinese supermarkets in the United States like soy sauce, pork, preserved vegetables, salted duck eggs, bok choy, Chinese sausages, mooncakes, woks, Chinese calendars, firecrackers, and so on were not available in Pakistan. Some items, like tofu and egg noodles, were made by one or two families, who sold them out of their homes.

None of the Chinese like me, born and raised in Pakistan, knew what Chinese things, ingredients, or culture really were or meant, because we were never exposed to them. We observed Chinese New Year, but nothing else. Marriage and death ceremonies tended to be Catholic, since most of the recent Chinese immigrants were Catholics. At the same time, some Chinese would add a Chinese touch to a wedding ceremony like the banging of the door to claim the bride, the tea ceremony before the elders, and so forth. Hence, in this Chinese vacuum, we operated as Pakistani-Chinese, using local ingredients to create distinctively Pakistani-Hubei, Pakistani-Hakka, and Pakistani-See Yip cultures. We could not recreate Chinese-Hubei, Chinese-Hakka, or Chinese-See Yip cultures. We had no choice.

Being Chinese in Pakistan was not considered a big deal. There is plenty of strife in Pakistan—Shia versus Sunni, Muhajir versus non-Muhajir—

primarily because of political and religious reasons. But belonging to any of these groups, or being Chinese, did not make anyone less Pakistani: we were all simply subsets of Pakistanis. Everybody lives in small communities, and everyone knows all the locals, if not by name, then by sight. Almost all the older Chinese families had been partially woven into the Pakistani fabric of life. So even though we Chinese were a minority in a South Asian Islamic country, because we were born and brought up in the neighborhood, we were considered locals. In daily conversation, people would call us Chinese, but that was only a term to refer to us. Nobody questioned the "Pakistaniness" of our "Chineseness," or vice versa. People accepted everything at face value. Life in Pakistan was already complicated and harsh enough, and no one had the time, energy, or the tools to differentiate between things too closely.

The closest I got to experiencing "real" Chinese life was when the Chinese embassy in Karachi occasionally invited the local Chinese to different events. Most of the time they would show Chinese movies and we, the local Chinese, would be invited, because we were the only Chinese around. They had no choice. The Chinese embassy in Pakistan was an important embassy because China and Pakistan are close political allies. We would all eagerly go for the free food and drinks before the movies. Anything free was a great attraction! I do not think we local Chinese went to these events because we felt we were Chinese or had feelings for China. Rather, we considered the events at the Chinese embassy a novelty, a chance to dress up and go somewhere "important."

I personally thought that the people from the Chinese embassy were different from us, because the embassy staff spoke to us in Mandarin, which most of us local Chinese did not understand. As far as I could tell, they did not speak English. I accepted that they were Chinese, but just as we considered ourselves a subset of the Chinese race, I considered them China Chinese. I remember that the first time I heard the expression "ni hao" (meaning "hello" in Mandarin), when the embassy personnel greeted us on arrival, I made fun of it because it sounded so strange. However, the language issue was not a big deal, because the guests could communicate among themselves.

Since I never spoke with any of the embassy people during our visits, I do not know what they thought of us. But based on their changing attitude toward us, I can only infer that they thought we Pakistani-Chinese were interesting and maybe strange. I must admit that we did not always behave courteously at these events. We would grab at the food as soon as it came out of the kitchen. Some older kids would even stand near the kitchen door, so that the moment the food came out, it would be gone. The food was delicious to us, because we local Chinese had never tasted such dishes before. The embassy must have imported all the Chinese ingredients. Also, sometimes we would mess up the cases of free soda that were distributed or just snatch the soda bottles from the hands of employees the moment they opened them. We did not stand in orderly lines. People often got drunk, because this was one of the few opportunities they had to drink alcohol, and for free, in a country where the sale of alcohol is largely banned.

In the beginning, the embassy people would serve food first for some events, and then show the movies. Then they realized that most people left right after eating and did not stay for the movie. After noticing this, they decided to serve the food after the movie. The children were very noisy and would go playing and running all over the embassy grounds. This restlessness was partly because the movies shown were in Mandarin, and none of us understood what was going on. Because the embassy personnel could not communicate much with us, they did not know how to contain our wild behavior. When I was young, the whole family would be invited for some of the events. Later on, the embassy would invite only adults. But whole families would still try to crash the events. To deal with this situation, the Chinese embassy would forcibly block the children from going through the gates, easing the situation a little bit. On reflection, I must admit that we Chinese-Pakistanis must have looked like hooligans!

When I was in Pakistan, I never asked myself if I felt Chinese or Pakistani. China was a remote country as far as I was concerned. I accepted that we were different, and I had no reason to feel anything for China. If I thought about it at all, I looked at China favorably, because in school and in our interaction with the locals, Chinese people were viewed as being good, smart, and hard-working people. The fact that China and

Pakistan were politically aligned may also have had some bearing on the favorable way we were regarded, because we heard and read a lot about "pak-cheen dosti" ("Pakistan-China friendship").[2] I was born in Pakistan and lived my life according to the Pakistani way. I accepted what came my way. I interacted with other Pakistanis most of the time— I dressed like them, ate the local food, went to the same schools, shopped in the local markets and bazaars, accepted the local culture, rules, laws, and so on—and was accepted as a Pakistani.

When I was eighteen, I emigrated to the United States. Earlier, my brothers had managed to win scholarships for higher education in the United States and then stayed on because of the opportunities available there. When my eldest brother became a U.S. citizen, he decided to sponsor the remaining members of my family, and we emigrated to America at different stages. Upon my arrival in the States in December 1986, I studied for the S.A.T., applied to universities, and was accepted by Scripps College in California.[3] In my interaction with students, faculty, and friends at Scripps, I consciously realized for the first time that I was different and came from a unique background. Nobody in Pakistan ever asked me where I was from, but here, people often did. When I said, "Pakistan," without fail I would get surprised reactions. My Pakistani accent and Chinese appearance confused the people I met.

In Pakistan, people do not think of themselves in hyphenated terms. The term Pakistani-Chinese, or for that matter, Pakistani-anything did not exist. Everybody acknowledges themselves as Pakistanis. But in the United States, I was forced to use words to identify my background. Thus, I started to describe myself as a Pakistani-Chinese-American and later on, jokingly, as a C.P.A. (Chinese-Pakistani-American). I could not just be a Pakistani (because I do not look like a Pakistani) or just a Chinese (because I do not speak the common dialects of Mandarin or Cantonese, but only a village dialect, with a Pakistani accent), or just American (because I do not fit the stereotypical, blonde-haired, blue-eyed image of an American).

It was the Chinese part of my background that confused me the most. I will never forget the time when a fellow student from mainland China, upon hearing that I was from Pakistan, at once exclaimed, "That means you are not Chinese!" and drew back from me. I was taken aback by her reaction because, ethnically, I am as Chinese as any other Chinese person, whether from China, Taiwan, Singapore, the United States, or anywhere else. I had always thought there were all kinds of Chinese, as my experience in Pakistan showed, and no matter what differences there may be, a Chinese was always a Chinese.

As more people asked me about my background, I began to truly question myself for the first time, and that is why I decided I needed to research my roots. The impetus for doing so was not that I felt being See Yip made me more or less Chinese. I never believed that one's clan, roots, or heritage makes one superior or inferior to anyone else. I believe that all human beings are alike, regardless of race or ethnicity; being different only adds to the diversity and richness of humankind. I had simply become curious about my See Yip heritage and wanted to add to my knowledge. Another factor in my search for my roots was my desire to meet some relatives. We did not have any relatives in Pakistan or in the United States, so while growing up, I often wondered what it would be like to have grandparents, uncles, aunts, and cousins. While I will never know what it is like to have grandparents, I realized that I still had the chance to meet some aunts and cousins.

I guess that after being in the United States, and being influenced by the prevailing attitudes about race and roots, it became important for me to find out more about the Chinese—especially the See Yip— part of my background. Being in the United States, and attending college here, I also learned to question everything, not just to accept what I was told. I wanted to know more. I learned that if I wanted answers, I needed to take action and not have the attitude I had been brought up with, which is "what will happen will happen" and wait for fate to intervene. If I did not know something, I should try to build my knowledge instead of being fatalistic and accepting.

In my search for information, I often asked around. Some people claimed they had heard the term See Yip, but did not know any more. Others mentioned the city of Toisan as being part of See Yip, while some Chinese-American students mentioned that their ancestors had come from Toisan but did not know about See Yip. I hit a similar wall when I asked ethnic Chinese from overseas, studying in the States. I posted a question on a Chinese chat board on the Internet but got very few concrete answers. I did some research on Chinese emigration to the United States and came across brief, cursory references to Toisan and Sze Yup. That seemed promising, but the authors did not elaborate. As I wondered all the more about See Yip, I told myself that in the near future, I would visit China and find out more about my heritage and roots for myself. I felt that this would be the only way to find the answers to my questions.

My wish came true in November 1995, when I first got the opportunity to visit my ancestral villages of Hu Then Lei and Khui Mei in China, with the financial assistance of the Durfee Foundation. The Durfee Foundation gives money to alumni of several colleges, including Scripps College, who want to carry out a personal project in China. A main criterion was that one had to have a deep personal reason for going to China. The project could not be for research, business, or academic reasons.[4] This seemed like the perfect opportunity for me. I applied, and was overjoyed to be selected as one of the recipients.

Once I got the final approval from the foundation, I set about planning my trip. In the beginning, I was a little confused and apprehensive, because, though I knew what I wanted to achieve, I did not know the exact location of the places I was going to visit. My parents could only tell me the village names in our dialect, and I could not find somebody who knew the names of the places in the official Mandarin to enable me to find the places on a map. I found out only that See Yip refers to four districts and that my village is in one of these districts. I wished I could take my parents with me so that they could be my guides, but the Durfee Foundation would only pay for me to go.

Numerous questions swirled through my head. Whom would I actually get to see? Would my relatives understand my Pakistani-accented version of the See Yip dialect? Are the places my mother mentioned still there? How has it changed since my parents left their respective villages? What would I find there? Would any family skeletons come out of the closet? Since, for financial reasons, my parents had never returned to China, their memories were time capsules of village life as it had been fifty years ago. But since that time, much had happened in China. The Republic of China had become the People's Republic of

China. The country had experienced devastating political upheavals. Now it is seen as a rising power. The 1990s saw China opening its doors to the outside world and people rushing in to pursue economic opportunities. I heard and learned much about modern China. Yet searching as I was for the "old" China, I did not know what to expect.

Nor could my parents enlighten me. My father had maintained contact with his mother until her death in the early 1980s, but with no one else. My paternal grandfather had died young, when my mother was still living in the village with them, and having left so long ago, my father no longer had any friends there. As for my mother, she had lost contact with her family. Since she is illiterate, she could not write to her family, and we had not known anyone in Pakistan except my father who could write Chinese. For private reasons, which she never elaborated on, my mother never asked my father to help her maintain contact with her family. I assume it could be because of the old-fashioned view that, when a woman got married she was no longer a part of her family but a part of her husband's family. Hence, my mother accepted her fate and, in addition to leaving behind her culture when she left China, she also effectively broke her ties with her family and village friends.

Nevertheless, with the goal of discovering my family's roots, I created a framework of my own. My mother had the address of her sister in Guangzhou (unless she had moved since my mother left China) and told me to use that as a starting point. I then asked a friend to help me write to my aunt. Fortunately, my letter reached her! After exchanging a few letters, thus opening communication between my mother and her family after more than forty years, I told my aunt about my upcoming trip and my need for her assistance. She wrote back saying she would be delighted to help me in any way she could.

I began my journey on November 30, 1995. As the plane left the runway of JFK Airport in New York, I felt my heart pounding. With a sense of pride and adventure, I embarked on my trip to meet and visit the people and places I had heard so much about. Finally, after all these years of wondering, wanting, and imagining, I was on my way to China.

After an overnight layover in Hong Kong, I caught the first train out the next morning. My port of entry in China was Guangzhou. As my train neared the Guangzhou train terminal, I felt very excited. Through the train window, I drank in the scenery whizzing by. I saw farmland, construction sites at different stages of development, and people—lots of people. Finally, I was on the soil of China, and my journey of exploration was about to begin.

At the train station, my aunt and her son were eagerly waiting for me. Since we had never met, I was a little nervous about whether we would find one another. Fortunately, I had an old photograph of my aunt, which my mother had carried with her when she left China. I recognized her at once when I came out of customs.

I discovered that while it was possible to communicate with my aunt since she spoke the See Yip dialect, no one else in her immediate family could really understand what I was saying. My aunt was originally from the village, but her husband and children had lived all their lives in the city of Guangzhou. They all speak standard Cantonese, the language of Guangdong province. The younger people speak Mandarin, the official language of China, as well. Fortunately, my aunt knew where I wanted to go and made arrangements for me to set out for my destination. The first and foremost thing I was told to do was to go directly to my paternal ancestral village to pay my respect to my ancestors. Not to do so would bring me bad luck. As a member of the Tham ancestry, my duty was to the Tham lineage. I did not have to pay homage to my maternal ancestors, the Lees, because I did not owe them any allegiance, since descent among the Chinese was from the male line. In deference to tradition, I decided to do as I was told and go where I was led, somewhere in the See Yip districts, located southwest of Guangzhou.

I finally learned the precise locations of my ancestral villages. See Yip refers to four particular districts comprising Toisan, Hoi Ping, Sam Wei, and Yin Ping. Within each district are numerous boroughs (clusters of villages) and individual villages. Both my paternal and maternal villages lie in Hoi Ping. My paternal ancestral borough is called Ou Sheng, which consists of five other villages. Villages were usually formed around last names, and all villagers are related in one way or another. Hence, Ou Sheng is the borough of the Tham clan. My paternal house, which had been built by my grandfather almost seventy years ago, is located in the village of Hu Then Lei. My maternal village of Khui Mei is located in the borough of Bart It Tui.

It took approximately three and a half hours by car to reach my paternal village. As we approached it, the first thing I saw was the village gate. When I entered the gate of Hu Then Lei for the first time, I felt a strange sense of pride and belonging—this was my family's village, and this was the place where my ancestors had lived and toiled for centuries. This is also where the Tham clan still lives. All the people who live there are Thams and are related to me through some branch of the Tham lineage. It was a feeling that I have never felt before. It was a feeling I had always wanted to feel when I thought about the Hubeis and Hakkas of Pakistan who, metaphorically speaking, lived with their clan in Pakistan, as my family never had. At the same time, I felt a sense of alienation because I was so different from the people around me. Here I was, an educated working woman with a bachelor's degree from Scripps College and a master's degree in international relations from Columbia University, and here were my relatives, poor and uneducated farmers, living in such backward conditions in China.

As I walked through my father's village, I saw that the houses were built in neat horizontal and vertical rows, with very narrow lanes separating one house from another. I walked through the lanes and was led to my ancestral house. Along the way I saw some dung sheds, goose pens, chicken pens, roaming chickens with their chicks, and yes, even a turkey pen. Somehow, I associate turkey with the United States. It was there, celebrating my first Thanksgiving, that I had first seen and eaten turkey. It seemed incongruous to see a turkey in China. Chinese turkeys! I started to laugh. Nobody knew why I was laughing all of a sudden, and I did not know how to explain my strange thoughts. They probably chalked it up to foreign behavior.

Before I reached my father's house, word of my arrival had already spread, and people quickly came to greet me. My relatives were fascinated to see me. What mesmerized them the most was the fact that I understood the village dialect. They could not fathom how an outsider like me, who had never visited the village before, could understand their dialect. It was strange to meet them for the first time and to realize that they were all my relatives. It was even stranger to realize that everybody who greeted me was also a Tham! Never having lived with or met any relatives before in my life, I felt quite overwhelmed to meet and greet so many of them at once. At the same time, while I knew that they were related to me through some branch of the Tham tree, I was conscious of the fact that they were not my immediate relatives. I did not have any paternal uncles, aunts, or first cousins. For that reason, while I was excited to meet them, I also felt some distance from them.

Most houses in the village were built in the same style. They were tall, angular, and rather severe-looking. My father's house was multi-storied, made mostly of red brick that, with the passage of time, had turned dark grayish and moldy. The top roof, which had been built with wood, had been eaten away by termites and had caved in from neglect and the ravages of time and weather. When the house was originally built, painters had been hired to paint the pictures of colorful flora and fauna and images of gods and angels all around the outer walls. Now most of the paintings were faded, and the paint was chipping. Nevertheless, I could tell that, besides the meticulous detail that went into the painting, much care had gone into the building of the house. Although it looked faded and old, it still exuded a certain beauty and presence.

My aunt tried to open the front door, but the lock stubbornly would not open. Since no one had opened the door for a very long time, something must have clogged or rusted. After a few more tugs and pushes, it gave way. Everything was pitch dark, and as I stepped in, my eyes had to adjust.

As I roamed around my paternal ancestral house, what struck me was its size. My mother had told me that when this house was originally built by my grandfather for his family, it had been one of the biggest and most beautiful houses on the block. It was approximately 3,500 square feet, with very high ceilings. Now it was almost empty. Most of the furniture and other household things had been taken away by the local villagers on the death of my grandmother about fifteen years ago. Only a few things remained—a few broken chairs and tables, my parents' bed, and faded, dusty photographs of my family that had been sent to my grandmother a long time ago. It was strange to see my family pictures in the house. Though I never knew my paternal grandmother, I thought it must have been hard for her to live alone in that house for such a long time. Never did she or my father know that when they parted about fifty years ago, they would never see each other again.

Today more than half the houses in Ou Sheng are locked up. In Hu Then Lei approximately 150 houses are locked up and empty because they belong to "absentee" families like mine. Present government policy encourages people to return to the villages, build new homes, and farm the fields. Current and prospective villagers are given land at extremely low prices. Thus, it is common to see villagers building new houses not just for themselves but for their sons and their sons' families. I saw numerous villagers busy laying bricks, cementing walls, or tiling roofs, proudly waiting for the day when they would be able to move into their own new homes.

Ancestor worship is an integral part of Chinese belief. Thus the first thing I had to do after seeing the house was to pay my informal respects to my ancestors and to "announce" my presence to them. All the villagers were eager to assist me. First, they cleaned the house, which was full of dirt and cobwebs, since nobody had lived there since my grandmother passed away. They also brought utensils for me to place my offerings of prayer cake and American chocolates and cookies. My mother had advised me to take some American chocolates, because my ancestors had never tasted American treats and would be delighted to eat some. She thought my grandfather would be particularly thrilled because he always had "discriminating" taste! I burned joss sticks and prayed to my ancestors. Further, in accordance with tradition, I informed my ancestors that I would return to honor them with a formal ceremony and celebration. Then I distributed the rest of the sweets and food I had bought to my relatives.

A few days after my visit to my paternal village, I set out to visit my maternal ancestral village of Khui Mei. The wife and children of my deceased maternal uncle currently live in Sen Sheng, a town not far from Khui Mei. Since I was going to be visiting Khui Mei in their company, I stopped by Sen Sheng first to meet them. We decided to walk to Khui Mei from there, since it would take only about forty-five minutes to do so. I was filled with expectations and excitement. All along the route while I was walking, I could hear my mother's voice in my head talking about Khui Mei, about how she used to walk to the different villages to run errands, and also the stories she related about each village. Once again, as I drew closer, I felt overcome with emotions and felt my heartbeat quicken. I could not believe that I was actually seeing what I had wanted to see for so long.

In appearance, Khui Mei resembled my paternal village, although it looked slightly smaller, because the village had been divided in the middle by a highway built by the government. Once again, word of my arrival spread like wildfire in the village. Everybody knew my late uncle's wife and came to greet her. In doing so, they were very curious to know who I was. They were thrilled to meet me. It seems that my mother was viewed as a village celebrity since she had the courage to marry outside the village of Ou Sheng and then settle far away from home. I was told that when one young girl recently married outside the village and was questioned why she wanted to marry so far away from home, she actually compared herself to my mother!

At this time, I also decided to pay my respects to my maternal ancestors, especially my maternal grandparents, uncle, and younger aunt. (Although this aunt would not be considered a Lee anymore after her marriage, I considered her a Lee because she was my mother's sister.) My maternal aunt assured me that I did not have to do this and that I would not suffer any bad consequences if I did not. She mentioned that I was a Tham, not a Lee clan member. I disagreed. I thought it was only fair that one pay one's respects to both lineages. Furthermore, since my mother had suffered so much, especially in having lost complete contact with her family once she left China, I somehow wanted to try to make up for that. It made me sad that her parents, brother, and younger sister had passed away during her absence and that she had not been able to pay her last respects to them. Therefore, I insisted on paying mine, and my aunt agreed to go along with whatever I decided to do. After all, I was the one paying for everything.

But I did have to follow Chinese etiquette. I could only "reach" my maternal ancestors through the male lineage of the Lee family. No members of my family, including my mother, may pay respects directly to their maternal ancestors, because we are not Lees. We lost this connection when my mother married my father and thereby became part of the Tham clan. Since my uncle was the only Lee son and no longer alive, my uncle's eldest son took over that role. He announced my presence by burning joss sticks and presenting offerings in front of my maternal ancestor's altar. I then also burned joss sticks and offered them a taste of American cookies and chocolates. Having opened these ancestral channels and satisfied both clan villages by paying my respects, I was free to do what I wanted. I could now rest assured that no ghosts would haunt me for not playing the dutiful clan member!

As I explored my paternal and maternal houses, and then the respective villages, I felt very emotional. Although my mother had always tried to explain her life in China, I could never picture what she was talking about. After all, my only experiences were Pakistani, and these were totally different from Chinese. Even my images of things were totally different from reality. For example, when my mother mentioned that she had to carry water from the river for use at home every day, I could only imagine her using Pakistani-looking pails. When she talked about village gates, the house, and so on, I could only imagine what they looked like. When I saw them for the first time, I felt as if I were watching a National Geographic program: fascinating, informative, and real. At the same time, a thought flashed through my mind. If my parents had not moved to Pakistan, I too, would have been a daughter of the village—working the fields, minding the buffaloes, collecting animal dung for fertilizers, and cooking with wood and dry grass! I wondered if I would have been happier in the village or in Pakistan. I could not answer that question. After all, everything is relative, and life in Pakistan was also very hard.

My initial visits to my ancestral villages were considered informal. I still had to pay formal homage to my Tham and Lee ancestors. To do this, I had to visit their respective grave sites, located a short distance from the villages. To be fair to both my paternal and maternal ancestors, I wanted to have duplicate ceremonies and to order two of everything. With the assistance of my maternal aunt, I went over the plans for the formal worship, which included holding a banquet for the entire village. Initially, I found this mind-boggling. Invite a whole village for a banquet? But then I was told that my relatives would buy all the ingredients (agreed on beforehand) and cook for themselves. I only needed to bring the roast pig.

All this involved money. I decided that while I would buy the exact same things for both of the grave site ceremonies, I would host only one banquet—for my father's village, since I am a Tham. Originally, the villagers thought that I was rich and therefore wanted to plan something very grand. But I told them to tone things down and to do things in moderation, because I did not have much money. In the end they believed me, probably because I was only a younger female Tham. Perhaps if my parents or brothers had gone, they would have been expected to have more money and to do things in style. Furthermore, I was not wearing a suit or any grand clothes, as they had seen other returning relatives wear. I was dressed informally in jeans. I brought enough gifts only for my immediate relatives—that is, my mother's siblings and their families. Since my father had no siblings, I did not bring gifts for my paternal relatives. For the village relatives, I only gave food items, and in some instances, a little money to those who had taken an active part in arranging the ceremonies and banquet. In my paternal village, I was asked if I wanted to make a small contribution to the village fund to build an embankment, and I did so in the name of my father. My maternal village relatives did not bother me as much, because I was, after all, a Tham, and not a Lee. They knew they had no claim on me.

When I went to pay my formal respects to my paternal ancestors, I headed toward the tombstone of my grandparents with all the required offerings, which included a roast pig, a goose, boiled eggs, cakes, and things my ancestors had liked in their lifetimes. The grave site was located at the top of the mountain, so that my grandparents could have good view of the river and the village. When we arrived at their graves, my relatives quickly cleared the area around the tombstone and arranged all our offerings. I burned joss sticks, bowed three times, prayed in front of the grave, and did what my maternal aunt told me to do. May my grandparents rest in peace forever!

After this ceremony, we went back to the village for the banquet. I did not stay for the whole event. Instead, the villagers cooked a little food for me and the people I had come with, and I left and let them enjoy the food on their own. The next day, I repeated the rituals for my maternal ancestors. However, in place of the banquet, I merely distributed the sweets and other food I had brought with me. Then I took the roast pig and other leftover food from the grave site ceremony to my late uncle's house in the city and had a small private family gathering.

During my six weeks in See Yip, I learned so much and yet so little. I had found a whole new world that was, at the same time, familiar. Bits and pieces began to fall into place. Names that before had just been sounds began to take shape. See Yip was no longer a name. It had become a reality. I had gotten to know something of my ancestral villages—what they looked like, how they had changed, the people, my relatives, their histories, the old culture, language, beliefs, and even old village gossip!

Now that I have visited China, I have a deeper and more personal understanding of my parents and of Chinese emigration in general. When my mother talks about her past or when I visit Chinatown and hear the older generation talk about their backgrounds, I know exactly where they come from and the nuances of what they are talking about. I see the past and present in juxtaposition, and it is a totally liberating feeling. It is hard to capture the myriad of emotions I felt and experiences I had during the short period I was in See Yip.

A saying in my village dialect truly captures the spirit of my trip: "Charp harn lei there farn hong sarng." This poetic, poignant, and humorous saying describes packing all one's belongings to visit one's roots and ancestral village. It would touch the hearts of See Yip people, who would understand its true essence.

In Search of Lin Jia Zhuang

MILAN L. LIN-RODRIGO

HAVING HATED MYSELF SO LONG FOR BEING CHINESE, IT IS STILL somewhat difficult for me to understand exactly why I went to China a few years ago to find my father's family.

It was not easy growing up Chinese in Sri Lanka, particularly in the countryside. My sister and I were the only "strange-looking" children in the whole village. Kids at school always called us names. It was I, more than my sister, who resembled our Chinese father. I was always called "cheeni," the "Chinese girl," which is somewhat similar to being called a nigger if you are a black person in America. I was Chinese only in appearance; neither my sister nor I spoke a word of Chinese, and we did not cook or eat Chinese food or wear Chinese clothes. Moreover, I always got straight As in Sinhala, the local language, and in Sinhala literature in school. Yet whenever somebody picked a fight with me, they would call me a "damn Chinese." There were other names: "flat nose," "yellow face," and occasionally "damn Tamil," after my mother's race, Tamils being a minority group in Sri Lanka.[1] The situ-

Milan L. Lin-Rodrigo is an instructor in the Sinhala and Tamil languages at Cornell University in Ithaca, New York. She is also a consultant with the World Bank and currently lives in Washington, D.C.

ation was not much different even at the boarding school I later attended outside the village.

I wanted to hide my Chinese identity in every possible way. I thought of changing my name. I grew my hair very long and dressed as a typical local. Later, I started dressing up as a Tamil girl; I always wore a *pottu*, a red or black dot, which symbolized the Hindu Tamil identity, on my forehead.[2] None of this changed the way I was perceived. Sometimes I thought that if I had been born in China, I would have been one of them and never laughed at.

In addition to the embarrassment of being different from other kids in the village, we were also regarded as illegitimate children, because nobody believed we had a father; nobody knew who he was or ever saw him visiting us. And, indeed, although my sister and I were in no doubt whatsoever about the existence of our father, for many years we ourselves and our mother did not know where he was.

My father came to Sri Lanka, then called Ceylon, in 1937 from China's Shandong province with a group of other Chinese traders.[3] He was already married, with a daughter, when he left China. His family owned farmland in Shandong, but it became difficult to work on farms after the Japanese invasions of north China in 1931 and 1937, particularly in Shandong, since the Japanese were very active in that province.[4] Like most other Chinese, my father came to make some quick money and return to his family; he had no intention of settling down in Sri Lanka permanently. However, with the meager income he received as a trader, it was not easy to save enough to go back as he had planned. Time went by, and the Communists assumed power in China in 1949. My father, like his fellow emigrants, feared returning to China, particularly when he heard horror stories about the ill-treatment of old people and landowners.

In addition, by then my father had remarried. My parents met each other just before the end of World War II. At the time, my mother was living with her eldest sister and her sister's husband in Anuradhapura, a town in North Central province of Sri Lanka. They knew my father only through business dealings. One day, my father, who was an itinerant cloth trader, was brave enough to ask for my mother's hand in marriage. My aunt and uncle were aghast; it was unheard-of for a local, respectable Tamil Hindu girl to marry a Chinese vendor. My mother seems to have been more liberal in her views, or perhaps she simply wanted to escape the ill-treatment she received from her sister and her brother-in-law.

I remember all the horror stories my mother told me about her past. She was the youngest in her family. Her father had died when she was about thirteen years old. Since my grandmother was busy earning a living, she left my mother in the care of her eldest daughter, my mother's eldest sister, who was well settled, with a husband who had a reasonably well-paying job. However, this sister was a mean and hot-tempered person who made my mother a virtual slave in her household. My mother was forced to take care of her sister's son and do all the housework while at the same time attending school. She was punished severely for every mistake she made. At the end of the day, after all the housework was over, my aunt would then make her husband test my mother on her schoolwork. Again, my mother would be caned if she made mistakes. It was all too much for her. She fell ill for months at a time, and eventually she could not continue with her schooling. She made several attempts to return to her mother but was unsuccessful. In the end, after meeting my father, my mother simply eloped with him and thus was not able to have a decent wedding or even have the marriage registered.

My parents initially went to live in Colombo, the capital of Sri Lanka. They rented a room in an area where other Chinese–Sri Lankan families lived, and my father gave up his itinerant life as a cloth trader. For one thing, as a married man, he found a wandering lifestyle difficult to maintain. Moreover, much of the cloth he sold was imported from China, and with the political instability there, supplies became uncertain. He therefore decided to join another Chinese friend in setting up a restaurant, and my parents moved to the faraway port city of Trincomalee, where I was born in 1945, and where my sister, my only sibling, was born a year later.

During the first few years of their marriage, my parents fared well. However, as time went by, my father lost all his savings, because he loved to gamble and smoke opium. Sharing as we did an apartment with my father's business partner and his wife, we did not even have a proper place to live. My mother became unhappy. She finally left my father, taking us children with her. She turned to her second sister, who was then living in the countryside of Western province, for help. My aunt took us all in. She did not have any children of her own, and so she became a second mother to my sister and me.

During this time, I remember my mother taking my sister and me on long bus rides to see our father. As I recall, those visits were not very pleasant, since my father had no proper home in which to entertain us. After my mother left, my father had started living in a small room in the restaurant itself. It had only a single bed and a bathroom, which was shared with all the other restaurant employees. Most evenings, a group of Chinese men would get together in an adjoining room to smoke opium and play mahjong late into the night.

My father refused to move to the countryside to live with us. He did not want to leave Trincomalee, where his fellow Chinese lived; he felt closer to them than to us. According to my mother, at that time, he frequently spoke of leaving Sri Lanka and going back to China. My mother did not want to risk the welfare of her two girls under these uncertain conditions. She therefore stayed with her sister in the countryside and did her best to bring us up and give us a good education. In this, she was fortunate to have brought with her the sewing machine that my father had purchased for her. This sewing machine was the first and only one in town at the time, and it enabled my mother to earn a living as a seamstress for several years. She taught me how to sew, and gradually I was able to start helping her. My mother was also able to obtain a piece of land from the government when it began distributing land to landless people. My aunt and my mother worked together on the land. With their hard work and help of a few others, we built our first home.

My parents maintained a correspondence for some time, but when I was about five or six years old, my father's letters, and the allowance he used to send occasionally, stopped coming. He never once visited us in the town where we grew up. He seemed to have decided that, with his poor language ability, traveling in the countryside of Sri Lanka would be too difficult for him. My mother went searching for him once or twice but could not locate him. The conclusion we all came to was that he had returned to China. This was the belief we grew up with until we rediscovered our father about a decade and a half later. The breakdown of communication seemed to have been due to a simple misunderstanding and the deception of the mail carrier. My father told us later that he had never stopped sending money to my mother. But instead of continuing to send postal or money orders, he had taken to simply inserting currency notes into the envelope with the letter. He claimed that he had taken care to inform us promptly of his many changes of address, but my mother had never received any of those letters or the money he sent. If his claim was true, someone in the postal system had discovered and appropriated the cash and letters.

To add to the social and financial difficulties resulting from my parents' ill-fated marriage, there was also a legal problem, which took some time to resolve. Since their marriage had not been registered properly, my sister and I had difficulty proving our nationality for official documents. Sri Lankan immigration laws did not recognize Chinese people as legal citizens even after many years of residency in the country. In addition citizenship was denied to the Sri Lankan–born children of fathers who were not Sri Lankan citizens; the fact that their mothers were citizens or that they were born in Sri Lanka did not count. We were categorized as people with no country. Obtaining citizenship in our case took much effort. Fortunately, although it was embarrassing that my parents were not legally married, it ended up working to our advantage. We could claim Sri Lankan citizenship based on the status of a single parent—my mother. Even this was not easy, because my mother's ethnic background was Tamil. Since her birth had not been properly registered, immigration officials suspected her origin to be South India, from where many Tamils had been brought to work as indentured laborers during British rule, and not Sri Lanka. We had to search for witnesses who could sign affidavits proving that my mother had been born in Sri Lanka. After all that hard work, we were finally able to register as citizens.

It was only when I entered the university that I began to realize that being Chinese was not entirely a drawback. I began to get some recognition for specializing in Sinhala language and literature, which was my undergraduate major. When I graduated, I was offered employment as a lecturer at my alma mater. Since I had citizenship by this time, I was able to accept the position, which was official recognition of sorts and gave me more authority. To my surprise, I was also approached by men who wanted to have permanent relationships with me. One major concern I had when growing up was that no one would want to marry me because I looked ugly and different. I began to enjoy the changes in my situation, realizing that racial and ethnic identity is not entirely independent of one's social position.

I began to understand the other reasons behind all that ridicule and harassment that my sister and I had suffered as children. We were not only outsiders in our village; we were also not wealthy. Moreover, unlike other foreigners, we did not belong to the English-speaking middle class. Simply being able to speak English fluently would have given us prestige, and we would have been able to avoid some of the disrespect and name-calling. Or, if I had been part of a complete Chinese family, rather than a product of a Chinese-local marriage, I wouldn't have attracted much comment. Even then, if we had lived in a major city, where most Sri Lankan women who married Chinese men settled, people would not have singled us out so much, since there were other foreign people in the cities as well.

During the time I attended the university, I made another discovery. Through some Chinese living near the university, I found out that my father was still in Sri Lanka and that he had never returned to China! After we had lost contact with him, he had tried many occupations, finally settling down as a dental technician in a small town in the southern part of the country. After some effort, I was able to reestablish contact with him. By this time, it had been almost fifteen years since my parents' separation. My mother and father both had their own reasons for what had happened. It was too late by then for any reunion between them.

I was saddened and confused about the past; however I was also somewhat excited by the fact that I had found my father. It took me some time before I could really forgive him for what I had gone through. My sister, who was less Chinese-looking than I was, had not been affected as much by having or not having a father; her problem was having an obviously Chinese-looking sister with a flat nose, narrow eyes, and the skin color of a boiled shrimp. A special bond gradually developed between my father and me. Later, when I was employed in Colombo, we maintained frequent contact. It became easy, because by then I had married a Sri Lankan man who was very accommodating—being, in fact, more interested in China and its political developments than I was. I would say that it was only from that time that my curiosity about my father's past and his family in China was kindled. However, I was unable to learn much. It was not possible to have a serious discussion with my father, since I did not speak any Chinese. My father understood all the three major languages spoken in Sri Lanka—Sinhala, Tamil, and English—to some extent, but it was very difficult to comprehend what he said in any of them.

Years went by, and my husband and I moved to the United States in the late 1970s. There I found myself among many more Chinese. Like me, some of them did not speak any Chinese. Unlike me, they did not seem bothered by it. They moved around as freely as everyone else, and nobody looked at them as if they were strangers. Seeing this made a big difference to me. I felt a sense of relief and independence. Like many other foreigners, I spoke English with an accent, but it was not a big problem, since my English was grammatical.

Nevertheless, my identity as a Sri Lankan was still confusing, not only to Sri Lankans but also to others who thought Sri Lankans were people with dark skin and sharp South Indian features. I surprised people when I introduced myself as a Sri Lankan: I had Chinese looks and my husband's Spanish/Portuguese-sounding family name, to which I had added my own Chinese surname, although I spoke neither Chinese nor Spanish.[5] On the other hand, I not only spoke Sinhala and Tamil well, but I also taught these languages at Cornell University. Some Sri Lankans in the States would widen their eyes and wrinkle their foreheads in puzzlement when I spoke with them in Sinhala or Tamil.

I let people guess my nationality when they asked me where I was from. Most of the time they took me to be a Chinese, Japanese, or Filipino—but never Sri Lankan. In some way, it made me feel sad, because it reminded me of the feeling of rejection I had experienced in Sri Lanka in the past, but it also gave me an opportunity to view the issue of ethnic identity in a broader perspective.

In 1985, just when I was planning to go to Sri Lanka and get all the details from my father about his family in China, he suddenly passed away. All I could find among his belongings was an envelope addressed to him, with a Chinese return address. I followed up from there. It turned out to be the address of his daughter in China. I asked one of my Chinese colleagues at Cornell to write a letter for me in Chinese, informing my Chinese half sister about my father's death. To my surprise, and also my joy, I received an immediate response from her.

From that time, I began to contemplate visiting China to meet her and her family. At around the same time, I had begun compiling information about the Chinese community in Sri Lanka. For this reason as well, I felt a great need to visit China, especially Shandong, where most of the Chinese in Sri Lanka originated. After some hesitation and anxiety about visiting a country that was unknown to me, and whose language I did not speak, I finally set off to China on Christmas Eve 1992. It occurred to me that this was not the most appropriate time for my first visit there; it was winter and very cold, but with my various teaching commitments it was the only possible time.

It was a long, tiring journey from Ithaca, New York, to Shanghai. By the time I landed I was exhausted, but I was also excited by the fact that I had arrived in a great country. I couldn't believe that I was really in China. As previously arranged, my nephews (my half sister's two sons) were waiting for me there, holding up a big nameplate with my totally non-Chinese name on it. They were to escort me from Shanghai by train to the town of Changyi in Shandong, where my Chinese sister lives. My younger nephew could speak a little English with the help of a dictionary he carried with him. The older one did not know any English other than yes or no. Our first meeting was rather restrained, perhaps because of the language barrier, but I wondered if there was more to it than that. Shaking hands with my nephews did not feel right. But I could not embrace them, as I would do with my sister's boys in Sri Lanka. My Chinese nephews were grown men, practically my age. However, we established initial contact, then got into a taxi and drove a long distance to a somewhat run-down hotel in which my nephews had reserved a room for me to spend the night.

From the moment I met my nephews, I had had a premonition that things were not going to be easy. And the frustrations surfaced almost immediately. The hotel we checked into did not have any heating, and hot water was available only for a few hours each day. Even though I suggested that we move to a better hotel and said that I would pay for it, my nephews refused to do so. It was not clear whether they were trying to save me money or simply did not want to bother; they did not explain.

Furthermore, while my understanding had been that we would spend one more day in Shanghai sightseeing, and then head to Changyi, to my surprise, my nephews had planned a longer stay in the city. It turned out that the families of two of my father's brothers lived in Shanghai, and my nephews had arranged for me to visit them. My father had never mentioned that he had any brothers, and I felt very uneasy about visiting them. I had not brought enough gifts for all of them. Finally, I simply pulled out all the presents I had and asked my nephews to sort out what to give to whom. I was embarrassed that those gifts were not substantial.

Next, confusion arose over the issue of train tickets. Although I had specifically told them before I left the States to buy the train tickets in advance, they had not done so, and they did not even tell me about it. Even with my Shanghai cousin's help it would take two days to get tickets. Finally, I called the American consulate for advice and managed to purchase tickets for the same day, at three times the advance booking price. Then, when we got to the station, I had a feeling that we would have to go to a special platform since we had special tickets. I told my nephew that we should find that platform; he did not take any notice of me. We went up and down the stairs with all our luggage for about twenty minutes before we found the right platform.

What struck me specifically at that point was the my nephew's reluctance to listen to me. I first assumed that it was because of the strange situation we were in, or perhaps because he did not properly understand what I was saying. However, as time went by, I noticed a general reluctance in men to take orders from women. Also, it became clear that I was expected to follow their instructions, since it was their country. I was not only the woman but also the foreigner, so they acted as if only they knew what was right and good for me.

After a twenty-two-hour train trip and an hour's drive, we finally arrived at my sister's house in Changyi at about nine o'clock in the evening. She was waiting there to welcome me, along with her husband, four of her sons, and some other relatives. My nephew introduced me to everyone. I turned to my sister. This was the moment that I had been waiting for, but I found myself uncertain of what to do next. I really wanted to hug her, but I was not sure if it was the right thing to do. Since I was the guest, I waited for a clue, at least a stretch of hand, but I did not see my sister moving to touch me. She simply smiled, nodded her head, and said something again and again to her son. I later gathered that she was telling us to sit down and relax, and have dinner. She thought that we would be very tired after a long trip. With my nephew's help with translating, I was able to exchange greetings and tell her how anxiously I had waited all these years for this moment. My sister replied that she did not see our father again since he had left her as a baby, but at least now she had gotten a chance to see me. Then she changed the subject to ask about my mother and sister in Sri Lanka. I gathered that she was not prepared for a detailed discussion about our father at this point.

My sister's place was a simple, two-bedroom flat in an apartment complex with basic amenities, but no hot running water. The place was warm enough and equipped with a television and the necessary furniture. As with many other working-class Chinese in the area, their housing was subsidized, and they had a bicycle for each member of the family. They ate and drank well. After a satisfying dinner, we spent some time talking more about our father and my family back in Sri Lanka. I expected there to be a lot of emotion as we started to talk about our father, but I did not see my sister express any particular feelings. She did not even remember him. That would make it hard to think about him with any emotion, I suppose. On the other hand, I thought, her lack of expression might be because, having been brought up in hardship, war, poverty, famine, and so forth, the Chinese in general may have learned to control their emotions.

I had to remind myself all the time that I had no right to pass any judgment on my relatives, since I had no understanding of the cultural context in which they were operating. Painfully conscious of this lack of understanding, I longed to be able to communicate more clearly and directly with my sister. This I attempted to do by trying to hire an interpreter who could better translate what I wanted to say to her during the five days I was to spend at her place. After many requests, a relative who had been introduced to me as my cousin brought a young woman who could understand and speak English fairly well—much better than my nephew. I felt very happy and spent time trying to find out about my sister's past and how she felt about our father and so on. The young woman was very helpful and seemed to be translating most of what I said to her, but I did not feel that my sister was giving me complete answers. Sometimes her response was simply, "It's all over now" or "There's no use talking about it," or things to that effect. Finally, I stopped pushing her any further.

I wanted the interpreter to accompany us the next day when we were to go sightseeing and shopping, and I offered to pay her for her time. This did not go down well with my sister or the others. Although the young woman at first agreed to return the next day, she backed off after a while, saying that she had to go to work. I was trying to understand the reason for her reaction. The only thing I could think of was that my relatives did not want to share family information with an outsider. Perhaps my nephew was also offended by my preference for the interpreter's English skills over his. I also suspected that it was not customary to pay someone for a favor like this, and therefore one could not ask her to do too much. I greatly regretted not having been able to learn Chinese as a child. One's ethnic identity is truly measured by one's language skills, more than by anything else, I thought.

During my first day at my sister's place, my cousin wanted to show me the shoe factory of which he was the manager. The factory also made winter coats, dolls, household linens, and other such items for export. Although my cousin held a good position, I realized that he had no intention of working much longer there. He planned to start his own export business, and he asked me if I could find some business contacts in America for him. He gave me a whole stack of photographs of all the products his factory made, as well as samples such as bedroom slippers. I did not think the quality of the products was very high. So far, they were exporting to places such as Russia and other Eastern European countries. I said that I would explore some possibilities. I also told him that my husband and I are typical academics and did not have any connections with the business world. I did not want to give him any false hopes.

My activities during the next few days were limited by the language barrier. I was not allowed to go out of the house alone; my relatives feared that I would get lost. However, my nephew had to go to work some mornings, so he was not always free to be with me. One day, despite several denials of my request to go out, I just left the house and walked to the nearby market to purchase some fruit. It only took me about half an hour to come back, but by that time, my sister's husband and the youngest nephew both had gone in search of me on their bicycles. They returned about an hour later and found me home. We all had a good laugh.

The high point of my journey to Changyi was my visit to Lin Jia Zhuang ("Lin family village"), my father's ancestral village, which was named after my father's family. My father's first wife was still living there. She had refused to move to the city to live with my sister, because she wanted to live in her own place. I was warned that she was mentally unstable and that therefore I should not reveal our father's death to her. She lived in a single room with no electricity or running water. My nephew told me that she had cut the electric wires off because she does not like electric lights. She was wearing at least five or six layers of clothing and was still was very active in her late eighties. She was still hoping that my father would return to her one day. I had to pretend that he was alive, but very ill and therefore unable to travel. I told her that I had been sent in his place. She was the only one who showed any emotions about the whole issue. She cried out and started reproaching my father for leaving her and not coming back. I had to explain that my father had had a very difficult life in Sri Lanka, being ill most of the time, and had never been able to save enough money to return.

I was told that my father's ancestors had settled down in this village in 1543. The genealogy had been maintained for generations. While I was visiting the village, everyone who had the family name Lin tried to approach me. The village headman, who was a Lin himself, brought me twelve long sheets of thick paper on which the Lin genealogy was documented. It was amazing to see how proud my relatives appeared to be about their ancestry. They repeatedly told me that the character for the name Lin was a very rare one. They claimed that this clan descended from aristocracy. It was also true that I could not find the special Chinese character that depicted this name Lin in many ordinary dictionaries. Only a few people were able to recognize it. When I was wondering how to get copies of these documents, my relatives hung those sheets up on the wall in a row and asked me to photograph them. What a great idea, I thought.

The visit to my ancestral village ended after a lunch with the families of several close cousins and a discussion with them about my father's life in China. I asked many questions, and it seemed that I received detailed responses. However, my nephew's translations were very short. It appeared that he did some gatekeeping, choosing what he thought was important and leaving out the rest. This took most of the fun out of the discussions. One of the older relatives was able to tell me about the hardships they faced during the war. He said that my father's family had all been farmers and had many rice fields, but that during the Japanese invasion they had been forced to abandon the land. He also said that most men, including my father, had had to do many different things to survive. At one time, my father had become a baker. He showed me a sample of one of those old loaves they used to eat during the war. Nothing brought enough income, and, finally, he said, my father decided to emigrate. I was saddened at the thought of my sister's mother—what a life she had spent separated from her husband for many long years, still believing that he was alive. All I could do was to compensate her with a considerable sum of money. She happily accepted what I gave her. After some photo sessions, we left my ancestral village.

My next problem arose over changing my traveler's checks into Chinese *yuan*. I had taken almost all my money in the form of traveler's checks, something my relatives were not familiar with. There was no bank in their town that could cash the checks, and we had to make a trip to a bank in a nearby town. My nephew expressed annoyance that I had not brought U.S. dollars with me. He told me that he could have gotten a considerably higher value for my dollars on the black market than for traveler's checks exchanged through a bank. I vaguely remembered that, in his letters, he had asked me to bring about four to five thousand dollars. I did not have that kind of money. I had only brought a little more than two thousand dollars in total.

The next task was to take my sister's family, my cousin's family, and other close relatives in town out to a restaurant for a meal. It made sense for me to celebrate with them. It was New Year's Eve, and I would be leaving them in less than a week to catch my return flight from Beijing. My nephew, as I expected, selected the dinner guests; altogether there were about twenty people. All went well until the end of the dinner, when I made the big blunder of trying to pay the bill. It was obvious that it was my treat to them, and I thought they would be proud of that, but for some reason they did not like my involvement in settling the bill. My nephew told me to settle the account at home and not at the restaurant. I must have hurt their pride; the custom was perhaps for them to treat me, the foreigner and the guest. My nephew's reluctance to let me engage in any monetary transactions in restaurants, shops, or in any other place became more apparent as we did more things together. It gradually became a pattern that he would pay for things that I bought for myself in shops, and I would settle accounts with him later.

After some days of sightseeing, the day came for my departure to Beijing. I would not be going alone. My sister and her two sons were to accompany me for the three days I was to spend there before leaving the country. At the train station, I said good-bye to the rest of the family. I did not know how a Chinese person would handle such an occasion. I wanted to say something gratifying and hug them good-bye. I particularly wanted to show my gratitude to the wife of my oldest nephew, who had been very helpful in finding things for me in town. I deliberated for a while before deciding that, whatever the Chinese custom was, I didn't care—I hugged her good-bye. She stiffened a little, but tears rose in her eyes. She muttered something in Chinese that I did not understand. My cousin had also come to say his farewells and to give me several of his business cards to remind me of his business deals.

With my cousin's help, in Beijing we had accommodation arranged in a subsidized hotel for government officials. Compared to the hotel I had stayed at in Shanghai, this hotel was a blessing. However, the employees at the desk and the other staff could not speak one word of English. My nephew was reluctant to ask them for any information about the sights that we wanted to see in Beijing. I could not understand this, since it was their first time in Beijing as well. My nephew said that he knew how to get to places, and there was no need to ask at the desk. His pride would not let him show others his lack of knowledge about things. I knew that things were going to be difficult, and I suggested that we move to another hotel where they catered to tourists, but as usual my request was ignored.

The next day, I arranged to meet a professor in overseas Chinese studies at Beijing University whom I had met at a conference in California. Fortunately, he could speak English and also had a phone in his house. My sister and the two nephews also came with me to meet him. For the first time since I had arrived in China, I was able to have a serious conversation with someone. I arranged to see him again the next day, to be introduced to scholars at the Institute of Overseas Chinese Studies. Since I had the address of the place and the directions to the institute with me, I could go by myself. I told my sister and her sons to go have some fun, because this meeting would be very boring for them. My nephew was not very happy about it. He said that I would get lost and insisted on accompanying me. I was thankful for his concern, but this time I did not let him get his way. After the meeting, I was also able do the necessary shopping and get back to the hotel safely. I could see the looks of surprise and relief on the faces of my relatives.

Our great expedition to the Great Wall came next.[6] The taxi we hired broke down halfway there. After waiting for about an hour and a half in the cold for a spare taxi to come, we finally decided to take another taxi. However, we had to close the deal with the original taxi driver. I suggested that we pay him only a portion of the original fee, since he had not completed the journey as promised, but my nephew started to argue against my suggestion. I was really annoyed to see him not defending me in a situation like this, but arguing for the driver. Was it a patriotic thing to do, to defend his fellow countryman against the exploitation of a foreigner? I suddenly remembered what he had said to me in Shanghai, when I was worried about leaving the hotel room unlocked. He said that this was China, and in his country, people do not steal. By the time we got to the Great Wall, it was fairly late. It was foggy, and we could not climb very far or take any good photographs. Despite all the disappointments, I was still happy and amazed to have seen it.

On our last day in Beijing, the question arose of what to see. The Summer Palace was a major attraction, but there did not seem to be much use in going there in winter.[7] I suggested that at least we should go to a nearby museum or a zoo, but that idea was not agreeable to the rest. I nearly lost my patience at that point. Finally, it was decided that we would go to the Summer Palace after all. It was a long journey, and we had to change buses twice to get there. I could not stop my tears while in the bus. It was difficult to enjoy anything in the snow. When we got back to the hotel that night, I was again close to tears. I wanted so much to share how I felt with my sister, but I was unable to communicate anything to her. I cried aloud, and for the first time I saw my sister crying as well. I felt a deep sense of connection.

The next morning, I asked my nephew to sit with me and to translate everything I wanted to say to my sister. I wanted to explain to her how I had felt about the trip—that it had been a difficult one for me, and that I wanted to apologize if I had in any way hurt her feelings. However, through our conversation, I realized that my message was not getting across in the way I had intended. I confronted my nephew and asked if he had told her exactly what I had said to him. He finally said that it was not so important for his mother to know everything. Frustrated, I decided that I would later get a friend to write her a letter in Chinese, telling her everything I wished to express.

There were numerous communication failures, culture clashes, and misunderstandings between my relatives and me during the two weeks I spent in China, and I have related only a few of them. It would have been much easier if I could have clearly communicated to them what

I expected from my visit, but I felt that it was not customary to do so. Similarly, I had no clear knowledge of what my sister and her family expected of me. I began to suspect that my relatives were disappointed in me. I tried hard to read their minds. Perhaps they had expected a rich relative who could buy them all expensive gifts, fly them to various places, and invite them to America. I was not that rich relative they had looked forward to meeting. Also, I was not the Chinese person that they had perhaps thought that I would be. Maybe most of the misunderstandings could have been avoided if I had only been able to speak Chinese. I am sure that this whole experience was as difficult for them as it had been for me. I must have shattered their conscious or unconscious expectations.

The day of departure finally arrived. By this time, my luggage was very heavy. I had many unwanted, bulky gifts that my relatives had forced on me at various places. One was a large calendar with scenes from China. Another was a heavy clay pot. Every time I admired something in a house, somebody presented me with a replica of that item. That's how I ended up with an apple peeler, half a dozen tea flasks, and some Chinese vases. Finally, I stopped admiring anything. Anyway, with all this luggage, I did not realize that I was over the weight limit. I was under the impression that since my journey had originated from the United States, I was entitled to two pieces of luggage up to seventy kilos each. To my surprise, I discovered that the rule was different in China. The airport officials were extremely rude and would not listen to any explanations. Finally, after missing my first scheduled flight, I managed to get onto the second one, after paying a large sum for extra weight. Thus, my journey ended as it had begun, with frustration and misunderstandings.

I hugged my sister hard and said good-bye to all. I felt an inexplicable pain inside me. I am sure she must have felt the same; after all, we are of the same blood. She wanted me to give her regards to my husband, my mother, and my younger sister in Sri Lanka. Her face looked pale, sad, and helpless, but I myself was helpless to do anything about it. Finally, I waved at them until I disappeared through the long aisle and boarded the plane. Despite all the sadness, I also felt a sense of great relief. I was freed of the tension and frustration of being unable to express myself.

It has been several years now since I made that trip to see my sister. I had promised her that I would come back again one summer with my husband, to spend more time with her. However, that promise has not been realized, as my husband and I do not have the money or the time to travel together. In the meantime, my sister and I have maintained a correspondence. I got someone to write some of the letters in Chinese, while others I wrote in English. I have kept her informed of the major events in my life. I told her about my husband accepting an offer of employment in Singapore a year and a half after my trip to China, and about my mother's death the following year. She also knew about my heart bypass surgery at the end of 1995, and that my husband had quit his job in Singapore to return to the States to be with me.

I received very kind and heartwarming letters from my sister, particularly after she heard about my surgery. However, once I informed my relatives that my husband had returned to the United States for good and now has a permanent job here, I suddenly stopped hearing from them. I have been sending letters and cards regularly. I even wrote to my cousin asking why I have not received any responses from my sister. My letters certainly cannot have gotten lost along the way, because my sister's second son works at the local post office and letters are addressed to that post office. I know that my relatives had hopes that my husband and I would settle down in Singapore for good. My cousin in particular thought that he would be able to establish some business contacts there. None of these things happened, and I wonder now whether their silence has anything to do with my inability to fulfill any expectations they may have had in this regard.

Reflecting now on my trip to China, I still cannot pinpoint any one reason or goal for having made that journey to meet my relatives. Mostly it was probably just to satisfy my curiosity about my father's relatives and his home country. I suppose that I wanted to visually witness that they existed and find out more about them. I also felt that I had a duty to visit them at least once; since my father could not return to China,

I thought that I owed his family this visit. Perhaps by establishing contact with his family and his country, I was also trying to stay close to my father, which I had not been able to do as a child. Somewhere in my mind, I must have also hoped that in China I would be better accepted than in any other country; or at least I wanted to put that idea to the test. It was also true that if all went well with my trip, I was hoping to gather some information for my manuscript on the Chinese who left for Sri Lanka from Shandong province, including my father. I knew this was not feasible on a two-week trip, but I thought I could lay some groundwork for my project and go back later if necessary.

Those were my hopes and expectations. I don't think that I will ever know now what my sister and her family expected of me, since I fear that I have lost them. I now realize that I should not have assumed that we would get on easily or that there would be a special bond between us simply because they are my relatives. However, despite all the disappointments and setbacks, I continue to cherish and be proud of this brief encounter with my roots. I consider this trip to be one of my big accomplishments. It has brought me peace of mind and joy in some fashion and has also given me new insights in my search for ethnic identity, helping to free me from my previous obsession with attempting to define myself in any one particular way.

No Roots, Old Roots

GRAZIELLA HSU

"L LOMA O L LODI?" MY FATHER ASKED IN HIS FUNNY ITALIAN. "DO you mean L as in Rome or L as in London?" We struggled to keep a straight face, but for him the question was serious—the articulation of the letter R didn't come easily to his Chinese tongue, and he used these two town names to differentiate between R and L. On special occasions, when visits of family members from around the world happened to coincide, you might hear Danish, Italian, Chinese, English, and French spoken around the same coffee table. This was one hilarious consequence of distant and turbulent circumstances by which two people of very different backgrounds were brought together, in the last years of World War II. The two met in Italy, and they were my mother and my father.

My mother is herself a mixture of cultures. Her grandparents, living in czarist Russia, were of noble families. After revolution broke out in 1917 and their hardship had become unbearable, her family, like so many others, fled the country in search of a better life and became scattered

Graziella Hsu is presently employed at the dance and theater department of the University of Copenhagen, Denmark, where she teaches, writes, and lectures on Western modern dance and Chinese dance and culture.

all over Europe. My grandmother ended up in Florence, where she was to meet my grandfather, an Italian aristocrat and lieutenant, making a career in the cavalry. They married, and in 1922, after they had moved to Vienna, where my grandfather had been stationed, my mother was born. The marriage, however, did not last long. Having moved back to Italy, my grandparents separated when my mother was four. Leaving my mother with her father, Grandmother left to join her mother in France, where she was soon to build up a new family with another Russian refugee. My grandfather, who preferred gambling and women to parenthood, was not in a position to take proper care of my mother. So my mother's maternal grandfather, who was very fond of his granddaughter, offered to become her legal guardian, assuming responsibility for her and her education. He, too, was a divorcé, having remarried in Switzerland into another well-to-do exile Russian family. He was consequently in a position to send my mother to a few of the most exclusive boarding schools in Belgium and France. Unfortunately, these good times came to an end when he died in 1937, and my mother had to leave school. She went to Switzerland to live with her stepgrandmother to get an education that would enable her to support herself later. She was then fifteen. Her future looked secure, when new turmoil shattered the well-laid family plans. World War II broke out in 1939, and my mother, being an Italian citizen, was forced to give up the governess training she had planned and return to Italy. At seventeen, she was thus stranded in Milan, alone, with few prospects, and speaking only French, since her early childhood Italian had faded into oblivion.

My father was born in 1913, almost on the opposite side of the globe, in the mountainous area around the coastal city of Wenzhou, Zhejiang. He was the fifth child and third son of a Chinese farmer in possession of his land. At that time, it was customary for children to help their parents in the fields. But in his early childhood, my father contracted a mysterious illness, which from time to time would cause his legs to develop open, inflamed sores. During these outbursts, he was hardly able to walk. Finally, he was excused from field labor and put to study instead. At the age of seventeen, he had learned enough to be able to start teaching. He found himself a job as a teacher at a distant village school farther down the mountain. He moved in with an aunt who lived closer to his new job. For four years, he traveled back and forth to school as best he could, only visiting his parents during vacations. How he managed these journeys with his afflicted legs has always made me wonder. Today, I wonder even more.

For reasons still unclear to me, it was decided that my father should travel abroad. It was 1936, a time of unrest, with clashes between Nationalists and Communists and an imminent Japanese invasion.[1] Grandmother did not want to let go of my father, the sickly darling son of the family. She would cry and claim that if he went, they would never see each other again. Sadly, she was proved right. But father did leave, on a big ship to Europe. Apparently, his initial intention was to pay a visit to relatives in Portugal, but fate had other plans for him. He mysteriously disembarked in Genoa, Italy. He was to remain in that country for nearly twenty years, after which he moved on to his final home, Denmark.

I picture my father, a young peasant lad of twenty-three, in an unknown Italian town, with no knowledge of any foreign language or of Western society. How he managed to fend for himself in those difficult prewar days is a mystery I still need to investigate. I can only speculate, since the two of us never had really serious talks about his youth. At least, I wasn't ready to engage in a quality conversation until it was almost too late, which I regret immensely.

How my parents actually met my mother still keeps shrouded in secrecy. She only agrees to reveal that, after having spent Christmas 1942 together, they ended up living together a few months later. In December 1943, I was born. At the time, my father was doing business, buying and selling silk ties or any other commodity he was able to lay his hands on. We managed well. In June 1945, my first sister was born, as if in celebration of the end of the war.

A few years later, when it had become safer, we moved from our wartime refuge in the mountains of northern Piedmont to the town of Bologna, where my father set up a leather goods wholesale and retail business. For a long time he was quite successful, and we lived comfortably.[2] Unfortunately, times changed again, business went bad, and in the mid-fifties my father thought it was time to look elsewhere for a new start. Denmark came up: a good friend of my father's had opened a Chinese restaurant in Copenhagen, a novelty at the time, and he greatly needed a chef.[3] Always a passionate and meticulous cook, a discerning lover and master of his native southeastern cuisine, my father decided to give it a try.

He went ahead alone to check things out—once again an immigrant in an unknown society. This time, however, he was armed with a reasonable command of Italian and a few words of French (which didn't help much back in those days, but he was always very inventive in communicating with the "natives"!).

Having found Denmark a promising possibility, he came back for us. The family reunited, and a new home was set up. Two more children were born, my youngest sister in 1959, and, in 1962, my only brother, the long-hoped-for son. Jokingly, I would later refer to them as "the Danish team" and to me and my sister, born in Italy, as "the Italian team."

Father was always very fond of children, so, disappointed though he may have been that I, his firstborn, was only a girl and thus did not really count in terms of Chinese family lineage, he was truly delighted with me. He would proudly carry me around as a trophy. Later, when I started to show a will of my own, cracks began to appear in our relationship. My mother has described to me how, when I was two years old, with my legs far apart to keep my balance, I would stand in front of him, defiantly yelling, "No, no!" in his face. I know he only wanted the best for us children, as most parents do, but the question was what that was. To him it was a good education, preferably at the university (a doctor or lawyer in the family would have been nice), getting married and having children, and achieving some degree of wealth: in short, becoming a respected member of society. Good old values still prevailed, especially in China, and maybe even more among immigrants.

From early childhood I was indeed fond of reading and studying; however, when at the age of six I saw the film *The Red Shoes* and dance suddenly entered my world, I was captivated.[4] "I want to do that!" I told my mother. She promised that I would be allowed to take lessons, but of course my father would not hear of it: I was to study. And I was too young to put up a fight.

Many years later, having finished high school and well into my language studies at the Commercial University of Copenhagen, I decided to take up dancing anyway. At first, acutely aware of my "old age" (nineteen being over the hill to start a dance education), I just wanted to have a taste of it. But soon I came to realize that there was no going back. So, in spite of lagging years behind, I managed not only to become a professional dancer but also one of the pioneers who, in the early 1970s, were instrumental in establishing modern dance in Denmark.

My father never wanted to know about any of this. He never saw me dance. Once I had left the path he thought was right and strayed into the dubious world of the theater, he began to avoid speaking about my professional life. When he overheard a conversation, he would ignore it or sort of smile with embarrassment, maybe at his own failure, maybe at my insubordination. He was resigned.

My personal life did not please him either. Much against his will and under the threat of being banished forever from my family, I left home at the age of twenty-one, the moment I came of age, to live on my own. Later, I was engaged in some long-lasting relationships, but I never had children. And as to wealth, you can forget about that! But I had the life I wanted and would not have traded it for anything. However, weighed against his values, nothing was really right. Nothing, that is, until I at last decided to confront my parental heritage.

"Cin', cin', cinesin'!" "Ch'eeez, Ch'eeez, little Chineeese!" Giggling young faces popping up outside the windows of our shop in Bologna, chanting in one breath their cheeky message, and darting off immediately, as if expecting the big bad wolf to come chasing after them. But I didn't feel like the big bad wolf, only like a puzzled little girl: Was I different? This is the only incident I remember from my childhood days in Italy—one flash of insight, but leaving no scars.

In Denmark, where we arrived late in 1955, I remember my schoolmates being terribly proud of having a foreigner in their class. During my first year at school, I was treated almost like a queen. There was always a bunch of kids gathered around me in the schoolyard, trying to make me say a few sentences in Italian, repeating them to the best of their ability. Almost every day, a trail of schoolmates saw me home, all the while trying to teach me new words in Danish. That I was different made them feel special.

I was fortunate to grow up in the days when exotic looks were perceived as something out of the ordinary, and therefore interesting. I wasn't exposed to the pettiness and hostility that escalating xenophobia tends to evoke in people today, Danes included. Nevertheless, eventually I wished to make the transition from being an exotic phenomenon to being an ordinary member of my community. This wasn't the case with my father. He always stayed "Chinese" in his heart, regardless of the surrounding society. Genuinely curious, he was amiable and jocular when interacting with it, but he didn't really participate in it. His home, his family, and his Chinese community were the real world to him. He kept cherishing his old values, refusing to accept that the situation of his children should be any different. Or so I thought.

But I was born and raised in Europe, my mother was not Chinese, and I was growing up in a period when women were fighting for and gradually obtaining equal opportunities and the right to make their own choices. I wanted to be part of all that. Embracing the values of a modern Danish society seemed to require dissociating from my father's culture, which I perceived as incompatible with my new one.

What I failed to see then was that breaking out of the narrow realms of my family, in search of my own place in the larger context of society, wasn't merely a question of adopting a new ethnic identity, but of acquiring an identity at all—it was simply part of becoming an adult.

For years and years, I postponed confronting my paternal heritage. When my brother and my then-husband decided to start attending evening classes in Chinese, I thought it was a good idea—for them. As for me, I didn't even consider it. It became a thing between the two of them, and soon among the three of them, when my husband started being able to write to my father in his own language! A formal exchange of notes began taking place. For instance, "Jintian bu yong gei gou chi, ta chi le" (no need to feed the dog today, he has already eaten). A petition by my husband, the wording stretching his Chinese vocabulary to its limits, had been solemnly submitted and was now being returned, endorsed with Father's confirmation that the favor asked of him in our absence had been granted and carried out, Father's characters written large and clear to accommodate his inexperienced reader. Gradually, I started to find it somewhat embarrassing that my husband, a Dane, knew more of my father's language than I did. Maybe I was a little jealous, too, of the intimacy this seemed to create between them.

Still, it took me several years before I was finally ready to venture taking classes myself. When I did, for the second time in my life I was immediately captivated. I persuaded my very busy husband to make time for a trip to China, and we fixed on the following June, in 1989. The military crackdown on Tiananmen Square that month, followed by some sad upheavals in our personal life, eventually shattered our plans.[5] I ended up by going on my own the next year.

In the autumn of 1990, I set foot in China for the very first time. I felt my heart pounding with . . . joy! I was so excited. Underneath my rebellious feelings toward my father, and therefore toward anything Chinese, had been a current of suppressed and contradictory feelings that now began to surface. Confronted with the faces and the figures in the street, especially the old ones of my father's generation, I recognized the stamp of the indomitable will to cope and endure, to get the better of hardship and privations, to adjust without losing confidence in the future—all so familiar to me. Suddenly, I could see my father, see what he was made of, where he came from, why he was the way he was.

Back from China, I decided to study Chinese full-time, and I enrolled at the university. Growing more and more involved, I had no choice but to let go of my previous life. I was submerged in the study of my father's culture, finally surrendering to the heritage I had been rejecting for so long. The more I learned and understood, the more I could "read" my father. I had finally found the key to genuine communication between us.

At first, my father almost ridiculed me, incredulous at my new initiative. Now I wanted to study? A middle-aged woman? He was trying to conceal his delight, I think, to avoid losing face. But he was proud! I learned from my mother, and later from my family in China, that he would boast of me, of my being so clever, having read so many books, and writing such pretty Chinese characters! I am glad he lived at least long enough to see me get my B.A.

We still had our fights, but reconciliation came more easily now. Drawing on a deeper understanding, I would soon find a way to release tensions with a laugh and a hug. There is a little garden in front of our house—"our house," because circumstances led me to rent a part of my parents' house when I was thirty-five and greatly in need of a roof over my head. I stayed on, which was not a wise decision at the time, since my living there gave rise to more fights. But in the end, my decision justified itself. For instance, we started growing tomatoes together, on a very small scale. He would water them, I would eat them. And we would discuss the prospects for our crops, as farmers do. Sometimes he might remember a detail from back home in China. I listened. The roses and the trees were important too; he had in his blood a deep love for anything growing out of the earth.

Sadly, this newfound communication between us was short-lived. One bright, sunny Sunday morning, in February 1997, what I had dreaded for so long finally happened. My beloved father died. The mysterious illness of his childhood had made itself felt one last time. Two years earlier, he had suffered the amputation of one leg, which chained him to a wheelchair for the rest of his life—two years of physical and mental pain. He felt incomplete as a man and tormented by the fact that he was no longer master of his own life. Unable to work on the house or in the garden, as he had always loved to do, he felt useless and humiliated. He thought of himself as a burden.

My youngest sister and I were with him at the hospital almost to the end. He was unconscious, but since his condition was stable, we went home at four o'clock in the morning for a short rest. I had only just gone to bed when the phone call came. He had passed away. We all rushed to the hospital—the next of kin as well as the relatives who had come from abroad to pay visits to "grandpa" at the hospital, everyone in shock.

But there were practical things to be done, phone calls to be made— to my sister, living in Africa, and my brother, who had moved to Beijing, as well as the many others all over Europe. There were funeral arrangements to be made. We were still at the hospital when the question came up: What kind of funeral was it to be? My mother and youngest sister wanted it more "our" way, my Chinese relatives theirs. We were facing a clash of cultures. I was stuck in between. As the situation became emotional, I had to soothe and comfort both parties, convincing them in the end of the only solution possible: it couldn't be one or the other. It had to be a mixture of both.

We proceeded accordingly. Then, three days before the burial, my brother and sister arrived. My brother, who, out of concern for my father's illness, had planned to move back to Denmark to look after him. My sister, who hadn't seen Father for almost a year, but was expecting his visit within the next few months. Stricken with grief for not having been present when Father died, they turned to the funeral arrangements for solace. Plunging themselves in body and soul, whatever we had already decided they found now not to be enough, not good enough, not big enough. And, first of all, it *had* to be as Chinese a funeral as possible! Even if Father had said that he wanted to be buried in Denmark, surely he would be pleased if it were done in the proper Chinese way! Hurt at first by their disregard of our good intentions, but understanding perfectly how they felt, the three of us agreed to let them take over. In fact, I myself had always imagined my father's funeral to be Chinese. Five years earlier, anticipating the inevitable event, I had made Chinese funeral rites and ancestral cults the subject of my first paper at the university. Now my study became our manual.

Hectic days and nights of preparations followed, with relatives pouring in from abroad. Hardly any sleep, many tears. But also laughter, when forgotten memories suddenly came to mind.

Then it was all over. No more panic and confusion when an important detail had been found missing. No more last-minute phone calls or shopping. The calligraphed banners, the white bands around our arms as marks of mourning, the gift envelopes with coins for luck, father's portrait adorned with flowers for the procession, the solemn music selected in lonely perusal of my music library in the small hours of the funeral morning—all had fallen beautifully into place.

Daddy's grave lay covered in flowers. Food and drink had been provided for him, incense and paper money offered, and burning candles made it all look peaceful, almost cozy in the dark.

Before returning to Zimbabwe, my sister mentioned that she might want to go with me on my next trip to China in the autumn. There had been previous talk of her accompanying Father to see his relatives on a last visit, but this she would only have done for Father's sake, for she had never really been interested in going to China. Thirty years ago, having found what was then colonial Rhodesia the ideal setting for a new start, she and her late husband, an Italian-American, settled down there as farmers. Step by step, they built up a flourishing business. Feeling fulfilled and perfectly contented with her life, my sister never considered her Chinese heritage. Now that Father had died, she suddenly felt that she might like to go anyway—to China, but, first and foremost, to father's birthplace.

In November 1997, our trip became a reality. Although my sister was traveling halfway around the world via Singapore and I was returning from a visit to Sichuan, we both landed at Beijng airport twenty minutes apart, exactly as scheduled. A promising start! We were so excited that we needed a cigarette to calm us down before we were even able to leave the airport. To allow my sister to become acclimatized before the visit to our father's village in Zhejiang, I had arranged for an introductory week of sightseeing in the capital and a trip to Xi'an. The scheme served its purpose: intrigued by what she saw, my sister became genuinely interested.

Then came the day. Sitting in the airplane, feeling that we were embarking on an adventure, we were alert and impatient. I was keeping an eye on the changing landscape below. What would Father's homeland be like?

In Wenzhou airport, again a cigarette! Euphoria made us giggle and joke. People kept coming up to us, two foreigners standing in the rain, surrounded by luggage, laughing and smoking: Did we want a taxi? But we kept sending them away, as if spinning out the time could possibly build up our expectations any higher! Finally, we were ready and rushed to a cab, soon on our way to Wenzhou. It was Sunday, late afternoon. The streets looked deserted, a rare sight in China. The rain was pouring down, and everything appeared browny gray and wet. Since the town area seemed to start almost at the airport, we imagined that we would soon be there. We were scrutinizing the skyline, looking for the tall building we anticipated our hotel to be. But the journey took much longer than we thought it would, giving us ample opportunity to look at the mountains outskirting the town. Somewhere up there, our ancestral village was waiting for us.

Once in our rooms, we rushed to the windows to enjoy the panoramic view of Wenzhou. The situation called for a celebration! Comfortably seated, we performed our "instant coffee and cigarette" ritual, looking at each other in high spirits. We were now waiting for our brother, who was to join us on this memorable expedition. Delayed by a last-minute job in Beijing, he couldn't be expected for a few hours, but because his Mandarin was so much better than mine, since he had been living in the capital for several years now, we decided that we would wait for him to make the first phone call to our relatives.

Going to China had originally been my brother's way of trying to come to terms with his roots. Being the only son, he grew up under the pressure of Father's hopes that he would one day marry a Chinese girl and produce a son to carry on Father's line of descent. My brother's foremost ambition, however, was to pursue a career as a musician, postponing family commitments until later. This had caused him his share of fights with Father. For years he had kept Father at a distance, insisting on his right to live the way he wanted. But in the end, after long travels in Africa, he changed his views, and, conscious of Father's old age and constant yearning for a grandson, he decided to go to China to study the language and to look for a potential spouse, to at least try to fulfill the dream that, in Father's words to my brother, "will make my heart sing for joy, like a little bird in the sky."

As time passed, what was initially intended to be a limited visit gradually became extended. Getting more and more accustomed to his new life, making new friends, and finding unexpected work possibilities, my brother reverted to his true profession as a musician, making Father's old country his new home.

In spite of his good Mandarin, when my brother finally did arrive, we still had to ask the chambermaid for help, since it turned out that the elders of the family spoke no Mandarin, only the local dialect. We arranged with our relatives to meet the following day, the exact time to be agreed on in a later phone call. Merrily, chatting and arguing as sisters and brothers do, the three of us went out for our very first meal in Father's hometown.

Waking up early the next day, I was looking forward to one of those blissful, quiet mornings when, slowly recovering your senses, you prepare peacefully for the challenge of the day. But it was not meant to be. At 8:45, my dear sister phoned me to announce that a number of relatives had occupied her room! I could tell from her voice she was trying to conceal with a smile how irritated she really was. She too likes to spend her mornings in quiet privacy. A quick phone conference followed: I should stop whatever I was doing, grab some clothes, and come to her rescue (needless to say, she speaks no Chinese at all). We would call our brother and have him do his morning routines as fast as possible, while we, God knew how, would entertain our relatives. He would then take over, so the two of us could get washed and ready to join everybody in the lounge, where proper introductions could take place. Roger and out. As soon as I could, I rushed into my sister's room, a dressing gown over my pajamas, only to find my sister in a similar outfit. Our relatives, of course, were nicely dressed. This was not at all the family reunion we had envisioned!

Well, the plan almost worked. When I was trying to sneak back to my room unseen—my brother having already set out for the lounge and my sister enjoying the shower she had rightfully earned—I was left the prey of a fresh contingent of impeccably dressed family members. Fortunately, one of them was an "overseas" cousin back home from France on a visit to his parents. Communicating with him in his new language, eventually I was able to point them in the right direction.

From the point of view of our relatives, why waste time making formal appointments? We would only be there for such a short time. Since our initial phone call, they had been busy calling one another to spread the news of our arrival (we had not been able to notify them of the exact time of our visit in advance). So, naturally, everybody was eager to meet us at last, having been waiting for this moment for so many years. In fact, they had been expecting us to visit them with my father, but unfortunately . . .

The three people in my sister's room were the eldest son of Father's elder brother and the eldest son of Father's youngest sister, accompanied by his teenage daughter. Fortunately, the daughter had learned

Mandarin in school, and she was appointed family interpreter. My sister and I had brought some photos of my mother and my two sisters' six children. Second Son's son (Father was Third Son) seemed rather moved. I liked him at once. Although he didn't actually look like him, he reminded me of my father. Time and again, the way he smiled, his body language, would bring sudden memories to life.

Later in the lounge, more cousins, uncles, and aunts. It was not an easy job to figure out who was who. The rest of the day we spent eating together, walking through the town together, talking together as best we could, experiencing to the full what it was like to be a member of a large family—we who had grown up practically knowing only our parents for family. Long ago, in Italy, I recall my sister and me meeting our maternal grandfather once, our grandmother twice, and mother's half sister maybe a few times. But they were all brief encounters. Our little family began and ended with our parents.

The following day was to be the highlight of our trip. Pickup time was set at 8:00 A.M. in the foyer of our hotel. Already a little wiser, I got up at 5:30. I wanted to make sure that I had enough time to myself to prepare for the big event. Surprisingly, the party was not gathered and ready until 8:30.

We walked to the nearest bus, which took us to the city terminal, where a rented bus was waiting for us. We started out with huge expectations. Food, drinks, and cigarettes had been brought along to last us the whole day. My sister and I were sitting by the window, our noses glued to the window pane, afraid that we might miss something. The town gradually changed into open country, and soon we were making our way up into the mountains. We followed a river, and everything became greener, wilder. As we came closer, we noticed clusters of white, horseshoe-shaped things scattered on the mountain slopes. Farther up, we passed through a number of little villages, where we would stop to pick up yet another relative. Each time, it meant a new round of introductions, chatting, and cigarettes. As we progressed, the road got narrower and narrower, until we reached a small bridge over what had now become a mountain stream far below us. We had to cross it to continue our journey around the other slope. However, the road there was merely a path and clearly too narrow for our bus to negotiate it safely: we had to get off. Our relatives, a dozen or more by now, most of them our age or older, did not mind walking or carrying our provisions the rest of the way, but they doubted that city people like us would be able to cope on foot. Again, my "French" cousin, a modern businessman, helped us out. Having brought his mobile telephone, he was able to procure an alternative: two tricycle-motorcars with a covered driver's seat in front of a three-sided box on two wheels, open at the back, handy for the transportation of pigs, crops, and merchandise— *and* humans, if they could manage not to slide out the back while climbing and bumping upward!

When the tricycles had taken us as far as they could, we had to climb the last steep bit on foot, under the careful surveillance of our relatives, who would rush to our rescue as soon as my sister or I made the slightest false step. Finally, we reached the first destination of our sightseeing tour, my grandfather's tomb.

It was a major concern of my father's that proper tombs should be erected for both his father and his grandfather. He lived only long enough to see the first one completed—and then only on video. Over the years, several suggestions and sketches had been sent back and forth between China and Denmark, since my father was regarded as the head of our family clan. He had kept rejecting them and demanding other solutions until he finally approved of one.

Now we stood there, awed by the fruit of his efforts. It was one of those white horseshoe-shaped structures we had noticed on our way. It was huge. It looked like a three-storied house lying down: three one-and-a-half-meter-high steps leading to a miniature temple, under which grandfather was buried. Below him lay his eldest son, leaving an empty story further below for Eldest Son's eldest son when the time came. Everything was richly decorated, with traditional symbols and illustrations inspired by the classics. In front of the steps was a little courtyard, with stone table and stools to accommodate the living when they come to visit the dead on Qingming for the ritual tomb sweeping of spring, or on any other important day.[6] The horseshoe effect was created by a two-and-a-half-meter-tall wall surrounding the whole complex. It opened through a gate to the east and a window to the south.

When the noise of our demon-repelling fireworks had died away, the only sound you could hear was that of silence. What a peaceful place for Grandfather to spend the rest of eternity, lying comfortably on the mountain slope amid the gentle breeze of the trees, overlooking the fertile terraces below, the evidence of his hard work and that of earlier generations.

Having paid our respects to the dead, it was time to care for the living. People were beginning to feel hungry—it was time to move on. I was still spellbound by the magic of the tomb site, so my memory of what happened next is a little blurred. Since the planning of our excursion had been left to my brother and the others, my sister and I only needed to follow their instructions, happy to go anywhere we were taken, seeing and absorbing as much as possible. So when the sign was given, we just followed suit, having no idea what was next. All of a sudden, we were at the foot of a small group of stone houses, separated by narrow lanes and paths, some of them so close together they were almost touching. Could this possibly be? The very next moment, I realized that I was looking at the house where my father was born.

I was caught off guard and could not believe that we were really there. Because my brother had been there before, he was not as affected as my sister and I were. We were dashing from room to room, having doors and gates opened, things pointed out—we wanted to see it all. You could tell that the house hadn't been lived in for a long time. Apart from a few things stored away here and there, it looked empty and neglected.

While we were running about, our relatives had been busy in a neighbor's house, cooking and arranging the food we had brought. The main room in the front of the family house had now been cleared and a table set up with benches around. Here we had our meal, seated in the cool shadow of the house, looking at the calm scenery below, of white houses and green mountains, shimmering in the midday sun of a late November day. Had it been anything like this when Father lived here? I tried to imagine him as a young boy. What did he look like, what did he used to do? Would he sit in the stillness of the house, by the window, when everybody had gone to the fields, diligently working at his Chinese characters? He had become such a master of the brush, and his characters were so elegant! Or would he quietly observe his aunts cooking in the kitchen, learning recipes that would make the angels sing? Or would he rather squat in a corner of the martial arts room, making no sound, watching his grandfather doing his exercises? His grandfather was a tall, strong man, and when Father's legs were so bad he couldn't walk, grandfather would carry him around on his shoulders. Father always spoke of his grandfather with love and admiration. That was why he made the promise to build him a stately tomb, a promise that his own children will keep for him.

Once the feeling of being one big family had been established, our relatives became more daring. They began hinting at the possibility of me or my sister helping this or that young cousin to go abroad, looking after them or even adopting them. I wasn't at all surprised, because that's what my father had done so many times before. Like many other Chinese emigrants, he always felt the obligation to help his family back home, and as soon as he had been able to, even as a young tradesman in Italy, he had sent them whatever money he could spare. Later, in Denmark, when his financial situation had improved, he helped some of the young members of his clan to emigrate and set up their own businesses in different countries. As the contributions to our relatives in China multiplied, their welfare, as well as that of their community, improved perceptibly. This was how my father earned his position as benefactor and head of his clan.

We had to disappoint them. Apart from our lack of aspiration to become "mothers," we had to explain how difficult it had become in our countries to get a permit to live there: unemployment, exploding numbers of fugitives and immigrants, and unstable political situations had caused restrictions almost everywhere.[7] We could see their hopes fade. Most of them gave up mentioning it; others were more tenacious, but eventually, they became resigned too. And thinking about it, who can blame them for trying? They just wanted what they thought was the best for their children.

The last few days were packed with family visits and family feasts. Some relatives only made it at the very last minute, just in time to say hello and good-bye. Before we knew it, we were waiting for a family friend to take us to the airport. Sitting there, in the hotel lobby, spending our last few hours together, we were wrapped in an atmosphere of mutual concern and affection, mixed with a little sadness. I, for one, would have liked to talk much more with the cousin I had grown particularly fond of, but language was still a hindrance. Sitting close to each other and patting each other's hands was all we could do.

It was time to leave. Hugs and handshakes all around—"We'll be back!"—and the car was on its way. We looked out of the rear window to catch a last glimpse of our family. It was raining again. They were moving slowly, keeping close together, huddling under one or two umbrellas, talking a little, their eyes turned in our direction. Soon we couldn't see them any longer.

On the plane, my sister and I didn't talk much. We were exhausted, but brimming with emotions and memories to last us a lifetime. We sat, keeping a little to ourselves, still savoring the experiences of the last few days, so far from the exuberant mood of four days earlier.

Yet another winter has passed. Through the window of my study, I see the old apple tree bursting with buds—flowers sprouting up from the soil everywhere. Spring is here at last, and soon it will be time to grow tomatoes again. Recently, my mother found an envelope with old photographs of relatives in China. Knowing of the book I am planning to write, she gave them to me. It is not an easy job to figure out who is who. We had such brief encounters. But they linked me to my father's world.

Growing up without belonging to a single culture, I have had a less than well-defined sense of identity during most of my life. Depending on circumstances, I have felt predominantly Italian, Danish, Russian, Scandinavian, and sometimes even Chinese. I perceived myself as lucky to be able to draw from so many cultural sources, and I refused to take sides in the ongoing competition for cultural supremacy within myself. I was a true citizen of the world.

The encounter with my paternal motherland reshaped this self-perception. Now I realized that to become a whole person, I still had to integrate one very important part of my cultural makeup, my Chinese heritage. Once I had recognized how much my thoughts and feelings were influenced by it, I came to understand myself better, and all the other bits of my cultural identity fell into place.

Before, I used to say, "My father is Chinese"; now I say, "I am half Chinese." And I say it with pride, with a sense of belonging to a great culture which—although I may not always agree with it—I have come to love and admire.

My roots are no longer blowing in the wind. Their long-time search for fertile earth to sink into has finally come to an end.

My Father's Land

MEILIN CHING

MY BACKGROUND HAS NEVER STRUCK ME AS PARTICULARLY unusual. It was only when people inquired that I wondered about it. Whenever anybody asked me where I was from, I was trained by my mother to answer: "I'm half Chinese and half Colombian." This same question-and-answer routine continues today, and, since I moved to Hong Kong a few years ago, it has had a further addition of, "But I grew up in the States." I am occasionally tempted to simply supply a one-word answer such as "Chinese" or "Colombian" or "American" but decide against it, since it would only confuse the interrogator even more.

My early childhood in the inner city of Boston was an extremely rich and fulfilling experience. I had friends of many different backgrounds: along with Caucasian Americans, there were blacks and some Latinos. There was a feeling of belonging among these people. Maybe I was too young to know what race meant, or perhaps it was because we were living among so many minorities that one's racial background didn't really seem to matter. Little did I know just how deep discrimination ran. I had no idea that this was a tense period in America, when bus-

Meilin Ching is a business development assistant with the Canadian consulate in Boston. She returned to the United States after spending six years in Hong Kong and mainland China.

ing of black students to white neighborhoods was being introduced to fierce opposition. The Vietnam War was raging on somewhere far away, beyond my imagination.

When I was eight, we moved from the multicultural inner city to the bland suburbs of white America. It was one step up the ladder, I suppose, but I recall feeling saddened by the dramatic change. Although the suburbs were considered better for many reasons, people's ideas and points of view appeared narrower there than where I had come from. I became aware of my physical differences for the first time in my life and felt the shame of thinking that I didn't quite fit in. The neighborhood was made up of mostly Italian and Irish Americans. With our Asian features and names, my siblings and I clearly stood out at school. Mostly, everyone was kind: the teachers, other classmates, and neighbors, but in every class there would always be the loudmouthed bully who would pick on the misfits for everyone to laugh at. One such bully would sit behind me and call out, "Hey, chicken wing, sweet and sour pork, egg roll . . ." They were all horrible jokes, making me into a hermitlike creature.

I remember crying in bed and cursing God for making me look as I did; if I had been born with blonde hair and blue eyes, surely everything would have been fine. I was sure that I'd get the top grades, be the most popular, and have the most friends. I wanted to scream to the world that I wasn't Chinese really, I was only half. And besides, my mother looked white. However, my name and the way I looked did not reveal my Colombian side—it made me Chinese, and I hated it. Looking back on all those painful memories, I regret that I could have ever denied my own heritage, to have allowed those silly souls to make my youth so miserable.

Most of those bullies never succeeded in getting properly educated and in moving forward in life. I ran into one just before high school graduation. He had grown into a thug with a drinking problem. He didn't seem to be very happy and actually went out of his way to say hello to me. I gave him an abrupt "hi" and walked away, deriving a certain amount of pleasure out of feeling that I was perhaps better off than he. I was going to college and to see the world outside my hometown. I had ambitions and plans for my life, whereas it seemed to me that his had just about ended. Who was the misfit here?

And so it was my Chinese appearance that would get the most attention, but ironically it was my lack of feeling for whatever it meant to be Chinese that eventually led me to Asia. I was searching for the one aspect of my background that I knew so little about. My brother and sister and I were always being asked if we could speak or read Chinese. Had we ever visited China? I sensed disappointment and puzzlement upon my usual answer of no. I knew absolutely no Chinese and very little about China. It was my responsibility to find out. I speculated about what it would be like to live in a place where not so much focus was placed on my appearance—a land where I would naturally blend in with the majority, a place where I believed I would feel more at home. I thought it would have to be somewhere in Asia.

Once my mother came home after a parent-teacher meeting and asked my little brother why he had told his first grade teacher that he had been to China—not only that, but that we had all been there many, many times. Why had he lied? He said with a straight face that of course we had, we went there every time we went to buy the large sacks of rice to fill up the rice barrel and to buy Chinese vegetables and spices not found in the local Stop 'n' Shop supermarket. He was referring to Chinatown and had easily become confused, believing that this was indeed China.

Chinatown was a mysterious place, especially seen through a child's eyes. Although it only comprised a few blocks, going there was really like stepping into another world. There were different sights, sounds, and smells. People there looked a little bit like me. It was where my father seemed to be the most comfortable, chatting with passersby in his native Cantonese, specifically in the Toisanese dialect.[1] My parents would take us there every year to celebrate the Chinese New Year and the Mid-Autumn Festival.[2] These were festive occasions with decorated streets and youths clanging rhythmically on large hollow drums and gongs. The colorful dragon dancing up and down to the flowing beat, and the deafening bursts of firecrackers, would further quicken the pounding of my heart.

For Chinese New Year, my father would bring home a hefty case of enormous round oranges; they represented gold and the fortune that was sure to come our way. We would welcome the New Year like so many Chinese in China, and around the world, with a clean home, a large family dinner, and great expectations. It was a time when we—my brother, sister, and I—were strictly forbidden to fight. We were also not allowed to shower on the first day, lest we wash away the good luck. This was not a problem, though, because we were also given money in a red packet *(lai see)*—something we eagerly looked forward to. These traditions and celebrations were all new to my mother, since she knew very little about China, her only connection to the culture being that she had married a Chinese man.

To me, everything Chinese was represented by my father; he was, after all, the Chinese parent. But paralleling my ignorance of the Chinese culture was the strangeness of never ever really being able to understand my father. He wasn't one to adapt entirely to living in the States, and some of his practices were atypical to those of mainstream Americans. My quest to find out what it means to be Chinese has also been a search to learn more about the man from whom I am descended and to understand what his life in China was like.

During my childhood I saw little of my father. He would come home late from work, when all of us were asleep, and get up after we'd gone off to school. We saw each other only over the weekend or on his occasional day off. Despite that, his position in the household was that of an emperor in his palace, maintaining constant control over his subjects, his wife and children. There was no chance for debate or argument, since he was "always right." We were constantly trying not to make him angry and to please him, but it was not easy. My brother and sister and I hold mixed feelings about our father; he was an austere man who was an extremely strict disciplinarian. He seldom opened up to us in talking about himself, his youth, or his birthplace. It almost seemed as if he wanted to forget about his past and keep everything covered up and shrouded in secrecy. His attitude was, and still is, very traditionally Chinese, and it seems that, even today, after so many years and so much distance and change, he is still living in premodern China.

Feeling much closer to my mother and her family, and well acquainted with this part of my background, there has never been a deficiency in my Colombian half. Many times, however, I have felt the emptiness of not knowing my Chinese relatives and more of the Chinese language. Because I look more Chinese than anything else and have a Chinese name, society almost expects me to behave in a certain Asian way or at least to be knowledgeable about these ways. Although people mean no harm, I occasionally feel pressured to be something that I am not.

There were, of course, other small sprinklings of Chinese culture that made their way into our household. My parents always eat with chopsticks, and my father regularly starts the day with tai chi exercises before reading the Chinese newspapers purchased in Chinatown. I am forever charmed by the sight of dumplings being made, since it brings back fond memories of my family seated at the kitchen table, taking part in the elaborate ceremony of preparing wontons by hand to make his famously delicious wonton soup.

But not all the food that he prepared was to our taste. Once my father brought home from Chinatown some very unusual-looking live birds. They lived on our porch for a week, and we became greatly attached to these new pets. Our companionship came to a sudden end when we returned from school one afternoon to find that the birds were no longer there. My father was cooking them in large pots over the stove, gleefully saying that tonight's soup would be yummy. Such events made me realize that we were no ordinary family on the block. After all, none of my classmates had to eat the so-called "delicacies" that we had from time to time. Years later, when I visited China, I realized it was an accepted practice to have live animals present before eating them, so one could be assured of the meat being fresh and probably also healthy.

We would call my mother at work, crying about this strange dish or the other that was for dinner. Other supposed delicacies—fortunately rare—were frogs and cow brain soup; the latter stank of dirty socks and strong medicine, and it permeated the house for days. My father would insist that we at least eat a few mouthfuls, but as soon as he got up to refill his rice bowl we would toss it onto my mother's plate. She sympathized with us and patiently tolerated my father's eccentricities.

There is an enormous difference in temperament between my parents. Because of this, there was always a marked change in our behavior when my father was home. My mother is a special friend to us all, but when my father is home, there is usually tension in the air. My mother was our ally when his expectations were too high and his rules too many. As teenagers we were not allowed to date or to go out to parties or to get phone calls from boys. My sister and I were forbidden to wear makeup and to dress up. These rules would have been fine if we had been living in a small village in China, but they didn't seem to make sense in the town I grew up in and the fashion-conscious high school I attended.

My mother understood our difficulties and would assist us when we wished to go out, behind my father's back. Although she meant to do well and to counterbalance my father's strictness, we were constantly getting mixed signals about what was correct. If my sister or I wanted to go to a party, we would strategically plan out the evening. My father would come home at around 8:00 or 9:00 P.M., by which time whoever had planned to go out would be long gone, all dressed up for a night of dancing and spending time with friends. He would naturally ask for the missing person, and my mother would casually reply that she was not feeling well and had gone to bed early. There would be pillows stuffed in the bed to make it look as if someone were sleeping there. This person would be let back in when my father was taking his evening shower or might just stay overnight at a friend's house. This was how we got around my father's rigorous rules.

To my sister's straight As, my father's response was always, "You should do better"; it was never good enough. He was trying to make us modest girls, and we were rarely commended for our accomplishments. He was constantly pointing out as examples the students who had come from China to study at Harvard and M.I.T., how plainly they dressed, but how intelligent and pure they were. I had an image of all Chinese as scholastically brilliant and moral. My father was quick to point out how bad Americans were: they drank too much alcohol, didn't study, and quickly drifted from their families. Later, when I first went to China, I remember feeling shocked at the sight of Chinese playing drinking games and getting very drunk on beer; I had grown up believing that Chinese didn't do such things. More recently, such undesirable vices as prostitution, corruption, and theft, which have been emerging along with China's booming economy, have further added to my disillusionment with my father's impossible ideals.

The languages spoken at home were English and Spanish—sadly, Chinese was put aside. It must have been difficult for my parents to include Chinese in the household conversations, since they communicated with each other in Spanish and my mother knew absolutely no Chinese. It was enough of a struggle just to learn English and to get by every day. My survival Chinese is based on the Mandarin I studied at university and from the little Cantonese I picked up while living in Hong Kong. I haven't found it easy, and I admire people who have learned to speak Chinese fluently. I eavesdrop on conversations in public settings, like buses, and although I can't understand most of what is said, I can usually identify a phrase or two. When locals instinctively address me in Chinese, whether it be a bank teller or someone asking for directions, I am reminded of my Asian appearance. Accepting the invitation to speak, I answer in disjointed Chinese, and a conversation usually arises. I gain a small amount of satisfaction for the bond achieved through such communication. At such times, I feel as Chinese as I could ever feel.

My cousins in Colombia joke about my father, saying that he is a person without a language. They say that he might have forgotten much of his Chinese because of limited use, his Spanish is very simple, and he was never able to learn English. Only my mother, brother, sister, and I can understand his words, his expressions, and forms of communication. After so many years together, we can guess what he is trying to say in his broken Spanish, when most other people are absolutely clueless. Whereas my mother learned English, my father was not able to. It was probably due to their personalities; while my mother is so friendly and talkative, he is cold and afraid of the world.

We would have to interpret for him on his errands. As children, it was hard for us to convey his meaning to strangers, especially when we didn't quite understand him ourselves. He would usually end up scolding us in his frustration, repeatedly saying that we were worthless and didn't know anything. However, sometimes his lack of English worked to our advantage. My brother and sister and I could talk about him even when he was in the same room. His pseudonym was "you know who" on those occasions.

As a child, my brother was not a very attentive student. He was a dreamer and an artist like my father. He would spend much of his time in class drawing when he should have been listening to the teacher. His first-grade teacher, Mrs. McGuire, didn't know what to do with him. She would repeatedly send him to the principal's office and complain to my mother. All this was in vain, since it made no difference to my brother. She realized that the only one who had the power to discipline my brother and to cause him to change his behavior would be my father. She insisted on having a meeting, after school, with my father. We were naturally very nervous and worried, since we always avoided getting my father cross. The dreaded day arrived; my brother, sister, and I were to accompany our father to school to meet with Mrs. McGuire.

My sister and I were to be the interpreters as usual. Since my father had no idea why he was there, he went with an open mind and a cheerful smile. On this particular day, he happened to be in good spirits. Mrs. McGuire began with, "I have called this special meeting to discuss the poor behavior of your son; he spends his time drawing, while I'm teaching." She continued, "And he never pays any attention." We carefully translated, "He's an excellent artist and student. Mrs. McGuire says she's happy to have him in her class." It was then that my sister and I realized the power that we held in translating. We would smooth out every negative utterance and soften it with positive words; to each comment, my father's smile grew. He began to pat my brother's head repeating: "Good boy, good boy." Mrs. McGuire became red in the face, and I guess she just gave up after that and couldn't wait for the school year to finish. Fortunately, this experience didn't seem to affect my brother's studies too greatly. Years later, he was able to receive a college degree in art and to earn his living as an artist.

When we were young adults, my parents treated us to a trip to China. This was in 1988, and it was the first time our family had traveled such a great distance, except for my father, of course. However, he had not returned to his homeland since leaving it thirty years earlier. We were to join a package tour for overseas Chinese, taking us to all the major cities of China. We traveled as lightly as possible and packed the most comfortable clothes: shorts, T-shirts, sport shoes—very basic attire. We dressed as if we were going to be roughing it, since we had heard stories of unsatisfactory hotels and service. We also didn't want to appear too ostentatious. At the time, China was in its early years of opening up to outside visitors. We were greatly humbled when we discovered that the tour provided accommodation at the most luxurious hotels in the area. They were splendidly decorated, with impeccable staff, and we felt very underdressed.

I fell in love with China on arrival. It seemed as if here was a place where I could fit in, where I could easily belong. Without opening my mouth, I could venture through tucked-away neighborhoods, not even receiving a second glance. I could bicycle through the crowded avenues and not be noticed. Although I was really a stranger, I felt a peacefulness within me that seemed so right. Looking back now, I wonder if I may have been just a little too naive in being swept away by the charms of an alien culture. Was the attraction there because I was part Chinese, or was it simply because I was on vacation and happened to be fond of the setting? We took romantic train journeys through the scenic countryside, glimpsing water buffalo and rice paddies, hearing the tinkling of bicycle bells, being charmed by the demureness of the young ladies in their pretty dresses. I was taken back to another time, before the age of large corporations, TV sitcoms, and fast food.

As for Hong Kong, although it was a sharp contrast to mainland China, being modern and full of skyscrapers, it was still able to maintain certain Chinese characteristics that captivated me as it had when I had first seen images of it in a Bruce Lee film. It was much more affluent and better organized than the mainland. The sight of double-decker buses, British post boxes, and portraits of Queen Elizabeth revealed that it was a place made up of several cultures. I was dazzled by the contrasts that Hong Kong offered. The bright neon lights in Chinese characters were not too far away from delicate vegetable fields in rural villages. All one had to do was jump on a ferry, bus, or train for an hour, and one could experience the other extreme: all the hustle of a big city and all the calm of a natural environment. Whereas China was strictly Chinese, Hong Kong was a mixture. At a dinner party there might be people from all over the world: along with Chinese and Britons, there could be French people, Filipinos, Africans, Indians, and of course, Eurasians. Being in the most international setting I had ever experienced, I once again felt as if I could belong here too, with so many people from different backgrounds

I did not know then that in the search for my roots I would later make Hong Kong my second home. Two and a half years after that initial introduction to this city, I returned. I came from Boston shortly after graduation, with a friend whose father had been living in Hong Kong for several years. My plan was to go to Taiwan to teach English while studying Mandarin, but a pleasurable stopover of two weeks in Hong Kong convinced me to return to it after briefly visiting Taiwan.

Now, the village that was my father's birthplace lies only a few hours away by bus from where I live. In the five years that I have been in Hong Kong, I have frequently thought of visiting it. Often I make plans to go and then cancel them at the last moment. I don't know where I would even begin, since I have little information to start with. My father had had no inclination to return there during our family trip, even though we were close by. Whenever I ask about it and announce that I will indeed go, he discourages me with, "Why do you want to go there?" and "To do what? It would be best if you didn't!" He claims that it would only be bothersome, because any living relatives would trouble me with demands for money.

During my first trip to China, and even now, I thought a lot about what my father might be like if he had never left. What might he be doing, and where might he be? His background had always been a mysterious puzzle that I have gradually tried to piece together. But the bits of information that I have collected still leave me with many more questions.

My father was born in the village of Toisan in the southern Chinese province of Guangdong. He must have come from a well-to-do background, since he attended a boarding school and lived in a large home in a period when China was very poor. My father once told us how one of his uncles had tried to flee from the Communists, carrying away with him heavy bars of gold. My father's father lived and worked in America for many years while my father was growing up, as was common in those days in their village. He had started off in California and had moved eastward to Ohio before settling in Massachusetts. My paternal grandfather would regularly send money back to his wife and children in China. He worked in Chinese restaurants, waiting on tables and laboring in hot kitchens. Undoubtedly, the money to keep my father in comfort came from my grandfather's hard work.

Chinese men employed in the United States at that time were not permitted to bring their families. They would be separated from their wives and children for many years. It was next to impossible for a Chinese person to go to the States even for a visit.[3] My maternal grandmother eventually died of cancer in Hong Kong, where she and my father had migrated after the Communist takeover. My grandfather had visited his family in Toisan, his hometown, three times before 1949, when the Communists came to power in China. When his wife died he could not manage to be there with her because he was very sick and had recently had one of his legs amputated.

With my grandfather's support, my father left Asia at the age of thirty-one, in the late 1950s. He was a handsome young artist, with big dreams of making it in America. It was for him, as for so many around the world, a promised land. He was leaving behind a poor Hong Kong for an entirely new life. Because it was very difficult for a Chinese man to immigrate directly from Asia to the States, the best route was through Central or South America. There was a Chinese man living on the coast of Colombia. For a fee of US$2,000 he would claim Chinese people interested in resettling in Colombia as his close relatives; my father was claimed as his nephew. This man must have alleged to have had quite a lot of relations, as most of the Chinese living today in Colombia, or who used it as a stop-off point to enter the States, have his last name, Ching. My father changed his family name from Yee to Ching, organized his traveling papers, paid the fee, and departed for Colombia.[4] The light at the end of the tunnel of this long journey was the reunification with a father he did not know and a sister twenty years older, settled with a family and living in Boston.

Things went amazingly well for my father in Colombia. As a Chinese artist, he was very much in demand, particularly among the rich, who appreciated and longed for culture. Examining old black-and-white snapshots of him in his glory days, before I was born, I am struck by how handsome and proud he looked, giving exhibitions of his artwork throughout Colombia, each of which was warmly received. Everyone was interested in this unique young man from far away. After spending a total of two years in different cities—Cartagena, Bogotá, and Cali—he ended up in Medellín, the second-largest city in Colombia. It was here that he would settle, meet my mother, and marry her five years later. My older sister and I were born in Medellín, a place that I would later regularly visit and that remains very dear to me.

My parents' meeting is a much-told story in our family. It took place in the main museum in downtown Medellín, El Museo de Zea, where my mother worked as an administrator and receptionist. Their contact started off as simple courtesy, which led to friendship; my mother would invite him home for dinners to meet her family. Whenever he visited, the neighbors would be called to take part in all the fun. He was probably the only Chinese person in Medellín at that time. He would cook wonderful Chinese dishes and teach them Chinese songs; they in return would teach him Spanish. He was an enchanting person, in a sociably comfortable environment.

I later discovered that my mother's family did not approve of my parents becoming romantically involved or of their eventual marriage. My grandfather did all he could to persuade his favorite daughter to assess the situation and to consider other suitors. After all, who was this foreign man ten years her senior? He was different, Chinese. He was fine as an acquaintance, but as a husband, and a father, who could know? What sort of a past did he have, and what were these plans of going to live in America and taking his daughter away? My grandfather gave my mother the opportunity to study in Spain for a year. This, he hoped, would be just what she needed to clear her head, become more worldly, and not think so much of this Chinese man. But it didn't work; my parents wrote to each other regularly. A year later it was my father who was the first to greet her when her ship docked in the port of Cartagena, and he accompanied her on the journey inland to Medellín.

After they married, they were accepted, and my grandfather was so pleased with his Amerasian grandchildren that he would openly say that we would be the most exceptional of all his grandchildren, speaking Spanish, English, and Chinese, being exposed to three very different cultures. Although my parents' courtship sounds romantic, their marriage always seemed a big struggle to me. They had many differences of opinion over how we should be raised.

In 1966, the year I was born, my parents moved to the United States, taking my older sister with them.[5] I was left in Colombia, in the care of my grandmother. One year later, when my parents had settled into their new environment somewhat, my mother returned for me. My brother was born in the autumn of 1968 in Boston, making him the only American-born person in my family.

Living in America was a reality that my parents were not prepared for. It was not easy adapting to a new land so far from home, where they knew neither the language nor the people. Like so many of the early immigrants to America, they were paving the way for a better life for the next generation. My parents had never worked very hard, until they moved to the States and had a family to sustain. Now they were to dedicate their lives to making it in America. In the early years, my father had to lower himself and work in a restaurant to earn more money. He would come home late at the end of a grueling shift to soak his swollen feet in Epsom salts and rest his weary body for a few hours. Meanwhile, my mother struggled with her studies and career as a social worker, in addition to bringing up three children, without the support and presence of her natal family.

I only have small bits of memories of my father's family. There was my paternal grandfather, whom we called Abuelito, meaning grandfather in Spanish, and my Auntie Got Yee and her children.[6] I hardly knew these Chinese cousins of mine, since they were several years older and always studying. Got Yee's husband had served in the U.S. Army during World War II. My very earliest memories of life were under Got Yee's roof; she would baby-sit us. A wiry Chinese lady with sparkling eyes and permed hair, she must have spoken to us in Chinese, but I can't remember if I ever answered in the same tongue. This contact only lasted for a couple of years, and then we stopped seeing Got Yee and her children, even though they lived so near to us, after an argument that led my father to cut off all communication with her. He claimed that she had stolen all my grandfather's money before putting him in a nursing home, but who will ever know?

Of Abuelito, my memories are of a pitiful-looking old Chinese man whose face would light up whenever he saw us. His two legs had been amputated because of arteriosclerosis, one just below the knee and the other entirely. He was living the rest of his life in an old folks' home. It was a sorrowful place smothered in disinfectant, which could not cover up the reek of sickness and old age. On entering the home, I would hold my breath as long I could. I couldn't understand how anyone could work in such a place, let alone live there. We would visit Abuelito, and although he was invited to live with us, he would always turn down the invitation, saying that it would be too much trouble. He would sit up in bed and chat in Chinese with my father, who would be seated beside him. My mother and Abuelito would politely communicate with nods and gestures. He was old and just waiting to die, which he did at the age of eighty. I was eleven at the time of his death, and it was at his funeral that my brother, sister, and I discovered a secret about my father's past that was so hard to believe.

At my grandfather's funeral and dinner we were reunited with Got Yee and the relatives we only saw on occasion. Two of them were people whose names we had heard mentioned before and whom we had come across at Got Yee's home in the past. We had believed them to be distantly related to us. However, on that day, they introduced us to their acquaintances as "my half sisters and half brother," which was rather confusing. It was in this way that we learned that my father had been married in China and had had five children from that marriage. He had only been a teenager at the time of his marriage, which had been arranged for him by his elders. By marrying my mother, he had disappointed and let down his family and his village. It was my grandfather who had seen to it that my father's Chinese family was not abandoned entirely, and who had assisted in bringing them all to North America. Most of them live in Vancouver, Canada. My father's first wife had contacted him and expected him to go back to her, but this had been futile. I once questioned my father about how it was possible to turn his back on his own children, but he always had an excuse for everything. His answer was that he had been too young at the time and that it had not been a marriage based on love.

My father seemed to me the worst hypocrite. He would lecture us all the time on how important it was for a family to be closely united, and yet he never showed us by example. I couldn't believe that he could completely ignore his own blood and be too stubborn to make peace with his sister and her family. He would tell us that China was the greatest country there was and that the States was unjust and bred low forms of society. We would retort, "Why don't you go back to China, then?" At this, his face would become serious and he would say that we couldn't answer him that way, that we simply didn't understand. Although he left China when the Communists came to power, he said that Communism had done wonderful things and that Mao Zedong was the greatest leader there ever was. He believed all the propaganda that he read in the Chinese newspapers.

I have come a long way since those days of heated discussions and feelings of alienation from my father. As an adult, I have made peace with him and can accept his peculiarities for what they are, without wanting to change them. He did, after all, come from a very different culture and from a time unlike my own. Accustomed to the finer things in life when he was a youth, I suppose that starting from the bottom in the States burst his grand bubble. He was capable of physically cutting himself off from his past, but it was still very much present within him, only with added glorifications of nostalgia. His greatest failing was in not being able to reshape himself to his new surroundings in the States.

Through living in Hong Kong, I have gained some understanding of my father and of his aspirations as a young Chinese man. In learning a bit about his culture, I perceive the origins of certain aspects of his behavior. Starting with nothing on arriving in Hong Kong, I can now also put myself in my parents' shoes and relate to the difficulties they must have endured when I was young, even though my hardships cannot compare to theirs. In Hong Kong, I can get by easily with English, and I also know that my stay here need only be temporary, since I can return to Boston at any time. Much to my regret, I realize that I am just as guilty as my father of not blending in with the local population. Living here, I have learned the extent to which it is always easier to fall back on what is most familiar.

When Hong Kong was still a British colony there was an added element of charm to its Britishness, which still persists, and it seemed an appropriate place for me, being a mixture of East and West. However, now I make plans to embark on yet another adventure: moving to the People's Republic of China to learn Mandarin. This is something that I have been longing to do for the last ten years, since it will expand my knowledge of China and Chinese culture. It is curious to realize that I have traveled in the reverse direction of my father. Although I am indeed a stranger to China, I feel a strong connection to its people. I experience a genuine human warmness in its simplest form. Even today, after many visits to the mainland, I always have a feeling of inexplicable nostalgia on leaving it. I hope to learn why and to unweave what China really means to me. This time I go to China with no set plans for departure.

Ears Attuned to Two Cultures

HENRY CHAN

MY EARLIEST MEMORIES ARE OF BEING PROTECTED BY MY MOTHER from Japanese bombs while fleeing from Guangzhou to Hong Kong and of the sea voyage from Hong Kong to Auckland, via Sydney. It was 1940, and I was three years old when we arrived in New Zealand to join my father, who was well-established there. In this way, I became the fourth generation of China-born males in my family to live in either Australia or New Zealand.

The first member of the family to set forth from our ancestral village of Sun-gai (New Street), Zengcheng County, in the southern Chinese province of Guangdong, was my great-grandfather, who had gone to help clear the bush in Queensland in the nineteenth century. He was followed later that same century by my grandfather, who established a country store in Wellington, a country town in New South Wales, Australia.[1] According to his obituary in the *Sydney Morning Herald* in 1934, he died a well-respected member of the community. Although he had

Henry Chan is a retired history professor and an honorary fellow with the School of Science and Technology Studies at the University of New South Wales in Sydney, Australia. He conducts research into the history of Chinese science and the history of the overseas Chinese in Australia. He lives at Echo Point in the Blue Mountains outside Sydney.

spent so many years of his life in Australia, his ties to his native village remained strong. I was eventually to discover that his bones had been returned for burial in the ancestral grave site in Sun-gai Village.

It must have been in part the money he sent back to his family that allowed each of his three sons to purchase a house in Guangzhou. All those sons eventually followed their father to Australia. I later discovered that there had, in fact, been five sons, but only three had survived to adulthood. In Chinese fashion, however, the dead sons retained their chronological place in the family. Thus the surviving sons were known to the next generation in the clan as "first uncle," "fourth uncle," and "fifth uncle." Only my fourth uncle was ever to return to China permanently. Fifth uncle remained in Australia, and the eldest son, my father, spent his life in New Zealand.

As a child, my father was sent to join his father in Wellington to help out in the country store. In his late teens, he returned to Guangzhou and married my mother. He stayed for two years and saw the birth of two daughters before returning to help his father in Wellington. He was later sent to establish a branch of the family business in Auckland, New Zealand, and did not return to Guangzhou and to his family until ten years later, after the death of his father. On this occasion, he again stayed for two years. I was conceived and born in 1937, in his house in Guangzhou. Shortly after my birth, my father returned to his business in New Zealand, again leaving his family behind in China; the restrictive immigration laws did not allow the rest of the family to accompany him to New Zealand.[2]

When I, the only son, came along, my two sisters were already twelve and eleven years old. In 1940, as the Japanese army advanced south, Chinese residents in New Zealand were able to sponsor their families to immigrate as war refugees. It was decided that my mother should go to New Zealand with her baby son, but my two sisters would stay in Guangzhou to take care of our grandmother. My mother died eleven years later without ever seeing her daughters again. And I would not be reunited with my eldest sister until thirty-four years later. My other sister died before any reunion was possible.

My father had a fruit and greengrocery shop in the Auckland suburb of Remuera, with a big garden and a second story, where we lived.

Occasionally, my mother's father, who was blind, would come to stay with us. He had a room in the basement where some of the shop workers also sometimes stayed. In the early twentieth century, my mother's father had migrated to New Zealand as part of the chain migration of the menfolk from his village. He usually lived in Wellington, the capital of New Zealand, where there was a large community of people from his village.

Similarly, in Auckland there were many Zengcheng people from Sun-gai Village and from my mother's village of Gua-lang.[3] There was a big store, Wah Jang, at the bottom of the main street, Queen Street, that was owned cooperatively by the Chans from Sun-gai and the Wongs from Gua-lang.[4] It was a kind of community center for Zengcheng people in Auckland, and I remember visiting it often with my parents. However, my Auckland childhood was lonely. I experienced an intense conflict between the education and atmosphere I was exposed to at the suburban public school that I attended as required by New Zealand law and the demands of my Chinese home environment and schooling. Very early on, I began to feel alienated from my Chineseness and to reject being Chinese. There were only two Chinese children in my school; the rest of the student body was solidly white Anglo-Saxon, from a very wealthy part of the city. My first day at school was traumatic, since I spoke no English at all. When the teacher asked me some questions, I jabbered back in Cantonese, much to the amusement of the rest of the class. I quickly learned English and spent much time in the bookshop next door to our shop and home, reading everything in English I could manage. I early on realized that knowing English made me more accepted at school; it meant I was treated as an equal. I was also to discover that English gave me some power at home, since my parents would often consult me about their English correspondence.

Outside school hours, my life was completely Chinese. My father spoke very little English and would not allow it to be spoken within our home. At the age of eight, I was sent to a Chinese school to study Chinese for three hours each day, four days a week, after finishing my normal school day in the afternoon. On Sunday mornings I was sent to the Chinese church, not for religious purposes but to attend the Chinese classes the church offered. Only Chinese friends of the family were

allowed to visit our house. There were only two other Chinese families living nearby, and since they were not Zengcheng people and were
business rivals, I was not encouraged to associate with them. As for
non-Chinese children, my father did not like me even to play with them.
Once, after school, a girl in my class invited me to her home, and I
stayed so long that I missed my Chinese lessons that day. The girl's
mother took me home and told my father he should allow me to play
with my school friends more often. My father was furious, and I can
still feel the awful beating I received that night for enjoying an afternoon with a friend who happened not to be Chinese.

My feelings of alienation from, and my rejection of, my Chineseness was most of all linked with, and intensified by, the growing rift
with my father. He was a thin and brutal man, ruthless and successful
in business, but with few friends in the Chinese business community
in Auckland. He was clearly disappointed that his only son showed no
interest in or aptitude for business but instead was a bookworm. I was
appalled at his concern with wealth and womanizing: his office walls
were covered with slogans about success and wealth and photographs
of his Chinese girlfriends. He flirted openly with the young Chinese
women who worked in the shop. I disliked his treatment of my mother's
blind father whom I was fond of but who was always driven away by
my father's treatment of him. Above all, I hated his treatment of my
mother, since I blamed him for the frequent miscarriages she suffered
in her efforts to produce another, more business-minded son for him.
My mother eventually had a stroke and, after two years, died when I
was thirteen years old. She also died brokenhearted that her struggle
to obtain permission from New Zealand officials for my two sisters to
join the family had not been successful.

It was chance that finally released me from my unhappy life with my
father—whom I blamed for the death of my mother—just when I had
been planning to run away from home. After my mother's death, I contracted tuberculosis, which kept me hospitalized for two years. The hospital authorities made it clear that, after my discharge from hospital,
I would require more care than my widowed father could provide. They
made arrangements for me to be fostered by a Scottish Presbyterian
clergyman and his wife, whose own family had grown up and left home.

I spent the last three years of my high school days in my foster home, and they were the happiest years of my childhood and adolescence. My foster parents gave me the love and encouragement that I had missed in my Chinese home. They encouraged me to succeed in my studies. I was helped and encouraged to make friends at school and among the young people at the church.

When I finished high school, I wanted to go to university. In this endeavor, I received encouragement from my foster parents. My father, however, wanted me to go to Hong Kong to marry; he had already instructed my sisters, who had by then moved to Hong Kong, to find me a suitable wife. He then wanted me to return to join his business instead of attending university. He disowned me when I refused to do so. My alienation from my Chinese family and my Chineseness became complete, and I would strive harder to become accepted as a yellow-skinned English New Zealander. England became my mother country, as it was for most New Zealand–educated young people in the forties and fifties. When I later went to London for postgraduate studies, I felt, like other New Zealanders, as if I were returning "home."

To my great regret, my father died before my university graduation and before I could attempt a reconciliation with him. He had sold his business and the family home and died a very lonely and obviously painful death from a perforated stomach ulcer, in a house that he shared with a white family in a run-down area of Auckland. Arranging his funeral, sorting out and disposing of his belongings, and settling his estate and affairs brought me back in touch with the Zengcheng community in Auckland, the majority of whom had not wished to involve themselves in the dispute between a father and son. Many in the community now gave me advice and assistance, and the Zengcheng people in Auckland gave my father a big funeral. On my way back to university, I also reestablished contact with my mother's father in Wellington, New Zealand. Moreover, after my father's death, my elder sister, who was now settled in Hong Kong, began to contact me. I also began to correspond with my father's one remaining brother in China, my fourth uncle in Guangzhou, and his sons.

All these events created turmoil in my mind. I was twenty-two at the time and was confronted with my family and Chinese past—a past that I found hard to come to terms with. My emotional turmoil and absences from my studies during that tumultuous year resulted in my failing all my university examinations. The flight of the "yellow-feathered Kiwi" was brought to an end, and I came crashing to the ground. However, I ultimately pulled through, and one of the happiest events in my life was to have my foster parents attend my graduation. After graduation, I taught in a high school for four years, then completed a master's degree and received an appointment as a university lecturer in seventeenth- and eighteenth-century European intellectual history. I married a non-Chinese colleague who was a specialist in English Renaissance literature, and with whom I shared a passion for Renaissance culture and humanist values.

New Zealand in the fifties, sixties, and seventies was a tolerant society. I did not encounter any overt racism directed at me or at Chinese people in general. The issue of my being Chinese never arose. At school and university I was accepted for the person I was. As a university teacher none of my students questioned my ability, although I was obviously Chinese, to introduce them to the history of their own culture, and I enjoyed lecturing on the Renaissance, Neoplatonism, Machiavelli, Erasmus, Bodin, Bacon, Descartes, Pascal, Hobbes, Locke, the seventeenth-century scientific revolution, and the eighteenth-century Enlightenment. I could read French, German, and Latin better than I could Chinese! I had begun to teach myself to read classical Greek. The making of a Canton-Kiwi was complete. Possessing both Chinese and non-Chinese friends, and experiencing no discrimination on the grounds of my race or skin color, there was little reason for me to be worried about my identity.

I was eventually led back to my Chinese roots by larger developments. In the early sixties, New Zealanders began to realize the importance of Asia, and the universities began to offer courses on China. Although alienated from Chinese culture, I had maintained some interest in it even during my university days. As an undergraduate, I enjoyed reading Chinese poetry and literature in English translation, and I had taken a few courses on Chinese history and philosophy. Then, in the early seventies, the New Zealand university at which I was teaching wanted to introduce Chinese history, and being Chinese I was expected to be able to teach it! After doing so for two years, I decided that it was time to make a systematic effort to recover and improve my Chinese language abilities. Asian Studies had begun to expand in New Zealand, and I wanted to study Chinese history in a more thorough way by undertaking a postgraduate degree in Chinese history overseas. This requirement to teach Chinese history was the impetus and the beginning of my long journey back to my Chinese identity.[5]

In July 1974, my wife and I and our fifteen-month-old son left New Zealand for London so that I could pursue postgraduate studies in Chinese history and begin Chinese language studies. We decided it was also time for a reunion with my elder sister in Hong Kong: my second sister had already died. My sister was fifty-three years old, and I was thirty-seven. We had last seen each other when she was in her teens and I was three years old. I had no recollections of her at all, but I had seen both old and recent photos of her. My two sisters each had two sons and two daughters, who were all in Hong Kong. At the airport in Hong Kong, I had no difficulty recognizing the Chinese family party that came to meet us—and the Chinese man with an attractive Caucasian woman and a baby would not have been hard for my sister to pick out. We rushed into each other's arms. We both shed many joyful tears and held each other during the taxi journey to the hotel in Kowloon. My family had arranged for an English-speaking friend, in case we encountered language difficulties, but my Cantonese did not take long to become updated.

However, despite the possession of a common language, this first family reunion was a disaster. For one thing, our one-day stay in Hong Kong was far too short. I managed to upset the family of my deceased sister, since I did not have time to visit their home or the cemetery to pay my respects to her. For another, I did not understand their expectations of me. Before leaving New Zealand, my wife and I had sought the advice of Chinese friends about gifts we might take to Hong Kong for my relatives, taking into account the limitations of our luggage (we were on our way to an extended stay in London) and the fact that we were not acquainted with any of them. The only gift I still remember taking was an expensive sheepskin rug for my sister and her husband, but our gifts were not appreciated by my nephews and nieces. One nephew was particularly rude and critical of his mean uncle from overseas, obviously unaware that although his uncle spoke Cantonese hesitatingly, he understood the language perfectly!

My wife and I were glad to collapse on the British Airways plane that took us from Hong Kong to London. My wife thought the reunion a nightmare that we had both endured: although she had not at all understood what was spoken, she had read all the body language and found my family greedy, grasping, and materialistic, with unreasonable expectations of what I could do for them. As for me, my romantic notions that the reunion would lead me back to my roots were shattered: I had not been adequately prepared to confront the gulf created by disparate cultures and thirty-four years of separation.

However, this initial visit did serve to make me aware of the large Chinese family to which I belonged from afar. A year later, on our way back to New Zealand from London, I effected a second reunion with my Hong Kong family. This time, we stayed for two days. A friend entertained my wife and son, allowing me time to get to know my sister and her family a little better. Unfortunately, this visit did not go much better than the first.

My sister took this chance to pour out her anger at having been left in China while her baby brother had all the opportunities overseas. She was angry at our parents for not doing more to see that she and second sister could join the family in New Zealand. Other parents had done so for their children, she said. She would not accept the fact that, by the end of the war, my sisters, who were already married, were regarded by the New Zealand authorities as independent adult children no longer eligible to immigrate on the grounds of family reunion. I told her that our mother had even traveled to the capital and had a special meeting with the prime minister to plead on behalf of her two daughters. The meeting had been arranged by a senior cabinet minister who was a customer in our shop. My sister now asked me to sponsor her and her family, or at least her sons, to come to New Zealand. I thought that my nieces, who had been much more agreeable and friendly toward my wife and son, were better prospects for immigration. My sister admitted that one of her sons did have some personality problems. She suggested, as an alternative, that I adopt her youngest daughter. My wife was furious to hear that I had promised even to look into the prospects of sponsoring my sister and her family to immigrate to New Zealand.

Difficult though this meeting was, it sowed the seeds for a third reunion. My sister had suggested that I should one day pay a visit to Guangzhou and our ancestral villages. She had just returned from a visit to Guangzhou, and she gave me news about my fourth uncle and some of my cousins in Guangdong. We left Hong Kong this time with more knowledge and information about my Chinese relatives, including the fact that my family still owned my father's house in Guangzhou. My sister gave me the title deeds to this house. That house would be the main topic of correspondence with my family in Hong Kong during the next ten years.

It was not until January 1984 that the opportunity arrived for another Chinese family reunion. In the intervening years, there was regular correspondence between Hong Kong, Guangzhou, and Sydney, where I have lived with my wife and son since 1976. The correspondence with my fourth uncle in Guangzhou and his sons gave me information about my family in China, and I developed a great desire to visit them in person. From my sister in Hong Kong, I heard more about my father's house in Guangzhou and was urged to officially claim it from the government as an overseas Chinese.[6] The house gradually developed into a major issue between my sister and me. Her anxiety to take me back to Guangzhou and my ancestral village partly stemmed from her hope that a visit to Guangzhou would enliven my interest in our family property in China. As I was my father's only son, it seemed that I had to be the one claiming the house for the family. In January 1984, accompanied by my eleven-year-old son, my sister and I made the journey to visit our extended family in China. For me, it was another important stage of my journey to rediscover the Chinese roots of my identity. It was also an opportunity to introduce my son to the Chinese roots of his Eurasian identity.

A very large group was waiting for us at the Guangzhou railway station. My mother's sister and her family had obtained the official permission that was then required to come in from the countryside to stay at the same hotel as my sister and me. My fourth uncle, almost in his eighties, was there with his four sons and some of their families. Several taxis took the Chan entourage to our hotel, where we were all properly introduced to one another. Though we were tired and still a little jet-lagged from the journey from London and Hong Kong, that first night in Guangzhou was a very happy occasion. I felt an immediate affinity with my large Guangdong-based family, and, having been in effect the only child in both my natural and foster families, it was good to have a sense of belonging to a large family.

An active program of sightseeing and family banquets had been arranged by my sister and fourth uncle. It was during this time that I was able to start piecing together fragments of our family history, linking them with and confirming the memories of what my parents had told me. It was only then that I discovered the fact that I was the fourth generation of the family to migrate to Australia. We visited my father's house, and my actual birthplace was pointed out to me. Our old neighbor, a schoolteacher, was still alive and living close by. She came to visit and said that she remembered me as a small baby and claimed that she had foreseen then that the baby would grow up to become a scholar! I was taken upstairs to my parents' bedroom, which must have been set up for the occasion, as an altar had been arranged with portraits of my father and mother, along with the photos of their tombstones in New Zealand that I had sent back to my sister many years ago. I looked out at the city from that second-story bedroom window and pondered what my life might have been like had I had been the child left in Guangzhou rather than my sisters. The previous forty-four years had been turbulent ones in China's history, and I wondered how I, as a young man, would have coped with events such as the Cultural Revolution.[7]

During sessions with my fourth uncle, I learned of his bitterness. He had been sent back to Guangzhou from Australia in the early 1930s to take care of the family while his other brothers made their fortunes, or squandered the family's wealth, overseas. Fifth uncle had ruined the business interests that grandfather had built up in Australia and wasted whatever family fortunes in Australia that remained. I did not know of, and therefore could not confirm, the rumors of the fabulous wealth of other members of the clan who had emigrated to the United States or to Fiji. But I was able to tell fourth uncle of the sad fates of his two brothers.

Ten years before, I had made the effort to find fifth uncle, who was living in Melbourne. Although I had never met him, I had no problem recognizing him when I saw him. His physical resemblance to my father and his lonely, bachelor existence in what, as a middle-class New Zealander, I regarded as a hovel, reminded me so much of what I imagined the last few months of my father's own life must have been like. I tried now to ease my fourth uncle's bitterness by reminding him that, nearing his eighties, he was surrounded by four successful sons and numerous grandchildren, whereas both my father and fifth uncle had died lonely deaths in their fifties and sixties, my father having disowned his only son for unfiliality. I thought my fourth uncle had been the most fortunate of the three brothers.

From my sister and my mother's sister, I was to learn another side of the family history in China, and I was reminded of the realities of conflict, rivalry, and dissension in a large Chinese family. My sister and aunt were annoyed by my seeming closeness and concern for fourth uncle and reminded me that he had mistreated my mother while she was living in Guangzhou, that he had been a tyrant who terrorized the women in the family, that he had taken the Chan family fortunes in China into his own hands, and that he had his greedy eyes on "my house" and wanted it for one of his sons! In the view of my sister and aunt, instead of comforting him, I should be seeking revenge and kicking the old man in the guts. As for me, I liked both my fourth uncle and my mother's sister very much and thought that their families had much better attitudes toward me and my son than my sisters' families in Hong Kong had ever shown us.

The day arrived for our journey into the countryside to visit my father's and mother's villages. It was a seventy-kilometer trip each way by hired minivan to Zengcheng County and back to Guangzhou. I was struck by the beauty and productivity of the countryside in Zengcheng, including my ancestral village of Sun-gai, as well as the squalor of the village itself, which apparently looked much the same as it had when I had left it as a baby forty-four years before. I was shown my family's temple, where the old villagers told me my mother would often bring me from Guangzhou whenever I was ill. From the family hillside grave site I could survey what, in the pre-Communist period, had once been the Chan estates. I thought how nice it would be to be buried there among my ancestors when I died or at least to have my ashes scattered there. I was shown the ruins of our family mansion that had been destroyed during war against the Japanese.

Then we moved on to my mother's village of Gua-lang, noted for its lychee trees. The village walls remained intact, and we could see the village watchtowers from afar as we approached. My maternal grand-parents' house was still standing. It was occupied by villagers, and there we learned as much about the Wong family as we had of the Chan family in Sun-gai. Further down the road was the riverside town of Xintong, where my aunt lived. The large family of children and grand-children of my aunt took to my son readily despite the language prob-lem, and the adults were left to reflect on the history of our families.

Our four days in Guangzhou came to an end with a farewell ban-quet in our hotel that I hosted for my Chinese relatives, a large num-ber of whom had come in from the countryside to meet me. I thought the visit to Guangzhou and my ancestral villages a happy success. I had gotten to know my Chinese family, recovered more of the family his-tory, and introduced my son to his Chinese family and heritage; and, although there had been moments of tension, I had been very com-fortable with my Guangdong families. I certainly had not sensed any cultural gulf between them and me, and my son had jumped any gulf he felt easily. I was overwhelmed by the generosity of my fourth un-cle and his family. Here is one trivial example: I had incidentally men-tioned that some of my Australian colleagues were researching Chi-nese peasant New Year prints and that I regretted, seeing the lunar New Year was approaching, not having seen any to buy. At Guangzhou Sta-tion I was sorry that my fourth uncle's youngest sons had not come to the station to say farewell. Just as we were to go through the barriers to the train we were called back, and my missing cousins presented me with a huge parcel of peasant New Year prints. They had gone to a great deal of trouble collecting them for me to take back to Australia.

But the feeling that I was still somewhat separated from my Chinese identity was reinforced by the day and a half spent with my Hong Kong family before returning to Sydney. My sister came back to the issue of the Guangzhou house. I learned that she had regularly returned to Guangzhou to collect "rent" on my behalf from the occupants of the house. She gave me a statement of her accounts and the proceeds of her "rent collecting" in Guangzhou while we were there. I returned both the statements and the rent money to her. Although I was fascinated by the idea of being an absentee landlord collecting rent from his property in a Communist state, I really was not interested in the house or in the rent from it. I had made inquiries with the Chinese consulate in Sydney and knew that everything was legal and that I could claim the house in Guangzhou, but Chinese friends in Sydney had warned me of the problems that might arise if I actually did so. I suggested to my sister that I should have the house transferred to her and that she should use the proceeds of the rent. She was not happy about that. She was also furious to learn that I had discussed with the Chinese consul in Sydney the possibility that any income I might derive from my family properties in Guangdong be used to fund educational development in my ancestral villages. She rejected my idea that the house might be more useful to my mother's sister and her very large family, since I thought their village living conditions unsatisfactory. It seemed to me that her major concern was to prevent the family property in Guangzhou from falling into the hands of fourth uncle's family.

A huge cultural chasm existed between my sister and me. She berated me for my friendliness towards the "evil" fourth uncle and suspected that I had agreed to help the migration of his sons to Australia, while refusing to help her and her family. She accused me of being prepared to help my mother's sister before helping my own closest relatives. Matters came to a head with arrangements for the family farewell banquet: the plans came undone when some of her family could not or did not want to attend. We waited a very hungry hour in the restaurant for one of her sons to turn up. There was bickering and argument; both my son and I were exhausted by the end of our trip. I would not visit my family in Hong Kong again until a happier reunion in 1999.

On my return to Sydney, I continued my studies of Chinese language, history, and culture and became immersed in researching the current and past histories of Chinese communities in Australia. When, in 1986, I was appointed a lecturer in Chinese history at a university outside Sydney, I became involved in Chinese community affairs. The local city was, and still is, one of the most Anglo-Saxon communities in Australia, with a small Chinese population of around five thousand. A new Chinese community association was formed the year I arrived, and I became a member of the executive committee and served as the president of the Chinese Association for two years. Despite the fact that the Chinese community was so small, it was diverse and terribly divided into factions according to place of origin: Australian-born Chinese or those who had settled in the city before 1960 made up about half of the Chinese population, and they spoke little Chinese of any variety; more recent Hong Kong migrants were multilingual, professional, and aggressive; Malaysian and Singaporean Chinese, who did not always speak Cantonese, did not get on with those from Hong Kong; a few from Taiwan speaking only Mandarin did much of the community work; and a small number of students and others from mainland China did not want to have anything to do with the local Chinese community at all.

A single example of the community's extreme divisiveness will suffice here. In the executive committee of fifteen, the only language that all but two of the members understood perfectly was English, but the language of the committee business was Chinese, predominately Cantonese, which about half of the committee did not speak, although most claimed to understand it, as I did. In the much larger and more powerful Chinese community associations in Sydney at that time, English was always the language of committee meetings, with translations and interpretation when necessary at general meetings. When I became president, I recommended that English be the language of committee meetings, with the minutes and business papers all being available in Chinese and interpreters provided for the one or two members who claimed they understood no English at all. The majority of the committee opposed the move, and I was made to hand down a presidential ruling that committee meetings would be conducted in English, though members could speak in any form of Chinese they liked.

The association depended on me and other English speakers to build up links for it with the wider community in the city but resented our preference for English and my recommendation that members of the community learn English. Perhaps some community leaders advocated the Chinese language to prevent any challenges from within the overseas Chinese community to their own power. Language is the key to cultural maintenance, but in an English-speaking society like Australia the language of power and influence is English. It does not surprise me that those Chinese community leaders most strident in their preference for Chinese over English owe their influence and power both in the Chinese and wider Australian community to their command of the English language. Whatever the case, my experience in the small overseas Chinese community reminded me too much of my experiences with my Hong Kong Chinese family, and it was a relief that an extended research leave, some of it to be spent in Beijing, gave me an excuse to get out of the politics of an overseas Chinese community.

It was through studying and teaching Chinese language, culture, and history and by mixing with the community of scholars involved in it, that I finally came to terms with my Chinese identity. That moment came at the age of fifty-five, during my visit in 1992 to Beijing, where I spent a total of twelve weeks. I was very surprised at how completely at ease and at home I felt in Beijing from almost the first moment, despite my obvious language limitations. The Mandarin spoken there was a language I had studied as an adult, and I was hardly fluent in it. However, from getting lost on the first day in the streets around my hotel in downtown Beijing, to finding myself proudly Chinese at watching the rising of the Red Flag, reaching the top of the flagpole as the sun burst over Tiananmen Square the morning before my departure, I realized that I had returned to my real motherland.

I returned to my university as what my Australian colleagues only half jokingly called "a reborn Chinese." On rereading some of my letters from Beijing to my family and Australian colleagues, I am surprised at the strident Chinese ethnic and nationalistic tone of some of them. Since 1992, I have been back to Beijing every year at least once, and each time I have felt as much if not more at home in Beijing than I do when I am in London. Certainly I feel more at ease in Beijing than I do in Australia or New Zealand. The fact that all my trips to China have been as a visiting scholar is probably one reason why I adjusted easily to Beijing and other parts of China. A transient guest is always well taken care of in China. Perhaps also the fact that in China I am ethnically a member of the majority, while in Australia I am a member of a minority group may help explain why I feel more at ease in China than in Australia. Further, many of my Chinese friends and colleagues prefer to speak or practice their English with me, which eases the language problem. But I have made some very close and long-lasting friendships with Chinese people young and old, some of whom hardly speak any English but who have helped me improve my Chinese language skills and taught me to be more Chinese. At conferences in China, some of the Chinese scholars I felt closest to spoke no English at all, but we felt an intellectual affinity, and even a bond, between us.

What does it mean to be Chinese? Some of my Australian friends and colleagues find me too Chinese, too reserved and inscrutable, reluctant to get too close, and disliking the social hugging and kissing they take for granted. Most of my Chinese friends find me far too Western: far too unreserved and frank and much too fond of physical contact! However, a visiting Chinese professor who recently came to work with me on a joint writing project, having observed me teaching Chinese history, commented that my greatest value as a teacher in China would be my ability to look at Chinese history and culture from a Western point of view, and Western history and culture from a Chinese perspective. In fact, I have become a cultural hybrid. And as a cultural hybrid, I will always be perceived and accepted in different ways by different people. But I have finally become at ease with my hybridity, and that is the important thing.

The flight from China back to Australia arrives in Sydney early in the morning. Each time I return from China, I watch the sun rise and bathe the Australian continent brilliantly red, and I feel the tug of the roots that were planted in Australian soil by my ancestors during the nineteenth century. At that moment, I know I shall soon be home with my family, and that home is really where one's family is living at the moment. But I also feel the need to nourish both the old and new roots of the family established in Australian soil. Having reached the Confucian age when "one's ears are attuned," I have come to realize and accept that my ears are attuned to two cultures.[8] I have two sets of spiritual roots that need to be continually nourished: those that take me back to England, Europe, and ancient Greece, and those that take me back to my motherland and to ancient China. I feel confident that the younger members of my family will continue to sustain the old Chinese roots while nourishing new roots wherever they may be planted in the future.

Guilt Trip to China

RICHARD CHU

"HOAN-NA GONG!" MY MOTHER WOULD CALL ME WHENEVER SHE heard me speaking in Tagalog, the national language of the Philippines. *Hoan-na* means "foreign barbarian" in our Hokkien dialect of Chinese; *gong* means "stupid."[1]

At an early age, I was already being constantly reminded of two separate identities: that of "our own" and that of the Filipinos. For, of course, the "foreign barbarians" that she was referring to were not us, the ethnic Chinese inhabitants of the Philippines, but the Filipinos themselves. The term *hoan-na gong* is often used by many older Chinese in the Philippines, whether China or Philippines born, who speak Hokkien as a first language, to chastise the younger ones who do not speak it and thus instead speak like Filipinos. I know that my mother said these words to me half in jest, but I could not help feeling a deep sense of shame whenever they were applied to me.

I was born in 1965, the only son of the seven children of ethnic Chinese parents. Reckoned on my mother's side, I am a third-generation Filipino. And, while my father was born in China, my paternal fam-

Richard Chu is a Ph.D. candidate at the history department of the University of Southern California. He lives in California and the Philippines.

ily's links to the Philippines go back several generations. As far as our family records show, my great-grandfather had traveled back and forth between China and the Philippines. But, as was the practice of many overseas Chinese at that time, only the men traveled overseas. Women, like my great-grandmother, were left behind in China to bear and raise the children. Therefore, my grandfather, my father, and all the other men in the family were all born in China but traveled to the Philippines as soon as they were old enough to work or help out in the business. Occasionally, they would go back to their home country, as my great-grandfather did in the 1920s to build a new house in the village. However, as conditions there deteriorated, especially after China's war with Japan in 1937, the family members in China moved to the Philippines.[2] My father was only seven years old when his family relocated to Manila in 1938.

I did not understand this until later, but one of the reasons my mother and those of her generation often looked back to and linked their sense of identity with China was the type of education they had received in their youth. My mother attended one of the many Chinese schools in the Philippines and other parts of Southeast Asia that operated under the supervision of the Chinese government.[3] She told me that they spent half the day studying in Mandarin Chinese, the national language of mainland China, and the other half in English. Most of their teachers, as well as their textbooks, came from China and promoted a certain view of the country. At the time, China was faced with threats from Japan and from Western powers.[4] To win both the financial and political support of the overseas Chinese, the Chinese government played up images of a great Chinese nation and its superior civilization in danger of annihilation by foreigners.

Moreover, for a long time, there were several constraints barring the Chinese in the Philippines from obtaining Filipino citizenship. The American colonial government implemented the Chinese Exclusion Policy in the Philippines just as it had in the United States.[5] This prevented many Chinese without Filipino citizenship from entering the country. Only people born in the Philippines could be considered citizens. To get around this policy, many Chinese entered the Philippines illegally. Others, like my paternal grandfather, bought somebody else's citizenship, and, as a consequence, changed their names. Thus, my paternal grandfather, whose real name in Hokkien is Ngo Tingseng, officially became Chu Ongco. Hence the surname I bear today. Furthermore, many Chinese already in the Philippines who wanted to apply for Filipino citizenship were discouraged by the exorbitant fees or were refused by the courts. On the other hand, the Nationalist government in China regarded all persons of Chinese blood, regardless of their place of birth, as Chinese citizens. It also allowed and encouraged the overseas Chinese to send representatives to hold positions in China's legislative bodies and often sent their officials abroad to visit the overseas Chinese.[6]

No wonder my mother and those belonging to her generation felt very close to China and still regarded it as their homeland. Many, like my own paternal great-grandfather, had always planned on going back to China when sociopolitical and economic conditions there improved and did not intend to stay in the Philippines their entire lives.

As with almost all children of middle-class Chinese-Filipino families, I was raised by a Filipino nanny who took care of me until I reached school age. As she played with me and fed me, she naturally spoke to me in Tagalog. I do not know whether my parents reacted with chagrin and horror to hear their only son speaking his first words in his nanny's language, as I have seen some Chinese parents react. But as I was growing up, my parents, like most Chinese parents of their generation, certainly wanted me to speak Hokkien. The language was more than a means of communication; it was also a way to bind me to what they perceived to be the ways and values of the *lan-lang*. Figuratively, *lan-lang* means "the Chinese people." Literally, it means "our people" (or "people of our own kind"). These two meanings are interchangeable, and typically the Chinese in the Philippines do not distinguish between the two.

And what were the ways of the *lan-lang?* One of the first traits that I learned to associate with the Chinese was thriftiness. My mother often told me how my father, in his younger days, used to sell rice cakes in the streets. Often, feeling very hungry but not having enough money to buy something to eat, my father could only afford to buy soda to assuage his hunger. According to my mother, this was the reason my father developed ulcers later in life. As she saw it, the fact that my father died of complications from ulcers at the age of forty-seven was mainly a lesson to me not to waste my money. Through the rags-to-riches stories that my mother told me about Chinese-Filipinos, I also came to connect working hard and being disciplined with being Chinese. "This is the reason why So-and-So rose up from being a shoe peddler in Escolta to become the biggest shoe manufacturer in the Philippines," she would say.[7]

Filipinos, on the other hand, were supposed to possess entirely different characteristics. When I wanted to buy something expensive, my mother would sometimes reprimand me for being extravagant like the *hoan-nas*. I have sometimes also heard parents blaming the failure of their children in their studies on the influence of Filipino culture. Clearly, for my mother and for many of the elders among the ethnic Chinese in the Philippines, Filipinos are, among other things, lazy and extravagant. I did not question the validity of this reasoning back then. Most of the Filipinos I met while growing up were domestic helpers and nannies. Or they were drivers, security guards, or laborers who worked for my family or for my father's business. Thus, in my mind, a *hoan-na* was someone who came from a lower socioeconomic background. It made sense to me that the Filipinos were poor because of their laziness and extravagance.

My mother was only acting like any other good Chinese mother. Her desire for me to avoid the ways of the *hoan-na* and to retain or follow the ways of the *lan-lang* came from her belief that it is by way of the latter that I would succeed later in life. To make us feel proud of our heritage, she would talk about the long, glorious history of the Chinese people, of more than five thousand years of civilization, and of great heroes and emperors. Being the only son in my family put an additional burden on me. It was my filial duty to try to follow and preserve the culture and language of my forefathers. Failure to do so was tantamount to ingratitude to them after all the sacrifices that they had made to give us, their descendants, a better life.

In their efforts to ensure that their children could speak Hokkien, my parents had to contend with the influence of environment. The disparity in Hokkien proficiency even among my siblings was a result of the different environments in which we grew up. When my parents first married, they lived in a large compound located in a major street in Manila's Chinatown. The compound housed my father's extended family, which included my great-grandmother, my grandmother, my father's male first cousins and their families, and my uncles and their families. Thus, my three elder sisters grew up surrounded by older Hokkien-speaking relatives and cousins their age. They learned to speak the language fluently and spontaneously use it when conversing with one another or with our parents.

However, starting with my fourth sister, then passing on to me and to my two younger sisters, Hokkien fluency deteriorated progressively. Just a few months after I was born, my parents, wanting to set up their own business and seeing that their family was growing bigger, decided to move. In the apartment building south of Manila where we relocated, I and my two younger sisters spent most of the time with our Filipino nannies and maids. By the time I started learning how to speak, my elder sisters were already going to school and had no time to play with us younger children. The younger brood in the family thus became more fluent in Tagalog than in Hokkien. Often my parents would speak to my three elder sisters in Hokkien, but when speaking to me and to my younger sisters they would unthinkingly switch to Tagalog. My fourth sister was caught in the middle. Sometimes my parents spoke to her in Tagalog, sometimes in Hokkien. It was in those moments when my two younger sisters and I would converse in Tagalog that my mother would use that epithet *hoan-na gong*. My second sister, Julie, tried to make sure that we learned how to speak Hokkien by making us say "Gua dio kong langlang ue" (I have to speak the language of our people) ten times afterward.

One of the ways in which my parents attempted to ensure that I maintained my Chinese heritage was to send me to Xavier School, an exclusive Catholic boys' school located in one of the new and posh residential Chinatowns of metropolitan Manila. Founded in 1954 by European and North American Jesuit priests who were expelled from China after 1949, the school quickly gained a reputation for academic excellence among the Chinese. It was in Xavier that I completed my elementary and secondary education. And that education, contrary to my parents' desire, helped me become more *hoan-na* than Chinese.

In part, perhaps, this process was due to the effect of a presidential decree issued in 1973 that called for the "Filipinization" of Chinese schools.[8] In general, the intent of this decree was to train students to become loyal and "true Filipinos." Among other things, it required the possession of Filipino citizenship by school administrators, the changing of the Chinese names of these schools, and the reduction of the Chinese curriculum to just two hours a day. In these two hours of Mandarin classes that we received every day for thirteen years, we were taught to read, write, and speak Chinese. However, none of us really became proficient or fluent in Mandarin, even though 90 percent of the student body at Xavier during my time came from Chinese families. At home, we never used Mandarin to speak to our parents. While at school, most of us hated the subject and managed to pass our tests only through memorizing. In fact, at the end of our Chinese education, only very few of us could utter even a single straight Chinese sentence with ease and confidence. With no motivation and no chance to practice it outside the classroom, we forgot our Mandarin as quickly as we had memorized it.

On the other hand, at Xavier, I continued to speak Tagalog with my friends and classmates, interacted and even lived with poor Filipino families and children as part of our service practicum and immersion programs, and, most important, learned to regard the Philippines as my home country. It was in my social studies classes that I was first exposed to Filipino history and culture. And, outside school hours, my classmates and I would spend weekends watching Filipino and American movies just like many Filipinos, enjoying the Filipino food that our Filipino cooks prepared at home, and participating in the many Catholic traditions that have become part of Filipino culture, such as Christmas or All Saints' Day.

In contrast, we felt lost when participating in Chinese rites and rituals. For example, during my father's burial, my elder relatives instructed me to carry his portrait behind my back immediately after they had sealed his casket inside his tomb. I was to bring it to the car that would take me home. There I was to place his portrait on the family altar. What I did not know then was that, while walking toward the car, I also had to shout and say, "Father, come home with us." I recall overhearing one of my aunts say, "How come he is not saying it?" In Chinese practices such as this, and in others that we were supposed to observe in burial, betrothal, marriage, or other life-cycle ceremonies, the Chinese of my generation hardly know the proper way of performing them, much less their origins and reasons.

But even as I increasingly assimilated into Filipino culture, I did not completely forget or abandon my Chinese heritage. Weekly trips to the Manila Chinatown to visit my relatives and to enjoy with my father a bowl of steaming hot noodle soup at a nearby restaurant, occasional movies from Hong Kong and Taiwan starring Jackie Chan or Lin Ch'ing-hsia, interesting stories of Chinese heroes I learned from school, yearly celebrations of the Mid-Autumn Festival, an acrobatic show from mainland China, and the constant reminder at home to speak Hokkien—all these balanced out the Filipinization of my identity and helped maintain my Chineseness.[9]

It was not until I reached college that I began to learn what it meant to be a Filipino among Filipinos. Behind the high walls of our homes and of our school, my classmates and I had actually lived a ghettoized existence, however much we may have come to regard ourselves as Filipinos. At the Jesuit university, Ateneo de Manila, I found myself for the first time in a predominantly Filipino community. It came as something of a shock to discover that many Filipino students there did not automatically regard me as one of them. Once during a discussion, when I made a statement about myself being a Filipino, someone cut in and said, "But you're not a Filipino, you're *Intsik*" (a term often used by Filipinos to refer to the ethnic Chinese and that has assumed derogatory connotations).

His words had a great impact on me and helped open my eyes to the cultural and other differences between ethnic Chinese like me and the Filipino majority among whom we lived. At the same time that I was developing a greater awareness of our differences, however, I was also being exposed to and drawn more intimately into the Filipino culture through my friendships with Filipino classmates. They invited me to their homes, and I invited them to mine. I met their families and participated in their social gatherings. In time, I felt very much at ease being around Filipino friends and gradually lost touch with my Chinese friends from high school. The cultural differences between my Filipino friends and me seemed to disappear as I also became more Filipino.

At university I also became heavily involved in extracurricular political and social activities. It was the time of the anti-Marcos movement, in the early 1980s, when people took to the streets protesting against his scandalously corrupt government. I participated in the numerous rallies, volunteered for the National Movement for Free Elections, which acted as a watchdog during the 1986 presidential elections, guarded the ballot boxes in the municipal hall after widespread fraud was reported, and lay down on the streets along with others to block the tanks of soldiers loyal to Marcos.[10] I celebrated when Marcos and his family fled the Philippines, and my heart burst with pride and hope for the new administration under Corazon Aquino.

My participation and involvement in this momentous episode increased my emotional attachment and commitment to the Philippines. The extent to which I had already identified myself with the Filipino people could be seen in my reaction to an incident at home. While visiting my mother one weekend, I heard her complaining about the maids and saying, "These Filipinos are really lazy." On hearing those words, I suddenly felt a pang of hurt inside my chest, almost as if she were insulting me and my people. But I did not say anything for fear of being reprimanded for defending the *hoan-nas*.

A year after graduation, I joined a newly formed organization called Kaisa Para sa Kaunlaran (United in Progress) that was founded by young Chinese-Filipinos.[11] The main objective of the organization is to help bridge the gap between the Chinese community and the Filipino community at large. Among our organizations' activities are a children's television puppet show that teaches both Hokkien and Tagalog, conferences and books on the Filipino-Chinese community and on the relations between China and the Philippines, and weekly visits to the Philippine General Hospital, where Kaisa volunteers bring food, medicine, and money donated by people of the Chinese community to hundreds of indigent Filipino families. We also coined the word *Tsinoy,* a combination of the words *Tsino* (Chinese) and *Pinoy* (a colloquial term for Filipinos), to refer to this new generation of Chinese-Filipinos who unequivocally regard the Philippines as their home and their country.

Yet despite all these activities, deep inside me the desire to be Chinese and to maintain my Chinese ways remained strong. Perhaps this desire arose only out of a feeling of guilt that I was never Chinese enough for my family. Probably the greatest departure of all from what was expected of me as a filial Chinese son was my eventual choice of profession. While in high school, I already knew that I did not want to be a businessman as my ancestors had been and that my interests lay in the academic world. Initially, I thought my mother would be proud of my desire to be a scholar, for wasn't Confucius, whom we call the Great Teacher, a role model for many Chinese? Didn't they teach us in school about China's long history of selfless and courageous Confucian scholar-officials?

However, the Chinese community in the Philippines is predominantly mercantile and entrepreneurial. Many parents, therefore, including my own, want and expect their children, especially their sons, to follow in their footsteps—that is, to take over the family business, or at least to start their own business. But thirteen years of liberal education under the Jesuits at Xavier and Ateneo had convinced me that being true to one's own calling and deepest desires was more important than making one's life fit other people's expectations.

So right after college, instead of helping out in the family business as my sisters had done, I went away to teach religion in a Jesuit high school in Cebu, a city more than five hundred kilometers south of Manila. Although my mother had never pushed me to follow her wishes, I knew that she would rather see me making lots of money than teaching students. Sometimes she would say to me, "I wish we hadn't sent you to Xavier." In her eyes, I had become a *hoan-na* through the liberal and Western-oriented education of the Jesuits.

More than anything else, it was this desire to expunge my feelings of guilt at not being Chinese enough that caused me to make my first visit to China, in 1987, as an exchange student under the Ateneo de

Manila University–Xiamen University Exchange Program. When being interviewed by the people at Ateneo about why I wanted to go to China, I told them that I wanted to serve as a bridge between China and the Philippines, that after a year and a half of study at Xiamen, a port city in the southern Chinese province of Fujian, I wanted to use the knowledge gained there to help improve relations between the Philippines and China. This explanation was by no means a falsehood; I was sincere. But the overriding reason for going to China was a desire to prove to my mother and to my relatives that I had not completely forgotten or given up on my Chinese identity. Even if I did not follow the path set by my ancestors, I could remain loyal to the *lanlang* heritage by using my academic career to study China, and be true to my roots by going back to visit the land of my ancestors. I also hoped to learn what it meant to be a true Chinese and therefore become more like the person my mother wanted me to be. Thus, on September 16 of that year, I, along with two other exchange students, boarded the plane to Xiamen.

The minivan that fetched us from Xiamen International Airport snaked its way through the narrow streets of Xiamen University. As I looked out its windows, I was struck by the sight of the men and women walking around the campus. The men had thick, unkempt hair and wore dark-rimmed plastic eyeglasses, white long-sleeved shirts, tight-fitting jean shorts, plastic or leather sandals, and ankle- or knee-length socks made of nylon! The women had either long or permed hair in wild wavy locks and wore thin, see-through dresses along with the same glasses, sandals, and socks that the men wore. At that moment, I felt as if I had been placed in a time warp, back to the 1950s. Right away, I had a strong impression of difference between me as a Chinese-Filipino and the mainland Chinese.

Later, it became apparent that tastes in style and appearance were only one of our many differences. Our worldviews and beliefs, our memories and experiences, our upbringing and education—all that constitutes the deepest core of our identities—had been shaped by very different sociohistorical and political forces in the last few decades, making it difficult for us to find common ground. I felt much more at home with my Filipino classmates and friends who were studying at Xiamen University than with the local Chinese friends I made there. Although I may look and speak Chinese, the gap that existed between my Chinese friends and me was too wide to be bridged by physical and linguistic similarities.

The local people who encountered us, the ethnic Chinese students from Southeast Asia, sensed the dissimilarities between us and them. They could tell at a glance, from the way we dressed, that we were not local. They could also hear the differences in our speech. The Hokkien dialect spoken in Xiamen and that spoken in nearby Jinjiang County of Fujian, where many of the Chinese in the Philippines originate, differ somewhat.[12] When I asked them to guess where I was from, they would often mention Singapore, Taiwan, Hong Kong, or some other country. Once I happened to overhear the conversation of the service personnel at our foreign students' dormitory. They were clearly talking to one another about the foreign students, including me and the other Chinese-Filipinos in the dormitory, and one of them referred to us as *hoan-na*. Immediately I felt stunned and insulted when I heard them, for I had learned to associate that label with derogatory meanings. But I was later amused by my own reaction, for never had I thought until then that I myself would one day be referred to as a *hoan-na*. Although the Chinese government, and some local Chinese, might constantly call the overseas Chinese "compatriots" or "brothers," despite our shared Chinese blood and language I realized that we were foreigners to them, as they were to us.

Yet perhaps this is not wholly true. I later discovered that the people of Jinjiang County, and of course of our village, feel a great deal more affinity with us than do the people of Xiamen, and I likewise felt the same way toward them. Two months into my stay in Xiamen, I paid a visit to my father's home village of Zengkeng, in Jinjiang County. Before making the trip, I met a professor at Xiamen University who was from the same region. When he started speaking Hokkien in the accent we use in Manila, I felt an instant connection with him—increasing the sense of anticipation that I was beginning to feel at the thought of being able to see my ancestral village.

The bus trip to Zengkeng, which took two hours, went smoothly.

We drove through wide swaths of farmland and stopped at small towns from time to time to pick up or unload people. As I begin to hear more and more people around me speak Hokkien in the manner that I knew from back home, I also began to feel more at home. But this feeling of smugness vanished right after I arrived at the village. For the motorcycle driver who took me from the bus terminal to the village started harassing me by insisting that I pay twice the amount of money that we had initially agreed on. When I refused, he grabbed my bag and wouldn't let go of it. I managed to yank my bag free and started heading toward the village, my heart pounding in anger and fear. Shaken by the experience, I felt my initial anticipation turn into anxiety. I had heard of stories of villagers and relatives in China trying to squeeze money out of overseas Chinese; I just didn't expect how brazenly some people would do so.

After a while, I calmed down. While walking along the narrow, winding dirt road toward what I thought was my great-grandfather's house as it had been described by my grandmother, I saw a man in his fifties coming my way. I asked him whether the house in front of us belonged to Ngo Tingseng. When he nodded, I told him that I was a grandson. He looked at me closely and said, "You must be Tian Hua's son." I was surprised. How could he have guessed correctly when I had never met him? But the association was understandable, for I am the spitting image of my father. As I nodded in agreement, this man explained that he had been a playmate of my father. He even recalled how my father loved to sketch, something that he was truly good at. Meeting this man and hearing his stories of my father made me feel at that moment that I was finally "home."

He held me by the hand and led me through the huge steel gate of my great-grandfather's house. As I entered the front courtyard, I was struck by the sight of the huge concrete edifice standing in front of me. Built by my great-grandfather in the 1920s out of labor and materials imported from the Philippines, the house had the architectural style of a Spanish colonial house. Two stories high with six large rooms on each floor, it also had a large open balcony on the western wing. It felt odd to find a house of this size and design in the middle of a remote Chinese village of six hundred people, surrounded by potato and corn fields. But as I was to discover later, while the village was still dotted by old, traditional Chinese-style houses, it also contained other Spanish colonial-style houses. They were all built by my great-grandfather, but none were as grand and imposing as his own.

The caretaker's wife came out to greet me, and after I introduced myself and explained the nature of my trip, she led me inside the house and prepared a meal. During the three days I spent in Zengkeng, I occupied the room that had belonged to my grandparents. In the room next door was hung, among other ancestral portraits, a photograph of my grandmother, taken when she was only sixteen years old. I was struck by the sight. She had been sixty-five years old when I was born.

The Wangs, the couple who had been taking care of our house for many decades, told me stories about my immediate ancestors and about how they had come to be the caretakers of the house. In 1947, when my great-grandfather realized that he did not have long to live, he brought his wife and some of his children from Manila to Zengkeng. He eventually died in November 1949. However, news soon went around that the Communist government, which had taken over the country a month before, was going to ban overseas travel. In their haste to leave the country, my grandfather and the rest of the family, including my great-grandmother, could not wait for the proper date to bury my great-grandfather. Before my grandfather left, he asked the Wangs to look after the house and my great-grandfather's body and promised them that he would return in a few months.

The months stretched to years, and then forever. For political and economic reasons, my grandfather never returned to China. Five years later, the Wangs received a telegram informing them that my grandfather had died and instructing them to bury my great-grandfather, whose body had been left lying in a tightly sealed coffin for all that time in the room that is now the ancestral room. To this day, the mausoleum that the Wangs built for him stands in the middle of the fields in front of the house.

This and other stories about my ancestors indeed made a deep impression on me. They reminded me of the great sacrifices that my ancestors had made to create a better life for their descendants and of their hopes of living together with their loved ones back in China. The empty rooms of my great-grandfather's house and his mausoleum have now become symbols of dreams unfulfilled and of the chasm that divides us from our ancestors. Although I had felt welcomed by the caretakers and by the villagers who had known my family and had initially felt that indeed I was back home, I slowly realized that this place could never really be to me the home that it had been to my immediate ancestors and that there was no coming back here for me except on occasional trips. Furthermore, I doubted whether even those of my older relatives who had been born in China and brought up to regard the country as their motherland would dream of returning permanently, either, even though they had managed to reclaim the house of my great-grandfather.[13] Very few have even visited Zengkeng at all. To their mind, it is a sleepy village that, until about ten years ago, had electricity only during the day, in contrast to the amenities that one enjoys in Manila. Even if the opening of China since the 1970s to the outside world, and their subsequent visits there, may have rekindled their patriotic feelings for the country, I suspect that most of them would prefer to live and die in the Philippines. Like me, they have grown deep roots in the soil of the Philippines. Like my great-grandfather, I would like to be buried in the land that I consider my homeland—but for me it is the Philippines, not China.

About half a year into my stay in China, the opportunity arose for me to visit my maternal grandfather's village, Keren, located on the coast just a few kilometers northeast of Zengkeng. My maternal granduncle, who lives in Manila, had reclaimed family property in the village from the Chinese government and had refurbished the home built by my maternal great-grandfather. He invited some relatives, including my mother and me, to visit Keren and stay in that house.

The house was almost as huge as my paternal great-grandfather's house in Zengkeng, but not as imposing or majestic. Its charm, however, was that it was made of red bricks. The village was also charming. It was a fishing village and thus faced the sea. I remember walking on a windy and cloudy winter afternoon along the rocky shores on which the houses of the village were built, gazing at the large fishing boats anchored by the shores and rocking as strong waves washed across the sandy beach. There, my mother told me, my grandfather used to swim as a young man.

However, in the three days that we stayed there, we were not able to see much of Keren. Except for that untoward incident with the motorcycle driver, nobody had bothered me for money or gifts during my visit to Zengkeng. I had made it clear to the villagers, by telling the caretakers at once on my arrival, that I was a poor university student. Word quickly got around, and no one came asking for money. But in Keren I was in the company of my great-uncle, who everyone in the village knew had money. He had made a fortune out of being a businessman in Manila, and he did not want to be besieged by relatives and villagers asking for handouts.

For this reason, we did not venture outside the house often for fear of being seen by them. Although the villagers knew that we were there, my great-uncle had instructed the caretaker to tell all visitors that he was out. There was some truth to this claim, for sometimes we were visiting the nearby city. But at other times, we were just hiding inside the house. On the last day of our visit, my great-uncle did see some relatives and give them money, but when the other villagers heard about this, and knew that we would be leaving soon, they wanted to see him too. Our caretaker told us about this, and we had to sneak out by a different route to our van (which could not be parked right outside the house because of the terrain of the place) to avoid meeting the crowd that was on the way to the house.

One important fact that I learned in China was a very basic one. While growing up, I had thought that all the Chinese in the world were rich, like the people I often met in Manila or other parts of the Philippines. I had been socialized into thinking that all Chinese, wherever they were, belonged to the same socioeconomic class, with its itinerant characteristics and ways of life. And though I had heard of China being "poor," it was still something of a shock to see Chinese drivers, waiters, and beggars when I first went there. Before going to China, I had never seen Chinese people working in the "lowly" occupations that only the *hoan-nas* take in the Philippines. Back then I associated being a Chinese with being a businessman or with being part of the higher economic stratum of society. In China, of course, being Chinese is not linked to a particular class or profession.

The effect, therefore, of my visit to China was to make me realize that my search for the identity of a *lan-lang* did not begin or end there. I had thought that by going to China I would discover the true meaning of being a Chinese person, and that maybe I could learn to become more Chinese. For wasn't China the place where we, the *lan-langs* in the Philippines, could trace our true selves? Weren't her people and her culture the standards by which we should measure our *lan-lang*-ness? Instead, I learned that there is no one true *lan-lang*. But this realization did not come to me until several years after my trip. At the time, all I knew was that I had left and returned to the Philippines without feeling that my identity as a Chinese-Filipino had changed. In other words, I did not identify with the Chinese mainlanders, even if we were of the same blood.

My trip to China did not, for the years immediately succeeding my return to the Philippines, expunge my guilt. I continued to feel different from the other Chinese in the Philippines, despite the fact that I had lived in China and learned to speak Mandarin better than most people of my generation. During family gatherings and with Chinese friends, I still felt that I was the different one, different because I had persisted in pursuing my academic career instead of becoming a businessman. And even if my desire to be a scholar had been partly inspired by the stories of Confucius and other great Confucian scholar-officials, I was too young then to question or understand the contradiction between what I had been taught in school and what society expected of me. All the male role models whom I saw and met back then were businessmen, not scholars.

The resolution to my feelings of guilt only came after years of studying Chinese history and the history of the Chinese in the Philippines as a graduate student in the United States. There, I learned that the question of identity—Chinese or otherwise—is a complex and multifaceted issue. Identity is not simply a matter of race, language, or nationality; it means different things to people of different ages, sexes, classes, ideologies, places, and times. Thus one's identity is capable of being constructed, invented, or manipulated. There is no single real and unidimensional *lan-lang* (or *hoan-na*) to speak of. Even within the *lan-langs* in the Philippines, I am beginning to see that we are all different from one another and that we cannot be bracketed within a single homogeneous group.

To this day, when my mother looks at the choices I have made with regard to my career, she still sometimes says, "You have stopped being like a Chinese and have become like the foreign barbarians." The only difference now is that hearing her say this no longer bothers me.

In Search of My Ancestral Home

MYRA SIDHARTA

GRANDFATHER WAS A PROMINENT FIGURE ON THE ISLAND OF Belitung, one of the smaller islands in the Indonesian archipelago. Guests were always welcome, and many came to stay for several days or even weeks. These guests were relatives—some only because they bore the same surname—or just friends. They were all Hakkas, a Chinese minority people, and most of them came from my grandfather's birthplace of Meixian, a county in China's northern Guangdong province.[1]

From my grandfather, his guests, and his servants, I very often heard stories of Meixian. Some were proud of the beauty of its natural surroundings, and others praised the handicrafts to be found there, especially the baskets woven from bamboo. According to them, the people from Meixian are the most intellectual and cultured of the Chinese people. My grandfather's guests would teach the children of our family songs which, according to them, were well-known all over the world.

I was born in Belitung in 1927, and when I was a child, the outside

Myra Sidharta is an independent researcher and freelance writer in Jakarta, Indonesia. She was a professor of psychology at the University of Indonesia for more than thirty years until her retirement in 1992.

world was entirely represented to me by the stories told by these relatives and guests, until I finally learned geography in school. These stories made me curious, and I used to ask: "If life is so good there, why did people have to go overseas to make a living? Why did Grandfather have to sell his little brother before coming here?" When my grandfather heard me, he would just sigh and say: "Don't ask so many questions. Go and learn your lessons, and one day you will become rich and you will be able to go to Meixian and see for yourself." I longed to do so, since I wanted to leave little Belitung as soon as I could and see more of the world.

The majority of the Chinese in Indonesia trace their roots to Fujian province in southeast China. Those of Hakka stock are the next largest group of Indonesian-Chinese, and most of them originated in Meixian. On the islands of Kalimantan, Bangka, and Belitung, the majority of ethnic Chinese are Hakkas who came to work in the gold and tin mines.[2] It was in 1872, at the ages of fourteen and thirteen, that my grandfather and his younger brother joined an uncle who had preceded them to the islands to work in those mines.

It had not been easy for my grandfather and his brother to make this journey. They were from a poor farming family, and life was particularly hard because their father had died a few years earlier. As soon as they were old enough to leave home, they decided, like many other Chinese at the time to seek their fortune overseas, in Southeast Asia. But they had no money to pay for their passage. My grandfather was the eldest of three boys. To obtain this passage money, and to leave some money for his mother, who was going to stay behind, the family decided to sell the youngest boy, who was then only four years old.

They tried to rationalize the decision by saying that his birth sign did not agree with that of his father, and that that must have been the reason their father had died. It was my grandfather who had to carry his little brother on his back to other villages to offer him for sale. All the while Grandfather said to him: "Don't forget that your name is Jinxin, your family name is Ou-yang, and that you came from the village of Guaizitu, near the county of Meixian. My name is Fuxin and second brother's name is Yixin. When you grow up you must come and visit us, and we will be united again." His mother had written all these names on the cloth into which Jinxin's clothes were bundled, but they were afraid that the cloth might one day get lost. Drilling the names into the little boy's memory might be more effective, my grandfather thought. Luckily, he found a family that, having no sons, was happy to adopt little Jinxin. Relieved, Grandfather returned home and, a few weeks later, he left with Yixin for a new life in Southeast Asia.

Grandfather told us this story more than once, but I think he did so because of its happy ending: many years later Jinxin found Grandfather in Belitung after a long search, and the brothers were reunited. Jinxin had also emigrated to Indonesia and settled in Jakarta, where he found work. When he had saved enough money, he set up his own rice noodle factory. Only then did he have the courage to visit his brother who, according to the stories he had heard from fellow Hakkas, had made it to the highest ranks on the island of Belitung.

In fact, fortune smiled on my grandfather almost from his arrival in Indonesia. He was too young to work in the mines, but he managed to find employment in a shop owned by a local Chinese man. While in China, he had acquired a basic knowledge of written Chinese, and, after a few years, he was hired by a Dutch mining company to be an administrative employee and, later, an interpreter. Thus he was spared from ever having to work in the mines. In his spare time, Grandfather continued to study the Chinese classics with the hope of one day being able to take the civil service examinations in China. This never happened: the classics-based examinations were abolished a few years before China's last dynasty, the Qing dynasty, was overthrown in 1911.[3] Grandfather became an active member of a group within the overseas Chinese community in Indonesia working for the overthrow of the Qing. In 1895, he married my grandmother, Chung Ah Kee, a local-born Hakka, who was then sixteen years old, and started his own family in Indonesia. He regularly sent money back to Meixian to support his mother and his younger brother, Yixin, who had returned to China because the warm and damp climate in Belitung did not suit him.

Until World War II, Indonesia was a colony of the Netherlands. Under colonial rule, all Chinese, including those born in Indonesia, were considered "alien Orientals" and treated as Chinese citizens.[4] It is not surprising, therefore, that Grandfather never stopped looking to China as his real home, even though he had become so well established in Indonesia. He kept one foot in China and the other in his adopted country. That he did so was perhaps most evident in the way he arranged his children's education. He sent five of them to a local Dutch school, while the other five received a Chinese education in one of the local Chinese-language schools. This practice of giving half the children a Dutch education and half a Chinese education was quite common among Chinese-Indonesians in those days.

My father was one of the sons who had received a Dutch education. At home, we spoke Hakka, except with my father, with whom we spoke Dutch as soon as we had a fair grasp of the language. My father worked as an accountant for the same Dutch mining company on the island for which my grandfather had worked. As the children of an employee, my siblings and I were allowed attend the school run by the company. It was a small Dutch-language school; the teachers were recruited from Holland, the curriculum was similar to that of the schools in Holland, and most of the pupils were Dutch. For our entertainment, my father subscribed to some Dutch magazines. Our command of the Dutch language was thus quite good, and so was our knowledge of Holland and Dutch culture. However, we seldom mixed with our Dutch classmates after school hours. They would come to our birthday parties, but most of the time they were confined to their homes. Most Dutch people were then very conservative and apparently afraid of "strange" influences on their children. They were especially afraid of the influence of the natives, whom they considered of a lower class than themselves. As for us, we would freely play with the children of Chinese descent as well as the Malay pupils from school. We also had many cousins and playmates outside our own school, who went to one of the two Chinese schools run by private Chinese associations or to a government school that taught in the Malay and Dutch languages. But we related well because we had one common language: the Hakka dialect.

During the Japanese invasion, both the Dutch and Chinese schools were closed. The Dutch teachers were sent to prison camps, but the Chinese teachers were not jailed. Some teachers had been recruited from China and had no relatives in Indonesia. My grandmother offered one of them, a single young woman, free board and lodging in exchange for tuition to her grandchildren. Thus, my Chinese-educated cousins could continue their education, and I decided to join them to learn Mandarin.

I made good progress, and my grandfather was very proud of me. Once, when I showed him my writings, he said to me: "Good, now you can show people that although you are Dutch-educated, you can also be a good Chinese." He said that he knew that we had been taught Dutch patriotic songs in school and was worried that we would abandon our Chinese identity. I assured him that going to Dutch school was only a means to advance in life, and that we had no intention of becoming Dutch. He knew it, but his Chinese-educated children were equally successful, and I thought that he may have wondered if there had been any point in having arranged a Dutch education for some of his children. He looked sad then, and said nothing, but I thought he might be thinking of Meixian.

Grandfather died a few months after this conversation. I once heard him saying to a friend that he regretted not having returned to Meixian. The war was then raging in China and in Europe, so he did not think that he would ever have the opportunity to go there again. And indeed, Grandfather never did return to, or even visit, his home village. When he took three of his daughters to visit China in 1933, they went to Beijing and Shanghai, but not to Meixian. The village was too far from the big cities like Hong Kong and Guangzhou, and transportation was quite a problem in those days.

I continued my part-time Chinese studies and learned more about China from a cousin who advised me to read books written by such authors as Ba Jin and Lu Xun, novelists who were active in depicting China's social problems in the first half of the twentieth century.[5] Of course, these books were too difficult for me to read, but my tutor and my cousin helped me to understand the stories. I was appalled by all the cruelties I read of, and it was only then that I understood what the people in China were going through. I decided to study hard, so that I could go to China to help them. What with my studies, and the stories I had heard from my grandfather, a visit to Meixan became a pilgrimage that I resolved to make in my lifetime.

When the war was over, I discussed with my father the possibility of going to China for further studies. He agreed with my motivations but discouraged my intention of further studies in China. The situation there was far from stable.[6] Moreover, he foresaw difficulties for me because I had not mastered the Chinese language well enough to study all the difficult subjects at the university level. But the situation in Indonesia had also become unstable because of the revolution for independence. Therefore, he suggested that I finish my studies in Holland, and I agreed.

Life in Holland was not easy: I had difficulties in adjusting to the different climate, food, and lifestyle. Luckily, I made many friends among other ethnic Chinese students from Indonesia. We formed a small group that came together once a week to discuss the political situation in China as well as in Indonesia. At that time, we considered ourselves marginal people. Officially, we were Dutch subjects, but we were Chinese by blood, by citizenship, and to some extent by language and culture. At the same time, Indonesia was our home; yet before the establishment of Indonesia as a nation, we had no claim to Indonesian nationality.

In 1949 China became a Communist country, and the independence of Indonesia was recognized in that same year.[7] One of the major problems we faced was that of nationality. We had to choose between Dutch or Indonesian citizenship. If we chose the latter we had to renounce our Chinese citizenship, because the new Indonesian government would not allow dual citizenship. We were forced to decide which country we truly belonged to. From the reports about China in the media, it became quite clear to us that China was not at all an attractive place to live, because we were so used to a different lifestyle. Thus, we decided that Indonesia was our home country and that we would all like to live and to work there. Together, we opted for Indonesian citizenship and resolved to return to Indonesia after we finished our studies.

I went back to Indonesia in 1958. I had studied psychology, and my husband had specialized as a neurologist. We were both needed to teach at the University of Indonesia, and we were happy that we could contribute to the training of students there. The political and economic situation in Indonesia was far from attractive, but we felt that we should help to develop the country.

Yet we were to discover that restraints had been imposed on our full participation in Indonesian society. Since 1950, the ethnic Chinese of Indonesia have been subjected to many discriminatory rules and procedures. A limit was placed on the number of such students admitted to the universities. It also became difficult for ethnic Chinese students to take up certain studies, such as those offered by the armed forces. On graduating, Chinese students faced job discrimination in the civil service, especially in the foreign service. For medical graduates, specializations in surgery and ophthalmology were not possible. And, in 1959, President Sukarno issued a decree banning all ethnic Chinese with Chinese citizenship from doing business in rural areas.[8] As a result, many Chinese decided to leave for China.

Another exodus to China occurred in 1965, when a coup to topple the Sukarno regime failed. The Chinese government was allegedly involved in the staging of this coup, and consequently the Chinese schools were closed and all literature in the Chinese script was banned. Thousands of students went to China, hoping that they could continue their studies there. Although we were not directly affected, we felt that a lot of injustice had been perpetrated against the ethnic Chinese. While many of our Chinese-Indonesian friends subsequently resettled in Holland, my husband and I stayed on and continued working.[9] We heard that in mainland China much unjust treatment was also being meted out to certain groups and classes of people, and I felt lucky that we were not living there.

In Indonesia, we mixed with people from all races and nationalities and had many friends among the native Indonesians. My husband had a flourishing practice, and his patients came from all parts of the country and belonged to the highest as well as the lowest classes of society. I myself, through teaching at the university and opening a children's psychiatric clinic, also had many clients who came to me for help. We never denied our ethnicity, and as ethnic Chinese we were accepted by all the Indonesians. Meanwhile, we gained an increasing appreciation of Indonesia and Indonesian culture and gradually came to feel more Indonesian than Chinese or Dutch.

Our first visit to China reinforced this feeling. Around 1980, China started to open up to tourists. We were curious about the sites that we had read about, such as the Great Wall, the Forbidden City, and so on, so my husband and I joined a tour specially organized for overseas Chinese.[10] We admired the beautiful monuments of the country and the cultural performances, but we did not like the treatment we received. The hotels we stayed in were not at all comfortable, and the service was poor. In the restaurants we were treated rudely; waiters would slam doors or put articles, such as cutlery or a bottle of soy sauce that we had asked for, down with a bang on the tables. We wondered what it was that had made them so angry and tried to correct our attitude toward them by being friendlier. However, it seemed that any request we made was seen as a criticism and as such was not acceptable. Of course, we compared them with the waitresses in Indonesia, who were probably less efficient and fast in their service but much more polite and friendly. However, we also knew that generalizing their behavior as being typically Chinese would not be fair toward the millions of other Chinese who might be friendly and polite toward us.

About half the participants of the group that we joined were from Indonesia, and some of them were of Hakka origin. One couple told me that they were going to Meixian after the tour to visit their relatives. They already had their visas and plane tickets. Back in Indonesia, they told us of their wonderful reception in Meixian. When I said that I would like to go too, they gave me some information about how to get there.

Such a trip would not be as easy for me as it had been for them, because our family had had no contact with our relatives in Meixian for a long time. The relatives I hoped to meet were the descendants of my grandfather's brother, Yixin, who had accompanied my grandfather to Indonesia when they were both young teenagers and who had returned to China after a few years because he had become sick. He had then been about sixteen years old. Grandfather had sent money home for him and their mother, and for the maintenance of part of the old family house that they occupied. After Grandfather passed away, Grandmother had continued to send money. Contact with these relatives in China lapsed after Grandmother's death in 1964, but this was not simply because she had been the main link with them. Only two years after her death, the Cultural Revolution broke out in China. With the antiforeign attitudes prevailing in China then, we considered it better not to contact our Chinese relatives for fear that they would suffer for having overseas ties.[11]

In 1982, after much work and preparation, I was finally able to visit Meixian. From my husband, I got financial support, as well as the permission to embark on this adventure: his signature was required by the Indonesian immigration authorities for me to obtain an exit permit. My mother, sisters, and cousins gave me all the necessary moral support and advice required for such a trip. Other relatives, such as my aunt in Singapore and my cousins in Belitung and in Hong Kong, provided me with more information about my grandfather. A genealogical book with information about the Ou-yang family from the fifteenth century to the present day also became a pleasant guide during my search. On the recommendation of a friend, I contacted the Hakka Association in Hong Kong. One of the members gave me a letter of introduction to the local authorities in Meixian. Thus, as prepared as I could be, I boarded a rattling plane in Guangzhou and flew to Meixian.

The guest house in which I stayed in Meizhou, the capital of Meixian County, was a very well-built old mansion. The fans in the high ceilings spread cool air. I rested for a while and then went out to contact the local officials. Apparently, they had already been informed of my arrival, and they gave me a warm welcome. When I told them that I wanted to see my relatives by the surname Ou-yang, and gave them the name of the village, they immediately called a man from the city office bearing the same surname. Luckily, this man knew of the family, although he was not a relative. He told me that he would inform my relatives of my arrival and ask them to see me the next morning.

Early the next morning, after breakfast, I was told that some guests wanted to see me. They turned out to be Yixin's granddaughter-in-law, a woman in her seventies, and two of her sons. She told me that her husband's father and younger uncle had passed away and that her husband was Yixin's eldest grandson. We had a look at the genealogical book, so I could make sure who they were and to which generation they belonged. At the same time, I could check whether they were really my relatives.

The woman—I was told to address her as "Sister-in-law Xiu"—showed her surprise that a female member of the family had come, and that I was by myself. I did not elaborate on my personal motives, but I told her that I wanted to visit the clan house and all the members. My friends, who had visited Meixian the previous year, had advised me to offer them all a lunch. Sister-in-law Xiu accepted my proposal that I host a lunch for the Ou-yang clan on the following day. After some calculations and consultation with her sons, she said that the estimated cost would be US$75.00 for a meal for about a hundred people. That was about the amount that my friends had paid on their visit, too, and I accepted their offer.

Meanwhile, I had formed a pleasant impression of my relatives. They were polite and friendly—not at all like the impression I had formed of the people in Beijing. They were dressed in a simple outfit, a white shirt and blue trousers, like the millions of Chinese I had seen on my previous visit, but they did not give the impression of being poor.

After this meeting, we went out for some sightseeing. Sister-in-law Xiu told me that there were many interesting places to visit, and she recommended a tour to a temple in the hills. After lunch, we returned to the guest house, and my relatives returned home. They told me not to go out, but I did not feel like sitting in the room for the whole evening. After all, I had not seen the town of Meizhou at all and was curious as to what it looked like. So, after dinner, I ventured out and asked a trishaw rider to take me sightseeing in the town. We agreed on the price, and off we went. To my eyes, the town looked like the many China-towns of Southeast Asia: standing in rows were shop houses, with porches in front where people sat down and merchandise was sometimes displayed.

There was also a park in the middle of the town where I saw people sitting and singing the mountain songs that I had heard as a child. A sense of nostalgia welled up in me, and I stayed there a while, before heading back to the hotel. I felt completely safe there, and I wondered why my relatives had told me to stay in the hotel.

The next morning a bus was waiting for me, and after breakfast I departed for a very important moment—the visit to my ancestral home, about a fifteen-minute drive from the town. We stopped in front of a large but simple brick building with a big well in front. It was not the original house where my grandfather had lived, but an enlarged structure, extended with the money my grandfather had sent back for the clan. His younger brother, Yixin, had been living there. Now his grandson, Man (Sister-in-law Xiu's husband), was head of the household of about fifty people, consisting of his family and his brother's family, including their sons, daughters-in-law, and grandchildren. Some other family members had apparently long since moved out to Meizhou or other provinces to work.

In the main hall was the ancestral altar table, and on the wall behind it was a board with the names of deceased male members of the clan. I could see the names of Grandfather and a cousin, who had died in infancy, but the names of my father and his brothers, all of whom had died after 1960, were not listed.

Sister-in-law Xiu guided me in a prayer at the family altar, and, when it was finished, a young man lighted a string of firecrackers that went off with a bang! I had officially entered the family home. I felt as if the clock had been set back half a century. Surely the house was not like my grandfather's house, but the activities I saw were very similar to those of his household. There were so many people, all of them my relatives, because they told me that they had invited all the members of the family with the same great-grandfather.

Sister-in-law Xiu's husband, whom I addressed as Brother Man, took me to see the house, and a small group of men followed. They showed me the kitchen in the back and two rows of rooms at the side, apparently used for bedrooms. It was for me an experience of déjà vu. The house looked very much like the houses in the mining villages of Indonesia, but much cleaner. Just as in my grandfather's house, the female members had arrived early to help in preparing the banquet. They were chatting happily, and a number of men just sat there watching, now and then making comments. The younger men were arranging tables and chairs, and the children were playing noisily.

They also showed me the compound where vegetables and herbs were planted for the common use of everyone living in the house. They had to build several godowns, where they kept supplies of rice, potatoes, and preserved vegetables and fruits. The rice fields were a few miles away, so I was not taken to see them. "Since the last few years we had to build these godowns, to keep our stock. Our harvest is so good now, that we have more than enough for our daily needs, and are able to keep a stock for the winter," Brother Man told me. He praised the agriculture department for supplying the farmers with good seeds and fertilizers, sounding very much like a person making propaganda for the government.

I got the impression then that my relatives were quite well-off now, which was in line with media reports that the economy in China had improved and that farmers, especially, were profiting from the progress. Two of Brother Man's sons had built shops in the compound, a hairdressing salon and a tailor's shop, and seemed to be doing quite well. With these two shops they showed that they were not confined to farming as their livelihood, but were also trying to enter the world of business and trade. That was good, because I did not have to feel guilty about not being able to help them financially.

We went inside, where all the guests had gathered, and the banquet commenced. I was seated at the center table with Brother Man and Sister-in-law Xiu and a few elderly people who did not live in the same house but had good relations with the family. Just before the banquet started, one of the men approached me and whispered: "I am sorry to ask you this, we know that you have already spent so much to give us this treat. But we would like to share our joy with the rest of village too. So, if you don't mind, we would like to rent a movie. It usually comes with a big screen that we set up in front here, and thus the whole village can come to enjoy with us. It is also our way of telling the people that one of our relatives, who has done well overseas, has returned." I asked about the amount needed and it was the equivalent of US$20.00, which I, of course, could not refuse. The movies were announced during lunch: two educational movies, not the ones that came from Hong Kong. I concluded from the applause that followed that the clan was very happy. Since this was the first time that a member of their family had returned, the movie must be giving them face in front of the village. Besides, the movie must be a welcome attraction; there was no television in the village.

The food was the familiar Hakka food served at my grandfather's home: steamed chicken, braised pork with salted vegetables, fresh vegetables, and steamed fish. It was delicious, except that the rice was a bit dry for my palate, which was used to the soft Indonesian rice. After a few glasses of red rice wine, tongues loosened, and my relatives started to tell me about the past, which had meant poverty for all of them. But now everything was fine again, and they were producing surpluses. They praised the economic reforms instituted by China's new government and above all, Deng Xiaoping, the head of that government and the architect of the reforms, who was also a Hakka, from Sichuan province.[12] All other Hakkas were also praised, including my grandfather, who had prospered overseas.

I found all this chauvinistic boasting about the Hakkas pretty boring so I was glad to mix with the women after the banquet. We were seated in one of the bedrooms, with some of the women sitting on the top of an old bunk bed. These women were spontaneous and possessed a lively curiosity. When one of them wanted to pour tea, Sister-in-law Xiu intervened and showed them a can of Milo.[13] Proudly she said: "We can buy this in the shops now; it is imported from Hong Kong. Let's serve this to our guest."

I didn't decline; apparently this humble drink was considered a luxury, reserved for special guests—it was a symbol of the hostess's good taste and status. When I took my first sip, I had the feeling that everybody was anxiously awaiting my reaction. So I decided to play my role and showed them with my expression that I was delighted.

They confessed that they were somewhat disappointed in my appearance. They had expected to see an elegant lady dressed in glittering clothes, as in the movies, and not one dressed in a T-shirt and jeans! They were also surprised when I asked them questions about social issues. They did not realize that so much news of China appears in the international media. For instance, when I asked the daughter-in-law of Brother Man why she was allowed to get pregnant again, when she already had a little daughter of two, she was both embarrassed and surprised: embarrassed because I had noticed her condition, and surprised that I knew about China's one-child policy.[14]

In fact, they asked me as many questions as I asked them, so the conversation became very lively in between my sips of Milo. I related much better to the women, who, in spite of their limited education—they had all attended elementary school only—showed a keen interest in the outside world. From the questions they asked, I concluded that they had read many books and listened to the radio.

At around 5:00 P.M. I had to leave them because I was expected at the mayor's office for a banquet, the last major event before my departure from China. The farewell from my relatives was very warm. They all told me that they hoped that I would return soon. I was happy to have met them all, my grandfather's family who had become my friends in such a short time. I was also happy because, in contrast to the experiences of my friends and other stories that I had heard, they did not ask me to come back with presents, such as electronic goods and luxury articles! When I saw them waving to me as I drove off, I wonder whether they had the same feeling I had had about visitors when I was still living on the island of Belitung. At that time, visitors represented for me the big wide world, and I had wondered then when that world would be mine too.

The dinner at the mayor's office was splendid. There were two guests of honor: a businessman from Singapore and me. The best Hakka food was served, such as smoked goose with garlic sauce, braised duck, barbecued pork, and much more. In his speech, the mayor praised the two guests who had come all the way from Southeast Asia in search of their roots, and expressed the hope that we would come back one day to help in the development of Meixian. They needed schools, a new university, libraries, and, above all, facilities for tourists, such as hotels, museums, and recreation centers. Better transport facilities would also be needed if these projects were to be realized.

On hearing this, the businessman replied that he wanted to see what he could do, and that he would consider returning to invest his money here. I, however, could not reply. I was not an entrepreneur, and I did not have the money or know-how to bring about such changes. The officials must have been very disappointed with me.

The next morning I flew home. Sitting in the bus on the way to the airport, I thought that if my grandfather were still alive, I could tell him that he was right. His country is beautiful, and the people are hardworking and friendly. I wanted to tell him that I had fulfilled my promise to visit his country and that, if I ever got the chance, I wanted to visit it again. However, I certainly also had to thank him for staying in Southeast Asia in spite of the hardships he had experienced, and for marrying my grandmother. Although we are not rich businesspeople, we all have enjoyed a good education, and we can look back on a fairly good life.

My trip to Meixian was made sixteen years ago, and China has changed a great deal since then. Many times I have considered going back to Meixian. Once I was quite close to a decision when some friends, who had attended a conference in another part of Guangdong province with me, told me that they were renting a car and were going to visit Meixian. I decided not to go, probably for fear that so much might have changed. Brother Man and Sister-in-law Xiu may not be around anymore, and the young women may now be less spontaneous and warm. I did not want to spoil the memory of that first visit when I had surprised my relatives and had made them and myself so happy.

My visit brought me back to my Chinese childhood in Indonesia, which is still so dear to me. I had the feeling then that the clock had been turned back and that I was visiting my cousins, who were staying in my grandfather's house. I still relish the moments of nostalgia that I experienced during my trip to Meixian. It brought me happiness to be with my Chinese relatives, but I was also happy to return to my own world. My world, the present-day Indonesia, has its problems and controversies, but that is the place where I work and feel most needed.

A Yellow American in China

BRAD WONG

WE HAD REACHED AN EMPTY CHICKEN COOP AND A FADED, WHITE-washed wall when the rear wheel of my motorcycle taxi spun and spun. It kicked up mud and made a deep groove in the wet earth. That morning there had been sporadic rainfall. A gray blanket of clouds covered what I remembered as a lush, green village with a bright, blue sky. An earlier downpour had turned a sloping path into a creek. The water rushed toward the houses. This path, along with a dirt road, is one of two ways to the outside world for this village of eighty people, tucked among rolling hills in a sleepy pocket of the new, dynamic China—one of the fastest-growing economic engines in the world.

My return in 1996 to my grandfather's village of Long An, just a few miles outside Taishan in the southern Chinese province of Guangdong, was a sharp contrast to my visit two years earlier. On the day of my first visit, the sun was shining. Peasants were harvesting crops of vegetables and rice. As a few barefoot girls giggled and scurried about, their parents and relatives relaxed under a large, sprawling tree that provided

Brad Wong is pursuing a master's degree in international affairs at Columbia University's School of International and Public Affairs. Previously he was a journalist writing on politics and illegal immigration, as well as a contributor to Lonely Planet Publications.

shade and served as the village meeting place. Life seemed idyllic. It seemed much less so now—perhaps because, apart from the oppressive weather, this time I was coming with a deeper insight into what village life was really like.

My first visit to the village was hectic, tense, emotional. I had accompanied my mother, aunts, and uncle to this place where their father had been born and raised. He left the village in 1912 at the age of seventeen to escape famine and turmoil in an area where locals have eaten tree bark to survive—and even today they look pretty thin. Armed with false identity papers declaring that he was a U.S. citizen, he went to live with two village relatives in California.[1] He would later return to China four times, to marry and to visit his family. After his first wife died, he married my grandmother in the 1920s, while he was still in the United States and she was in a nearby Taishan village. He eventually brought her and his three daughters to the United States in the 1930s.

Life was difficult for them, but they managed. Before World War II, my grandfather sold vegetables from a truck to nearby restaurants, ran a lottery in Oakland's Chinatown, and worked at a grocery store in the area. and During the war, he worked at the Alameda Naval Shipyard. He eventually managed to save enough to open Great China, a restaurant of his own in Oakland, California. In Oakland he raised a family of six daughters and one son.

My grandfather died before I was born. But he used to tell my mother that the village and its rolling hills—which locals say resemble a dragon's curvy back—were paradise. To a romantic, Chinese villages can indeed look beautiful with their carefully sculpted rows of crops. Bundles of green vegetables sprouting from the brown earth provide a crisp, sharp, yet soothing contrast for the eye. Peasants carrying buckets of water slung over their shoulders, balanced by a bamboo pole, symbolize a hard but honest day's work. I often thought that country life was ideal, perhaps more meaningful than the whirlwind of the West and my suburban life. It seemed pure and uncomplicated.

But it only looks like utopia—especially through the eyes of someone who never has to do the work. In reality, the manual labor involved with village life can make a body ache and age faster, and a person's hands bleed within minutes. I learned that lesson when I tried to live that kind of life myself. My grandfather had no choice. He was a peasant. I know that older Chinese immigrants often don't dwell on the abject poverty they escaped or what they have done to survive. The memories are too painful. There is no use, many say. So they remember the good.

One thing my grandfather did not tell his children about was the house where he was raised. On our 1994 trip, we saw it for the first time. After we walked down a narrow village alley, between faded cement homes and with the stench of manure in the air, we finally saw it—a brown brick-and-mud hut with a low ceiling and shingle roof. A small, dusty courtyard lay in front. A large plastic sheet covered the doorway, and tall weeds stood nearby. As my mother, aunts, and uncle peered over the plastic sheet into the small, dark room, they caught a glimpse of their father's former life and its cramped confines. It was the only remaining room of what appeared to have been a two- or three-room house.

Looking through the doorway of the house, we discovered that the villagers had kept water buffaloes in the tiny room. A pile of manure was in the corner. We stood and inspected everything in the courtyard. Villagers crowded around and stared at us, the American-born relatives. We were both familiar and foreign. We had Chinese faces but wore Western clothing and spoke a different language. My mother and her siblings stood in awe, wept, and asked questions. We were finally seeing the conditions my grandfather had left—and the place where our family had begun.

My father's side had a similar experience of leaving China and settling in the United States. His ancestral village is closer to Guangzhou, the booming capital of Guangdong province. His parents left during the 1910s and 1930s, stayed at the Angel Island immigration center in San Francisco Bay, and eventually settled in Oakland to run a market.[2] By that time, my mother's family was running their restaurant in the city's Chinatown.

With my parents having been born in the United States, I grew up a third-generation American, knowing little about my Chinese heritage. I was born in 1968 and raised in a northern California suburb with clean streets, nice homes, and safe schools. In my neighborhood, there were few Chinese-American families. At local stores, school functions, and weekend soccer games, it was easy to spot my parents in a crowd: they were the ones with the straight black hair. As a young boy, I gave race and ethnicity little serious thought. At one point, I was even under the impression that these were things that one could change at will. So one year I thought I would be Chinese-American, the next year I thought I would change and become Caucasian, and the following year I thought I would be African-American. I didn't realize a person's race and ethnicity never change.

Because my neighborhood was predominantly Caucasian, I spoke English at school and at home. My sister and I attempted to study Cantonese at a local Chinese school on Friday evenings so we could communicate with our grandmothers, who were our only surviving grandparents. They spoke no English, and, unfortunately, I never gained much more fluency at Chinese school than to say, "I want an order of fried noodles."

But my Chinese face led to certain experiences that many other Chinese-Americans share: people thought I could not speak English, some blamed me for the 1941 Japanese attack on Pearl Harbor, and still others made disparaging comments about Chinese and Asians in front of me. They didn't appear to think anything of it. And even in the 1990s, after generations of Chinese-Americans have strived for equal treatment and respect, and some have excelled in politics, academia, business, art, and literature, people still ask me where I'm from.

As a college student, I began to study Asian-American history and politics. From socially conscious relatives and thought-provoking professors, I learned about the Chinese-American experience, beginning with the first Chinese immigrants' arrival on the West Coast. In part, these experiences fueled my curiosity about what China in the 1990s was like. If I stood out in the States, would the opposite be true in China? Could I fit in with a billion people with black hair? What would I find? That became my quest. China—truly a foreign place for me, but the link to my ancestry—lurked in the back of my mind. After that first trip to China with my mother and her siblings, I decided it was time to experience what my ancestors had known.

After traveling through different Chinese provinces in 1996, I contacted local officials in Guangdong and told them I wanted to work in the fields so I could understand China. I told them I didn't want to visit my grandfather's village again just then, because I wanted to avoid relatives asking me for money. Also, my grandfather's village is too poor to accommodate a guest. As I talked with the officials, they kept reminding me that peasant life was too hard. I told them I wanted to experience it.

So the local officials took me and my translator to another village a few miles north of Taishan City (Toisan in the local dialect). It was right off a new highway, and by Chinese standards it was prosperous. Many overseas relatives send money back, locals sell food at the free markets, and there are a few small factories. To me, the place looked tidy but run-down.

They paired me with a local village chief, a skinny, graying man who enjoyed smoking cigarettes. As chief, he had a motorcycle and a relatively spacious cement home for his family. He managed some small factories and farmed a few acres of land, giving some of the crops to the government in payment and selling the rest at the township's free market. He had been a farmer for more than thirty years. And from left to right, his green fields blowing in the wind were lush and beautiful. Our task—on my first true day as a peasant—was to clear about fifty yards of overgrown foliage in the irrigation ditches.

As he handed me a shovel, I noticed it was a long bamboo pole with a metal spade attached at the end. He showed me how to first loosen the mud and then chop through the plant roots. He would follow and scoop the underbrush out. So I kicked off my sandals, rolled up my green People's Liberation Army pants, and felt mud ooze between my toes.

For the first few minutes, I was fine. I thought the shoveling wasn't as hard as it looked. After all, I was young. With my shirt off, I periodically stopped to wipe sweat from my forehead. But, in a matter of minutes, pressure from gripping the bamboo pole started to rip my skin and blister my fingers and palms. My hands became tender and raw.

I was embarrassed and said nothing. When we rested, I kept my arms to my side and my palms away from their sight. I just kept working, trying to help. But my translator soon noticed that I was gripping the shovel delicately to alleviate the pain. He pulled my hands up. About a dozen blisters had formed. Some had already ruptured my skin, and blood was starting to drip down my palms. I looked at my hands in disbelief, not realizing this could happen. "Let's have a rest," the chief finally said. It was late afternoon, and he decided it was time to eat dinner. It also was a polite excuse to stop me, an international guest, from hurting myself any further.

Later, at a banquet with some government officials, my translator recounted my experience in the trenches. He also held up my bloody hands. The people sitting around the table looked at me in bewilderment. They probably wanted to know why I sought such hardship. In many cases, perhaps because of few opportunities, Chinese people say they're used to jobs that may be backbreaking or mind numbing. While the job may be their only way to survive, the saying may be their only way to rationalize their circumstances. But deep down inside, I don't think anyone ever gets used to being a peasant. My stint as one lasted only a few days.

Yet despite this experience and knowing that my relatives might ask for money, I still wanted to revisit my grandfather's village. I wanted to see again, and more clearly, the life that he knew. So, on that summer day in 1996, I showed up to visit relatives in the tiny village nestled among brown and green mountains. This time, only a translator accompanied me. Of the relatives we had met previously, only my distant cousin's mother, second wife, and son were home.

Their dark gray clothing seemed to match their mood—and that of the day. Because crops were growing and the rainy season prohibited picking or planting vegetables, my cousin and other village men were searching for factory work in various cities. Only elderly women, mothers, and children remained. Some huddled around a low table and played cards to pass the time.

My cousin's mother was sitting under the same large tree that I remembered from my 1994 visit, when she spotted me and my translator. She ran over to greet us. "How are you?" I asked with a smile and in the little Cantonese I knew. After we shook hands, she opened the door to their tiny house. Inside, flies covered the straw-burning stove, cement floor, and chipped table—the same one my family had sat around discussing my grandfather's life two years earlier. My cousin's wife appeared and greeted us. A son about five years old wandered into the room, clutching a plastic bottle of water with a goldfish in it. Flies had descended on him too.

Throughout the village, chickens were running loose. The stench of manure filled my nose. With little money, my relatives often cannot pay their electricity bill, so there was no fan to circulate the thick, humid air or power the lights. A little daylight entered through a ceiling window in the otherwise dim room.

Sitting on wooden chairs, we talked politely about one another's families and everyone's health. My cousin's mother explained that work was scarce. This was the first time my cousin had been able to find some in a while, she said. Two of her granddaughters were unemployed and stayed in the village. She cared for three of them. As peasants, they work when they can and wait when they must. Because they need field workers to survive, many have escaped the country's strict one-child policy.[3]

After chatting for a few minutes, I asked to see my grandfather's house again. My translator and cousin's mother stood by and talked in the village dialect, which I cannot speak. I had no idea what they were saying. I looked around and noticed that leaves from some big trees I saw in 1994 were gone. The courtyard looked more barren. I snapped a few pictures, but raindrops started to cloud the lens. With rain continuing to fall, we quickly returned to the house.

My relative and translator continued to talk. He finally turned and looked at me. She wanted financial help. Instead of immediately asking for money directly, though, she first described her reality—how she and her son take care of so many people in the family, and how one of her grandsons wants to get married. There was no room in the current house for him and his future wife to live, she said. Also, one of her granddaughters was a college student who can speak English. She needed work. My relative added that every year her family cleans my great-grandparents' hillside graves. The cleaning is part of a spring festival at which relatives worship ancestors, honor them with flowers, and pray with incense.[4] My translator told me the total dollar figure of her requests and explained what other overseas Chinese have done in similar situations. The translation was clear.

She wanted a loan to build a new three-story house on the site of my grandfather's hut. She asked for immigration help so that her English-speaking granddaughter, who knows no one in the United States, could live and work overseas. And, for all those years of grave cleaning—an important task in a Confucian society where respect flows upward to elders and the deceased—she requested compensation from the overseas relatives.

I was the conduit. I understood why this seventy-six-year-old woman with a silver-streaked bob who had worked decades in the fields was asking for help. The blistering sun had turned her skin leather brown. She had wrinkles, spots, and creases. Thin clothing hung off her skinny, frail frame. Traces of dirt covered the face and legs of her grandchild, the boy playing with the goldfish in the plastic bottle.

I looked at my cousin's wife. Her skin also was rough and dark from the sun and wind. Insects hovering in the fields had bitten her legs, scarring them. After years of wading through mud and ankle-high water, fungus had turned the skin under her toenails brownish yellow. And here I was, sitting in their hovel, as my translator wiped mud off his Western athletic shoes.

My relatives live a substantial distance from the nearest city center and its free market. While they have more food than they did twenty years ago, the distance to the market essentially bars them from selling what they have grown and prospering like others. Given all this, it was easy to see how my village relative could view me as a wealthy person who somehow could produce miracles. In her eyes, any relative with enough money to fly twice from a place that literally means "beautiful country" in Chinese to his ancestral home must be rich.

In part her request stemmed from a tradition of overseas relatives helping those who remain. In the south, where there has been a mass exodus to foreign countries, new schools, houses, stores, and cement roads dot the rural landscape. The money comes from those emigrants and their children whose lives have improved. And the peasants often boast about gifts of overseas money. They may be simple, uneducated people who toil in the fields. Some urban residents may treat them as

second-class citizens. But many have wealthy relatives who have succeeded in another country. As a result, these peasants have "face;" they
have prestige.

My relatives' request was not new, but more explicit. It blossomed
from an earlier hint. In a letter after the 1994 visit, they said that they
were happy to meet us. Their family was fine. But village conditions
were the same. By default, on this trip, I became the stateside family
representative. That experience was new for me. When I was growing
up as one of the youngest American-born relatives in my family, I re-
lied on my mother, father, aunts, and uncles as the council of elders to
resolve family issues.

Still, my village relatives' plight worried me—the crowding, the filth,
their future. My concern was somewhat ironic, because I could hardly
communicate with them and didn't know them well. They are not direct relatives. But their lives reminded me of my grandfather's experiences before he left—or at least what I imagined them to be.

Seeing their lot also made me realize my own prospects. As a U.S.
citizen and a visitor, I could leave the country any time I wished. But
their few options included working in the fields, sitting in a tiny village house waiting to harvest crops, or searching for factory work. If
one of them was lucky or maintained good relations with local officials,
the person could ascend to the plum job of being a factory manager
or working in an office.

So on that day, after hearing their requests, I told them I would pass
the information to my family. Inside their house, around their table,
I gave my cousin's mother and wife enough money for three of them
to buy food for one month.

I later asked my translator why the government cannot provide for
the welfare of its citizens—or at least offer some type of help. Peasants
make up more than 70 percent of the country's 1.2 billion people. Why,
in this case, was the responsibility falling on a relative? The government has no money, he said. Or, as I thought later, it funneled resources
to other priorities. Sometimes, he added, visiting relatives receive so
many requests for financial and immigration help—and it becomes so
grating and constant—that they stop visiting. Even he perceived me
as a millionaire. He frequently referred to me as rich. Once he threw

out the phrase, "You can pay, because you're a rich, wealthy overseas Chinese" when we were eating with some of his friends. He jokingly patted me on the back.

As lunchtime approached that day in the village, my relatives invited me to stay and eat. But after seeing their circumstances, I decided to invite them to a restaurant. My cousin's wife stayed behind to look after her son.

By car or motorcycle, the nearest township with a restaurant is a quick drive from the village. But the motorcycle taxi had left, and there were three of us. Few buses or vehicles ply the road to the township. So, in a steady downpour and humid weather, we huddled under umbrellas, slogged through mud, and eventually reached the new cement road that would take us to a restaurant.

The walk was new for me. Since I was used to arriving in the village by hired van or motorcycle, the trek seemed long. Without a vehicle, we faced puddles, rainfall, and stagnant air. My hiking boots did not get excessively muddy, because we walked on the new cement road built with overseas Chinese money. Still, my feet and hair became wet. My glasses soon became blurry with water spots. As we walked, we passed roadside stores, crops, and other brick villages.

I constantly looked back at my cousin's mother to make sure she was OK. At her advanced age, she shuffled more than she walked. I kept thinking the walk was a burden on her body and her feet. But I forgot that she frequently walks to the township to buy goods. And, with so much physical work in the fields and village, a walk to town is easy for her.

Along the way, she occasionally talked with my translator. She explained what she does when my cousin is away from the village looking for factory work. She feeds the water buffaloes, which help with farming. She also plants rice and corn. Once, when she was farming, a water buffalo knocked her to the ground. But she did not suffer any injuries, she said. She just stood back up.

The walk to the restaurant took thirty minutes. I had no way of knowing if the restaurant we chose was good, or if it was going to be special for her. It looked like a large, open village building with people eating. She said she had never been there.

To celebrate the homecoming of sorts, I told my translator to order pork, beef, chicken, and a fish. All are rare and costly for peasants. But it was a special occasion. Midway through the meal, I noticed she was not eating the vegetables we ordered. I pointed to them and said they were delicious. "I eat vegetables every day," she responded. That fact had slipped my mind. With so many meat dishes, she carefully wrapped the leftovers to share with her grandchildren.

After lunch, we rented a truck to take us to a nearby village. She wanted me to meet her granddaughter, the one who could speak English. When we arrived at the house where the granddaughter was supposed to be, she was not there. So we waited. Like a nervous parent, my cousin's mother constantly kept looking out the door, hoping that she would appear. She eventually grabbed an umbrella and searched the village for her grandchild. By late afternoon, there was no sign of her, so we decided to leave.

The three of us walked to the roadside, where my translator and I caught a three-wheeled scooter taxi back to my hotel. She waited for a bus. With her eyes fixed on us, I told her I would give my family her request. She did not say much. "When will your parents and relatives visit?" she asked. I told her that I didn't know. "The American relatives must be busy," she said.

Before I returned to California, I went to the village two more times to share money and wish my relatives well. My family and relatives in the States had contributed enough dollars for them to buy food for three months. And, strangely enough, during all those visits, I felt like an immigrant myself—new, curious, unaware, somewhat timid, and, in a way, helpless.

I often think about all the opportunities I've had because my grandfather left his tiny, village house. I also think about some basic questions: "What if, by chance, I ended up a peasant who had to ask a visiting relative for money to survive? What would I do?" I would probably talk about crowded conditions, low-paying jobs, and lack of opportunities too.

Now that I have returned home, I am happy to hear when a friend or businessman donates money—occasionally thousands of dollars—to build schools, roads, and houses in China or when a friend decides to go there to teach English, a marketable skill for Chinese workers. When we can, my family sends money to the village.

In the West, we often view China as exotic, as having a repressive government, or as a new commercial market with boundless consumers. Sometimes we adopt it as a trendy "new" culture for our food and fashion. But the longer I stayed and learned about people's hopes, plights, and circumstances, the more I realized that China is a striking contradiction. Its rich history, culture, art, and cuisine are renowned. Yet for me, it is one of the saddest places on earth. I often wonder if I made a mistake by stepping across that border. Sometimes when I think about China, my thoughts and memories become too painful. But perhaps there is no use in worrying about something if nothing can be done. That mighty Western bravado and can-do spirit that I and other overseas Chinese have cannot solve everything. So as I think about the Middle Kingdom, I just try to remember the good.[5]

I'm not sure if I'll ever go back. My grandfather never had that option. He had the pressure to provide for his family in a new country. After bringing them to the United States, he never returned to his ancestral home. So for me, returning is a luxury I'm uncomfortable thinking about.

As I think about all my China experiences, I'm left with that one feeling of longing for a place that I love but yet don't want to romanticize because life can be so hard. It's odd. In both China and the United States, I can be accepted—and I cannot. The feeling can be difficult to describe. And ironically, my visit to my grandfather's village—where I thought I could fit in, but learned that I couldn't—underscored this truth more than I could have imagined.

When I'm around Westerners, my clear English and stateside education and outlook allow me to do something that many Chinese immigrants, like my grandparents, could never do—instantly communicate with Westerners and enter their conversation. And traveling and living in China are probably the best reminders for me of how fortunate I am to be a U.S. citizen and have the opportunities and freedoms that come with living in the West. But when I'm around my Chinese friends, or even among the masses in China's streets and countryside, a profound sense of comfort washes over me. I'm uncertain why. Perhaps it's all those faces or all that black hair—and the fact that I can blend in and be at home, although the country is not my birthplace. And perhaps it's because I always have the peace of mind of being a U.S. citizen.

I suppose when I'm with my Chinese friends, I feel comfortable because they view me as an instant family member, not as a stranger, not as a foreigner. They share with me, instead of assuming something about my face, culture, and background. All this prompts me to pause and think: these people are just like me in many ways. And after growing up in a suburb, where I often stuck out, that's a reassuring feeling. But I know, deep down inside, that we are still different in ways that I probably don't understand.

I suppose that's the beauty of it.

One Family, Two Fates

CAROLYN KOO

AS I HURRIEDLY STEPPED FROM THE CAB, MY AUNT SUDDENLY
appeared before me. In the dark, rainy Shanghai night, she said, "I'm
sorry, love, but he died this afternoon." I felt nothing, except that I
had come too late, despite the rush to catch the plane, the express tourist
visa, the ride from the airport to the house where my mother had spent
her long-ago childhood. There was nothing left but to trudge down
the alley into the house of mourning. It was the same alley where he
had stood so many times waiting for me, the last time in his dapper
new blue wool hat. It was strange not to see him there now. I tried to
console myself by picturing him as he'd been on my other visits—
shuffling slowly into the alley, supported by his cane. Occasionally, he
would greet a neighbor, but that was just a distraction. He would really be waiting for me, his granddaughter, anticipating my arrival as
much as I anticipated arriving. It was too late to see him again, but not
too late to know that I had done my best to forge a relationship with
him.

My flight to Shanghai that night in April 1995 took only two and a

*Carolyn Koo is a journalist in New York City with TheStreet.com, a financial news website. Be-
fore returning to the United States in the summer of 1998, she lived in Hong Kong for six years.*

half hours from Hong Kong. In reality, however, my journey to reach him and my family's past had taken much longer than that.

I had paid very little notice to my Chinese heritage during much of my childhood. I was born in the United States in 1970 and grew up in a suburb of New York City, where Chinese faces were few and far between. Although I realized that I looked very different from my Irish American and Italian American classmates, I didn't think much about it. Looking back, my childhood perceptions of my Chineseness emerge mostly as unrelated vignettes: I hated being dragged to dirty, smelly, crowded Chinatown for our monthly grocery runs, though I liked all the food we brought back. Like almost every other Chinese American I know, I did not appreciate my Chinese school experience, mostly because it involved extra work and Saturday classes. I felt superior because my parents could speak our secret language of Shanghainese in public and no one knew what they were talking about; we were privy to a secret code.[1] Compiling my family's genetic history for a fifth-grade biology class was one of my easiest assignments ever—for time immemorial, everyone related to me had black hair and brown eyes. And, once, on the bus when I was in fourth grade, an eighth grader taunted me with the derogatory epithet "chink," because I wouldn't vacate my seat for him.

That was the extent of my awareness—it was enough to know that we were Chinese but American too, and both had always seemed completely compatible, even complementary. My parents encouraged that perception, and my brothers and I accepted it. In fact, what consumed me was not China, but Europe and all things European. I collected pen pals—from England, Sweden, France, Germany, Northern Ireland, Luxembourg, and Greece—with the grand dream of one day touring the Continent and the British Isles and visiting all of them. My fascination with the British royal family, born during the Queen's Silver Jubilee in 1977 and cultivated during the early Princess Diana years, transformed me into a young expert royalist of sorts; it baffles my British acquaintances even today. Even as I ignored China and Asia, I was determined to see Europe and became a student of European foods, languages, peoples, and culture.

Once in a while, visiting my maternal grandmother would provoke thoughts of my grandfather, known to some as "Shi Di" and others as "Joe." As long as I could remember, my maternal grandmother had lived alone on Long Island, but I also knew that she had a husband, my grandfather, who resided in China. Why did they live apart? I had no idea. Why did no one ever speak of him in my presence? Again, I didn't have a clue. Admittedly, I didn't give it all that much thought. I was too busy trying to get As in school, practicing the piano, and reading my royal family books.

Then, one day in September 1980, my parents told me we were going to the airport. I fairly danced with excitement at the announcement. As a child, I loved going to the airport, because it fed into my yearning for travel to faraway places. I would stand in front of the departure screen, fascinated by the planes taking off for London, Paris, São Paulo, Tokyo, Stockholm. If I had realized the significance of our trip to the airport, I would have been even more excited. But I didn't. I only understood that my grandfather, who had lived in China all his life, was moving to the United States. He would be reunited with his wife and daughters, whom he hadn't seen in almost thirty years.

At John F. Kennedy International Airport, I immediately spied my favorite grandmother, my mother's mother, and ran to embrace her. Gna-Boo (the term in Shanghainese for maternal grandmother) seemed as cheerful as usual. Other relatives were there, too, including sixteen-year-old Jim, whom a football injury had consigned to crutches, and eleven-year-old Adam. The gathered family stood expectantly, waiting for the passengers to make their way down the runway. Then he was there, a proud, gray presence. And no one knew what to say, but tears streamed down my mother's face. My younger brother, Steven, said that's when he first realized that tears could be happy as well as sad. The Huang family was reunited.

We had no way of knowing then that he would return to Shanghai—for good—in just over a year.

Why and how this long-awaited reunion came to such a pass I would not begin to understand until very much later, and never fully, even though Gna-gong (the Shanghainese term for maternal grandfather) didn't disappear entirely from our lives after his return to China. For ten years, until he sustained a hip injury after getting shoved off an inevitably crowded Shanghai bus, he made annual sojourns back to the States. But his visits were stilted, formal affairs, usually just dinner, and then he'd be off to see friends we didn't know. He never stayed with any of his family, which was just as well, because none of us ever knew what to say to him. And he never visited his wife, my grandmother. I always came away from these meals full of unanswered questions about the trajectory of his life, but an implicit taboo prevented me from satisfying my curiosity during the entire decade of his visits.

Prompted by my interest in the shadowy figure of my grandfather, some time in my early teens, I started to put together a family tree. After badgering relatives all over the United States and in Singapore for birth dates and birth places and full names, during the course of a few years, I gained a reputation as the family chronicler. Eventually, when I had culled all the information I could from the relatives I knew, I reached an impasse. The next frontier for historical research would have to be China itself, and I formed vague—very vague—notions of one day learning Mandarin well and going there to finish the thing off. Tracing my genealogy, incomplete though it was, opened my eyes to the Westernized nature of my family's background. My paternal grandfather served as General Electric's Chinese liaison in Shanghai, so his English was fluent and his contact with foreigners, especially Americans, frequent. When the Communists bore down on Shanghai in the spring of 1949, my grandfather packed his wife and children off to Hong Kong on one of the last flights out of the city. Later on, his four sons all went to the States for college—my father in 1957—and settled there.

On my mother's side, the Huang family hailed from a tiny village in Taixing County in northern Jiangsu province. A land-owning clan of minor importance, and counting a government official who had passed the first level of civil service examinations among its members, the Huang family relocated from its ancestral roots to Shanghai when my grandfather and his three sisters were old enough to attend school. Gna-gong spoke English fluently, and his children—my mother and her sisters—all studied at English schools run by missionaries in Shanghai; my eldest aunt claims she never spoke anything but English to her father while growing up and, indeed, two of my aunts knew English well enough to work as English-language tutors on moving to Hong Kong as teenagers.

But perhaps my grandfather's best, and favorite, foreign tongue was French. He learned the language early on, after moving to Shanghai and enrolling in a school run by Jesuit fathers from France. Apparently he spoke French to my aunt the day he died, saying, "J'ai tout oublié parce que je n'ai pas eu l'occasion de pratiquer cette langue" (I've forgotten all my French because I haven't had a chance to practice). I recall attempting to impress him with my high-school-level French on one of his visits to the States. He immediately responded in as beautiful an accent as I'd ever heard, with vocabulary much beyond my comprehension. It was the last time I ever tried that.

In college my interest slowly turned from Europe to Asia. I chose to double-major in history and Asian studies, and my courses in Chinese language and history were a natural enlargement of my personal interest in my family tree. During my four years at Williams College in Williamstown, Massachusetts, I continued to research my heritage. Since my paternal grandfather had died when I was seven, and my paternal grandmother was afflicted with a form of Alzheimer's disease, little was known about my father's family. But my mother's side was easier to research. Having discovered that some of my maternal grandmother's siblings had studied at Boston University and at Oberlin College in the 1920s, I searched for—and found—records of their existence in school archives. I became ever more curious at this time about those relations that I still had in China, especially my maternal grandfather.

After four years of working with professors who ably stimulated an intellectual interest in Asia and a revival of interest in my family tree, it seemed a natural choice on graduation to gravitate toward China. Having sacrificed my opportunity to take a junior year abroad, I thought it would be folly to give up the chance that presented itself now. Indeed, I felt almost a sense of mission. I was lucky enough to attend a college with ties to Asia—Williams College and the Chinese University of Hong Kong's United College had established a student exchange program in 1961, and the program had gradually expanded to allow Williams alumni to teach English at the university. Truthfully, I had very little desire to teach. Journalism had become my field of professional interest, and if I had remained in the States, I would undoubtedly have pursued a career as a television producer. But everything else seemed perfect. It was the opportunity to go to Hong Kong with a job and housing. Hong Kong was not mainland China, but the mainland was only a stone's throw away. And certainly, living in modern Hong Kong seemed much more palatable than facing the hardships of China.

At that time, I had no responsibilities to anyone but myself, so I could just pick up and go. At last, I could achieve my goal of seeing the world. I'd travel and have the adventures I'd always dreamed of. But just as great an impetus was the opportunity to connect with my grandfather by learning about him and becoming acquainted with him. I knew just enough about him to find him intriguing, and what I didn't know tantalized me. Also, I began to understand then how events beyond anyone's control had worked to divide Chinese families like mine, even when its members could finally be together again. The resulting sense of loss was not confined to members of those generations with immediate experience of those events.

And so I shipped off to Hong Kong in August 1992, looking forward always to my first visit to Shanghai. During my first nine months in Hong Kong, I took great advantage of the territory's proximity to most points in Asia and eagerly went about collecting stamps in my passport from the region's immigration officers. I visited Bangkok, southern Thailand, Singapore, Macau, and the major cities of eastern China, and bubbled over with plans for future trips, before taking in Shanghai for the first time. And, in preparation for that momentous journey, I reimmersed myself in my family's history.

As the scion of a land-owning family, Gna-gong was brought up to live a life of leisure. It's said he was spoiled by his mother and his sisters, which was probably true. What only son wouldn't be? Because he already had the means to live comfortably without having to work very hard, any business he engaged in was only a hobby. He dabbled in businesses—he held the General Motors franchise in Shanghai and imported their cars. He also owned a factory that manufactured military uniforms. My grandfather also made sure there was ample time for the pursuits he loved, especially gambling and mingling with the Shanghainese elite, be they gangsters like the legendary Du Yuesheng or politicians like Chiang Kai-shek and the Soong family, and foreigners from all over the world—Frenchmen, Germans, Englishmen, Americans, White Russians, and Jews—who gathered to make that city one of the most cosmopolitan of its time.[2] He had a penchant too for fast cars, and over the years he drove a Buick, a Cadillac, a Willy's jeep, and a Sunbeam motorcycle. I'm told he souped up the jeep and drove it at tremendous speeds down the crowded streets of Shanghai.

In 1932, my grandfather married my grandmother, Li Gwan Mei, the best friend and classmate of his favorite sister. It was a love match, unusual for that era. I've always taken great pleasure in their wedding photos, with my grandfather, all six feet of him, as handsome as a matinee idol in his Western-style suit, and my petite grandmother at his side, an entire foot shorter than he, virginally beautiful in a white wedding gown with white flowers and a veil over her dark hair.

This was life in 1930s and 1940s Shanghai. Those were turbulent years for the nation and city, as China engaged in war with Japan and civil war between the ruling Nationalists and the renegade Communists.[3] Those years were to prove fateful for my grandfather and his family. They were the waning years of the old China, and shortly after the Communist Party took power on October 1, 1949, the world changed irretrievably for the Chinese nation. I often think of Margaret Mitchell's *Gone with the Wind* in this context, a movie that captured the Chinese imagination and resulted in the naming of countless Vivians and Scarletts and my own Aunt Bonnie. In the book, the civilization of the old South is swept away, gone with the wind, after the Civil War, resulting in a new world with different rules, and those who were too caught up in the ways of the old society were "winnowed out" as well. The same could apply to China after the Communist Revolution, when the civilization of old China, with its warlords and landlords, was swept away and replaced by a new landscape, a landscape in which those who could not adjust were marginalized and thrust aside. That happened all too poignantly to my grandfather.

The Communists assumed power in 1949, and Gna-gong, of course, stood for everything the Communists railed against. And so, in February 1951, officials knocked on the door in the middle of the night and politely asked if my grandfather would accompany them to the police station. Outside, armed soldiers waited in an army vehicle. His wife and daughters would not see him again until that reunion at Kennedy Airport many years later.

The next day, Chinese New Year's Day, my grandmother ran from station to station with a bedroll, change of clothes, toothbrush, and towel for my grandfather. But she found no news of him, and the family feared he had been executed. Every day after that, my mother's cousin trudged to the city's main police station and checked the daily posting of firing squad victims to see if my grandfather's name was on it. During that time, my thirty-eight-year-old grandmother's hair went gray, and my great-grandmother aged visibly. Finally, after seven months, a letter came from my grandfather. He had been sentenced to hard labor at a camp in bleak Qinghai province in northwest China—the land where the Chinese leadership exiled its worst criminals and dissidents. My grandfather was neither. He was a man of few political loyalties, with more interests in the pleasures of life than in anything else. The means that allowed him to lead an easy existence had also permitted him to move in a world of people reviled by the Communists. Those accidental ties led to his downfall. Three and a half years after his arrest, he was charged with supporting imperialism by having sent his four daughters to a religious school run by foreigners. He would pass ten winters in the Chinese equivalent of Siberia.

While he worked off his sentence, his family slowly filtered out of the country. His eldest daughter, Lucy, only seventeen, left first, in September 1951, and headed to Hong Kong. Fifteen-year-old Ruby, the second daughter, soon followed. After six years, his wife and third daughter, eighteen-year-old Bonnie, were next. And last, in 1959, my mother, Anne, only fourteen at the time, boarded a train bound for Hong Kong.

My grandmother was roundly criticized for her decision to get her family out. At the time, my grandfather's three sisters accused her of abandonment. Perhaps it was. But, given that China would soon descend into ideological madness, it was a timely and courageous move on my grandmother's part. Certainly, it's one I thank her for often. My grandmother tells me she wanted to flee as early as 1948, to Hong Kong, or Taiwan, or even to the Philippines (where her sister's husband served as China's consul general), but that my grandfather stubbornly resisted, insisting that all would be well in China. Actually, my great-grandmother may have understood my grandmother's prescient motivations, since she, too, had considered leaving for Hong Kong with my mother. But she was a mother first, and she changed her mind at the eleventh hour, remaining in Shanghai in a show of support for her beloved only son.

When Gna-gong finally emerged, stooped and broken, from Qinghai and returned to Shanghai, one daughter was married and the mother of two in Singapore. Another was married to an American in the United States and a new mother. His wife and two other children, including my mother, were in Hong Kong, with no thought of returning to China. When he came home, it was to his mother and sisters, in the old family home in Shanghai.

It's not surprising that the second phase of my grandparents' marriage was unsuccessful. My grandmother came into her own in the States and proved herself to be a tough, independent woman. I often wonder what else she could have become if she'd been encouraged and properly educated. She attained a proficiency in English, learned to drive (indeed, she taught me), cooked, sewed, knitted, worked at Macy's, traveled, and generally learned about the world. I think she wasn't ready for a man to reenter her life, even if that man was her husband. My grandparents hadn't seen each other for thirty years, yet it was expected they would be as compatible as they had been when they wed in 1932. But my grandfather was a stranger, from the moment he stepped off the plane.

Though theirs was a love match, even its first phase had hardly been ideal, since my grandfather quickly proved he was no family man. He stayed out late, usually without my grandmother, who bore four girls over the space of ten years and wanted to lead a healthy lifestyle so that she could one day give him the son she knew he wanted. She never did. Thus, toward the end of the 1940s, when the Communist threat grew ever stronger, my grandparents' marriage gravitated further and further away from the joyful flush of their wedding day, becoming less the stuff of fairy tales and more in line with the realities of a Chinese marriage. Part of me believes that my grandmother must have been halfway glad to free herself of the unhappiness of her marriage and move to a new life in Hong Kong and the West. I gather that her husband's very presence served to squelch her independent spirit because he expected her, in 1981, to be his wife of 1951. And I'm sure there was no little resentment at the fact that she'd left him, even if it was to further the prospects of their family in the United States.

While working in Hong Kong, I made three visits to Shanghai during my grandfather's life, and they were all happy ones. I took my first trip, in May 1993, with the greatest anticipation. On that inaugural visit, my grandfather came to pick me up at my hotel, and I remember how dignified he seemed in the lobby of the Hotel Equatorial. We then went to the house—the house my mother had grown up in. It was located in the city center, near Jing An Si, formerly called the Bubbling Well Temple. Located along one of Shanghai's famous alleys, on Yuyuan Road, the house was a four-story brick affair, sturdy on the outside but fallen into disrepair over the years. There my grandfather lived, along with his youngest sister, his older sister, and two of her children, plus the family of one of the children. There was also one son of my grandfather's half brother, and the second wife of that same half brother. It was a household of nine. That, combined with other relatives in the city, came to a staggering number of new people to meet. Over the next few days I was treated to a cavalcade of relatives and home-cooked food—those are my most distinct memories. I got great joy from finally being able to match faces to the names that I had scrawled over the years on my family tree.

The warm welcome that my relatives extended to me on that first trip was to hold steady over the years on all my subsequent visits. Everyone—from my mother's great-aunts to their children and grandchildren—treated me as a member of the family. I'd heard of that sense of shared kinship enveloping others. And I was pleased to feel that I had an adjunct, truly Chinese, family, which made my identification as a Chinese-American that much stronger. Of course, when

I say they treated me as a member of the family, I mean they welcomed me with open arms and eventually allowed me to stay in their house, despite their protestations that the bathroom facilities weren't what I was used to, that is, there was no hot running water. They would allow me to do the odd errand for them, but still I was not allowed to help in the kitchen, where my great-aunts and one of my mother's cousins would seemingly spend all day cooking for me. There were endless delectable homemade meals—from standard fare, such as noodles and dumplings, to delicacies such as fried shredded eel, now one of my favorite dishes.

On my second visit to Shanghai a year later, I still recall with amusement and pride my grandfather's memorable encounter with my travel companion and friend, a blond-haired, blue-eyed Minnesotan named Carrie. I knew that my grandfather had always been a man with cosmopolitan tastes and attitudes, and foreigners did not faze him. It was the same for so many Chinese men who had cut their teeth in 1930s and 1940s Shanghai. So when Carrie entered the home on Yuyuan Road with me, I anticipated no communication difficulties. We spoke in English, but since Carrie had lived in Bremen for a year, she and my grandfather conversed in German for a short time. Most amusingly, though, Gna-gong entertained Carrie with his imitation of a strong Brooklyn accent. I beamed with pride when I heard him wowing Carrie. After all, how many Chinese-Americans had grandparents who could speak perfect English and French, as well as converse in other Western languages *and* do accents? I loved it that a man who had rarely ever left China could know so much about the rest of the world, especially since China had been closed to that world for much of his life.

Unfortunately, although my grandfather's command of languages revealed much about his privileged pre-Communist background, he was reluctant to say anything about his past, even when asked questions point-blank. He disavowed any contact with Du Yuesheng, the infamous and powerful Shanghai gangster, though I'd heard that my grandfather had called upon Du to clear the streets of Shanghai for his father-in-law's funeral procession. He made very little of his acquaintance with the Soong family. I realized soon enough that he didn't wish to dwell on events that happened long ago, and so I acceded to his wishes and stopped asking questions, as much as it frustrated the historian within me. However, Gna-gong did make amends. Knowing how important the family tree was to me, during one visit he presented me with the great gift of an official family tree going back twenty generations, a precious document indeed. Eventually, he also acceded to my request to visit the grand house he had designed and built in Shanghai in the 1930s for the family; one of my mother's cousins was dispatched to take me to the intersection of Amherst Avenue and Columbia Circle (now Xingfu Road and Panyu Road) to see it. The house is now in the hands of the Chinese government.

It bothered me then and still bothers me a little, especially now that my grandfather has passed away, that he never opened up to me. But I respected his decision, and, when I think about it now, try not to regret my lack of aggressiveness when wondering about his glittering, pre-Communist life and the hard years of his time in Qinghai. More important to me is the knowledge that he appreciated my visits and perhaps grew to love me. After all, I was his granddaughter and the first member of his family to return to China and visit him. I know I never replaced my second cousins, who grew up with him, in his heart, and it was folly to think I could have, given the short amount of time we spent together. But I'm confident that Gna-gong cared about me. Altogether too few of his children and grandchildren really loved him, so my willingness to visit and spend time with him was valued.

I must admit that I was happy when he acted like the grandfathers of middle America that I watched on TV while growing up: he warned me against eating food from street stalls and cautioned me about the preponderance of pickpockets on congested Shanghai buses. I remember, too, falling sick on Nanjing Road and taking refuge in the Hotel Sofitel lobby, watching from my prone position on the couch as my family, hobbling grandfather included, rushed in to bring me to a doctor. Thus, well before the time I had made my third and last visit to Shanghai before his death, I felt I'd achieved that goal of connecting with him as his grandchild.

By the time my grandfather passed away, I felt that I'd done the best I could to become close to him and spend time with him. Therefore,

I had few regrets. He was gone, but I was left with his legacy—all those other relatives I'd discovered and come to know as family over the years in my quest to find him. But precious though this legacy is, it is far from being all that he has left me. In 1997, I made another trip to Shanghai to visit my relatives. My great-aunts were, predictably, cooking yet another meal for me, and, predictably, I was banned from the kitchen. It was the perfect time, I thought, to visit my grandfather's room, still kept as it had been during his life, and say good-bye. One of my great-aunts gave me the key, and I creaked my way up the stairs.

When I unlocked the door, the musty air inside assailed me. After a few moments of adjustment, I turned to look at his photograph sitting on the wooden bureau. On either side sat a vase with artificial flowers, straining to add an air of respect to the scene. My grandfather looked vaguely worried in the photo, as if events of the moment were not to his liking. It was an appropriate expression, I surmised. This was a man whose life had not gone according to plan. I sat for a few moments in the chair before the bureau but didn't know what to say or think. So, in the Shanghainese way, I turned from the sentimental to the practical and focused my attention on his possessions in the room.

There was a wooden desk next to the window with three drawers, all difficult to open. Against the far wall were trunks and boxes galore. I made a thorough search, and, in those drawers and boxes, and piled stack on stack atop the trunks, I found dictionaries—Chinese/English, English/French, and French/Chinese. There were scraps of paper in my grandfather's handwriting, with translations of English words and phrases like "etymologist," "referendum," "presumptuous request," and "falling leaves settle on their roots" into Chinese. Copies of *Time* magazine from the mid-1980s, *Paris Match, L'Express du Monde.* Workbooks put out by the U.S. Information Service on life in America, with appropriate vocabulary terms. A workbook issued by the Australian government with an introduction by Robert Hawke.[4] A booklet on life in France. The Lord's Prayer in Chinese and English, hidden away in a Dutch cigarette tin. A bilingual copy of Guy de Maupassant's short stories in French and Chinese from 1979.

I was stunned. Only then did I fully understand the truly cosmopolitan nature of my grandfather. Here was a man who wanted to reach out to the world. This spirit was cultivated during the glory days of Shanghai, and it was something he never let go of, through war and revolution and a decade of hard labor.

I'd like to think that he saw some of this spirit in me and felt close to me because of it. I finally really understood that, beyond our blood relationship, he and I had a real connection—far more than just being Chinese, we both had a desire to be citizens of the world. This was the commonality with him that I had searched for and finally found.

In My Father's Shadow

WILLIAM SHANG

THROUGHOUT MY CHILDHOOD AND ADOLESCENCE, MY FATHER impressed on me that China was my "real home." It was, however, a home from which he had chosen to exile himself for many years and which, consequently, I had never visited.

I was born in Tokyo in 1957, when my father, Shang Zhen[1] (Shang Chen), was already seventy years old, though still fit and quite stylish. In my eyes, he was not a general, provincial governor, mayor of Peking and Tianjin, chief of staff, or any of those things he had once been, but just my dad—the figure around whom our very complex household of eight revolved.

My father came to Japan as the senior Chinese representative to witness the execution of General Hideki Tojo and other Japanese war criminals, and his last post was commander in chief of the Chinese Occupation Army in Japan. Rather than return to China, where he would probably have been assigned to command one of the war zones in the

William Shang is a research associate at the Centre of Asian Studies at Hong Kong University specializing in late-eighteenth- to mid-nineteenth-century Western paintings of China and Southeast Asia. Until his recent move to Hong Kong, he was a researcher at the Research Department of the Tōyō Bunko (Oriental Library) in Tokyo for more than a decade.

187

civil war that was raging between Nationalist and Communist forces, my father retired in May 1949. For a high-ranking and devoted military man, this was a bold move. It was one he chose because pointing a gun at his brothers and sisters went against the beliefs that had been instilled in him during his days at the Baoding Military Academy. A few months later, a Communist government came to power in mainland China and established the People's Republic of China (PRC). The defeated Nationalist government of the Republic of China (ROC) that he had served fled to the island of Taiwan. Not wishing to actively serve either regime, my father stayed on in Japan, acting as a senior adviser to the Chinese diplomatic mission in Tokyo, a position he officially held until he passed away in May 1978.

Apart from my father, my Japanese mother, my two older sisters, and me, our household consisted of my father's personal secretary, the personal secretary's mistress, and my father's Chinese mistress, Hamama.

My father's secretary was someone I trusted and talked to, since he always seemed have the right answers. He provided faithful service to my father for more than forty years, until my father's death. Like many other former Nationalist soldiers who could not, for the foreseeable future, return to their families in China, he had taken a mistress, a Japanese woman who had spent her childhood in northeast China. Many years later, after my father's Chinese mistress passed away, this woman would attempt to take her place as the first lady of the house.

In fact, our household was like a scene from a movie depicting a wealthy, decadent Chinese family typical of the nineteenth or early twentieth centuries, with servants, concubines, mahjong games, banquets, and garden parties with the affluent members of society. On the surface, everything seemed perfectly calm, but in reality, with its petty quarrels and power struggles, things were chaotic, to say the least. Our family was like a time bomb, with the most ridiculous incident being enough to trigger an explosion.

We ate dinner together as a family, but at breakfast and lunch, my father and Hamama ate in the dining room, while my mother, sisters, and I ate in the kitchen. When my father was not around, Hamama would throw her weight around, trying to control the household. She was the oldest woman, both in age and in terms of companionship with my father, and fiercely protective of the position this gave her.

Living with Hamama, who made personal attacks on me and my sisters, was not easy. I remember that whenever Hamama was upset over our lack of interest or response to what she had to preach, she would abruptly end the conversation with obscenities. And, despite her own status, whenever she had the chance, she enjoyed telling us that my parents were not married.

But from a child's point of view, our tolerance was most severely tested when my father's friends came to visit. As a normal practice, they would bring sweets or other things for us children. My father would call us to come and greet the guests, after which we usually made a beeline back to our rooms, since we knew that what followed was going to be adult talk—politics and military stuff. As to the gifts, my father assumed they were in our hands, but actually they were usually taken straight up to Hamama's room and stored under her bed. When we next met the same guest, we wouldn't say anything about the gifts, never having received them in the first place. Later, the guest would sometimes ask my mother or my father's personal secretary about whether we had received the gifts and why we had said nothing about them. Perhaps they were curious about my father's policies on home discipline or manners.

One day, when I came home from school, I noticed something different about the atmosphere. My mother, my father's personal secretary, and his mistress were in the kitchen talking about Hamama's "under-the-bed-storage," which my father had discovered. It was an embarrassing moment for my father, since his discipline had been questioned, and especially since he had found out about it through a third person. From that day, Hamama began informing us about the gifts we had received so that we could politely thank the guests. But in the end, nothing changed; she still took everything up to her room as before.

Even as a child, however, I understood Hamama's need to hoard things. It was the result of her upbringing, when she had never had enough food. According to her, she had been born into a large family in north China. Desperate to make ends meet, her parents had sold her to a brothel when she was thirteen years old—or perhaps even younger. She had met my father in Tianjin in the 1930s and had lived with him ever since. Her ties to her family broken, she was totally dependent on him. Back in the old days in China, my father hired private tutors for her education, but she never put her mind to studying. She was petite, and I always thought she must have been very attractive in her youth. But her uncultured manners and dogmatic attitude reflected her sad childhood.

We were left to protect ourselves from Hamama until her death during my junior year in high school. As a result, we grew up tough and sometimes aggressive. To my father, most of our run-ins with Hamama must have seemed unimportant. One of my father's famous sayings was: "When a dog barks at you, are you going to get on your knees and bark at the dog? That's her mentality. So don't let trivial matters bother you." As for my mother, perhaps she wanted to protect us from mistreatment, but more than anything, she was inclined to abide by my father's rules within the household.

My mother was the youngest of the adults in our home. She had met my father while working at the Chinese Diplomatic Mission in Tokyo during the occupation days right after the war, when she was only in her twenties. My father had been married twice before, but these relationships did not affect our Tokyo household. My father's first legal wife had passed away in childbirth, leaving two sons, who were both living in the United States by the time I was born. My father's second wife was also living in the United States, with her family. It must not have been easy for my mother, a Japanese newcomer in an already complicated and established Chinese family structure. But she was nonchalant and did not let Hamama's existence or her presence affect her in any way. Having borne my father three children, with me as the only son in this Tokyo household, my mother could be sure of his unceasing attention and care.

One of my father's policies that I respected was his equal treatment of his children. He gave my sisters the same education as he gave me, his son, and he treated me as well as his other sons. Being retired, he had more time to look after me and watch me grow up. Once, when my half brother visited us in my sophomore year in high school, we all went out sightseeing, and during lunch I was leaning on my father and touching his bald head, wondering when I, too, would become bald. Later, my half brother told me that when he was my age, he hadn't been able to talk or act the way I did in front of our father. He had never even dreamed that anybody would be able to do those things to him. So all along I knew that my father was trying to act like a normal parent in the Tokyo household, even though, because of his age, I didn't expect a normal father-son relationship. He didn't teach me to play catch or throw a football or go bowling on Friday nights. I never wished or expected him to do anything like that. Just seeing him confident and satisfied with his own accomplishments (he had been born to a poor peasant family from Hebei province), and seeing other people looking up to him was enough to cause me to respect him.

Whenever a new Chinese ambassador arrived or a delegation passed through Tokyo—whatever the occasion—officials came for a visit. For my father, these visits might simply have meant a friendly chat or meeting with former subordinates or old buddies, but for me they exemplified the glories of his past positions. Seeing my father's old photographs, military uniforms, and medals and listening to his wartime stories made me want to follow in his footsteps. But when my father sensed this, he vehemently opposed my desire to pursue a military career. One day he told me that a military establishment should be built solely for the purpose of protecting a country from foreign enemies or attacking invaders and that soldiers are trained to fight, but only to carry out their missions against the invaders. Too many soldiers would lead to unnecessary battles and war, unfortunately sometimes against one's own people. He emphasized that the most ludicrous aspect of war was the involvement and sacrifice of innocent civilian lives. He certainly wasn't about to add manpower to that establishment. I was only in junior high school at the time, but his words, coming from experience, made perfect sense. I was forced to change my goal.

My father's expectations of me were probably similar to those of any other Chinese father at the time. He suggested careers in medicine, law, and education, with an emphasis on helping and working with the common people, which must have been lacking in the China that he had known. At home, he insisted on a strict Chinese lifestyle. I don't think my father ever expected to stay in Japan permanently or expected or wished that any of his children would do so.

It must have been a dilemma for my father, educating his children to be Chinese while living in a country with a different culture and language, and further complicating the situation by sending us to the American School to improve our opportunities. All during my years at the American School, I wondered about being a Chinese national living in Japan and what I would be and where I would live later on in life. Within the household, whether it was my father's intention or just a matter of convenience, we usually spoke Chinese, although we children spoke in Japanese with my mother. My mother, who had had no command of Chinese when she met my father, managed to pick it up by ear, becoming fluent over the years. With the Chinese language came our indoctrination about our roots. Perhaps my father knew the difficulties of overseas Chinese living in Japan, where Koreans and Chinese are often looked down on. Or maybe he wanted to take us all back to China when the time was ripe or thought that we would live in the United States on completing our education. After I began attending the American School, my father spoke to me in English more often than in Chinese until I entered high school, when it became hard for him to think in English because of his age. He probably wanted to provide me with an English-speaking environment. All along, my father might have realized that it would be difficult for me to fit in, either in China or Japan.

Attending the American School had a greater effect on me, linguistically and culturally, than perhaps any other influence in my life. However, in terms of identity formation, it was confusing. It might have been easier for me if I had been enrolled in a Japanese school in my district or in a Chinese school somewhere in Tokyo. I distinctly remember the contrast between the modern, high-quality Western education at the American School and coming home to a nineteenth-century Chinese household. I think this contrast made me stay away from home as much as possible, and, when I was home, to stay alone in my room. In this sense, athletics was a savior, a way to offset my frustrations. Most important, it kept me off the streets. I spent most of my time playing football, lifting weights, and participating in other sports such as wrestling and track and field. Contrary to the typical Asian view of sports—that they are a waste of time and a distraction from academics—I found the experience quite useful in the long run, teaching me to work in harmony with others without completely losing myself. The other thing I learned, maybe not directly from athletics but as a result, is to stick to the basics, no matter what I do.

When, in 1975, I went to attend LaVerne College (now the University of LaVerne) in Los Angeles, sports eased the transition to college life and a new country. I had never been overseas before, but I felt at home as soon as football practice started. In fact, I had a feeling of being liberated. I had finally reached the place where I felt most comfortable, in terms of language and culture. Some people thought I had grown up in Hawaii, while others assumed that I was raised in the Los Angeles area. I never tried to act like a local student, but after attending an American school, my thought processes seemed to be similar to those of the rest of the students.

I might never have left the United States, the land where I felt so much at home, had an anticipated, but still momentous event not occurred during my junior year at college. In May 1978, my father, who hadn't expected to stay in Japan permanently, died in Tokyo at the age of ninety. His sojourn in Japan could nevertheless be regarded as temporary, because his body was to be laid to rest in China. The government of the People's Republic of China proposed to give him a state funeral at the Babaoshan Revolutionary Cemetery, where heroes of the Chinese revolution are buried, and my mother, my sisters, and I were invited to come to China as his official family to attend. Thus, my father's death was the occasion for my first visit to China, the country I had been taught to think of as home.

As we made the final descent to Beijing Airport, looking out the window, I felt uneasy with the darkness below. But the excitement of coming home for the first time was overwhelming, enough to undo my apprehension. When we landed, airport security and military officers boarded the plane and told us to wait until the other passengers had disembarked. Ignoring the passengers' inquisitive stares as they deplaned, I looked out of the window, trying to get a glimpse of my country. Minutes later, with anticipation, I was finally on the gangway. We were met with the flashes of the New China News Agency camera crew and bright television camera lights. Waiting beyond, to receive my father's ashes, was an entourage of Communist Party officials, military officers, and my father's old friends. I balked at taking my first step off the plane.

Although it was a premature assumption, as we drove along Chang'an Avenue, Beijing's main thoroughfare and sped by the Beijing Hotel and through Tiananmen Square heading to the cemetery in the western section of the city, I felt that this was the real encounter with my home— that I had at last reached the land of my roots. Things I had read about China and heard from relatives and my father's friends were all coming back at once. I remember my first sight of Tiananmen Square and thinking that here was civilization and culture. And later I was informed that the hall in the oldest wing of the Beijing Hotel was where my father had hosted cocktail parties back in the 1920s.

The memorial service for my father was conducted by the Chinese Communist Party. This was my initial meeting with the Chinese leaders whom I would read about in newspapers and magazines and see on the news for many years to come. Deng Xiaoping was the most senior of the officials in attendance.[2] The service lasted for several hours, but, more important than what was happening at the moment, it finally dawned on me that my father's legacy was allowing me to find my roots in the most extravagant manner.

That I was here in China, as a citizen of the People's Republic of China, came about because, four years earlier, my father had switched his citizenship from the Republic of China to the People's Republic. His decision wasn't political, as some people might have imagined. His allegiance had always been to the Chinese mainland rather than to ideology, whether Nationalist or Communist. He had refused ever to set foot in Taiwan, which he never considered his home, and forbade us to do so either, even though our ROC passports were issued by the government in Taiwan, and the Chinese embassy in Japan to which he acted as advisor was an ROC embassy until the Japanese government normalized relations with the PRC in 1978.

What I think my father wanted to do when he changed his passport was to see China again before he died. He was eighty-six years old, and time was running short. Actually, my father had had several prior opportunities to visit China, having been invited by Premier Zhou En-lai and later, by his former colleague, General Fu Zuoyi some years earlier.[3] But it was not until 1974 that he judged the political climate to be favorable enough for a visit. I later heard from older overseas Chinese about the day my father went to the PRC's Overseas Chinese Association in Tokyo to apply to go to China. They likened his visit to a thunderbolt from a clear sky. The broader impact was tremendous for other overseas Chinese living in Japan and even in the West. Chinese officials considered him the highest-ranking ex-Nationalist official living overseas and noted that China had set its sights on receiving him in style to prove to other overseas Chinese that they, too, would be welcomed. Indeed, his visit did influence many others to return.

For his first homecoming, my father was scheduled to fly to Hong Kong and cross the border into mainland China. But the Chinese diplomatic mission in Tokyo intercepted clandestine information concerning a possible assassination plot, and the route was changed to have my father take the test flight, with the Japanese deputy minister of transport on board, on a new air route between Tokyo and Beijing. At the time, I was more interested in this test flight than in the significance of my father's return. I'd heard that the pilots of the Japanese and Chinese airlines were to exchange controls in midair, meaning Japanese pilots had the controls over Japanese airspace and the Chinese pilots over Chinese airspace. I certainly didn't understand the importance of my father's visit until I read the morning paper following his arrival in Beijing.

Now, during my own return to China, it was the historic sights that most interested me, since they reinforced the proud feeling of being home that I'd had ever since arriving. I could sense the time and effort that the Chinese officials had put into making us feel comfortable. Although it was a bit propagandistic, their planning and execution certainly impressed me. We were shown the sights in Beijing and taken for a three-week trip around the country.

During this initial trip I had my first meeting with a relative in China: my cousin, the daughter of my father's only brother. I hadn't known anything about my relatives in China before this visit. However, my half brother had been looking up our relatives in China for four years or so. He happened to be in Beijing on a business trip at the same time we were in town and took me to our cousin's place one evening. This cousin was a graduate of Qinghua University's department of engineering and worked at a hydroelectric plant in Beijing.[4] She was the bookworm, scholarly, reserved, and aware of the consequences of having overseas relatives. During the Cultural Revolution, because of her overseas connections, she had been relegated to driving the city bus along Chang'an Avenue and would often joke about how familiar she was with the streets of Beijing.[5] Several years after the Cultural Revolution, she was reinstated to her former position and instructed younger engineers.

In later visits, I remember my cousin studying English and Japanese even after her retirement, while looking after her grandchildren. Somehow, she retains the motivation to expand her knowledge. I heard many stories of Chinese relatives demanding that their relatives bring them household appliances from the West, sponsor them to live abroad, and so forth, but my cousin never asked us for anything except that we meet her every time we visited China. Throughout the years she told me interesting stories, helping me understand why I was treated the way I had been by my parents and Hamama. So I have a very positive impression of my relatives in China.

After this first visit to China, I returned to finish college in the United States. I began thinking about attending school in China, for the experience, and to explore and come to terms with my identity. I also wanted to learn more of the language, for I could converse but couldn't read or write. But, first, I earned a master's degree at Columbia University's School of International Affairs, spending six years in all studying in the United States. When I finally left America, in 1984, it was to carry out my plan of studying in China. At the time, I thought that I would be away from the States only for a year or two. I wonder sometimes whether I would ever have left the land where my education had groomed me to feel most comfortable if I had known that, in leaving, circumstances would take me in other directions and that I would never return to America to live. Placed in that predicament again, I would probably do the same. I had to search out my roots and come to terms with my Asian background—with my Chinese citizenship and with the Japanese culture I had grown accustomed to over the years.

All along, I knew that the China I had seen—a dozen times by the time I went to study there—was not the "real" China. Rather it was a superficial version, composed of senior officials, black limousines, extravagant dinner banquets, and resorts, unknown to most Chinese. What I expected from my planned one-year stay in China was to be treated more or less like a local student and to be able to talk to such students, albeit with some precautionary reserve on their side. After all, like them, I was a citizen of the PRC. For my own identity fact-finding mission, I did not want any special treatment.

From the start, I was told by the embassy in Tokyo to enroll at Beijing University. I was given no choice in the matter of schools. And, while the Chinese officials kept their word and did not assist me unless I specifically asked for help, I was not able to live exactly like a local student but was instead placed in the university's foreign students' dormitory.

In the end, I couldn't fulfill my expectations of getting close to the local Chinese students. In part, this was because of the Chinese system of constraints, designed to keep foreigners and locals from interacting too closely. Local Chinese who visited foreigners, for example, had to leave their ID cards with the watchman at the door and fill out forms in triplicate before being allowed past the lobby. It felt like being locked up and not having any access to the outside world.

Later, I began to restrict myself from even attempting to mingle with local students. Whenever I did have a chance to speak to them, they always wanted to talk about leaving the country or to practice their English or Japanese. Even the Chinese immigration officials could not understand why I was still legally a Chinese citizen. I was always asked the same question: "How come you haven't changed your nationality? Living overseas in either the United States or Japan, it would be easier to use an American or Japanese passport." What really bothered me was that China's propaganda machine was always calling for patriotism, love, and construction of the motherland, yet no one there could even see the point of being a citizen of China if the opportunity arose to become a citizen of someplace else.

The truth was, I found that I had little to say to the local Chinese students and felt much more comfortable with the foreign students I lived with. After some months in Beijing, I began to realize the complexity of Chinese identity, especially the gap between mainland Chinese and overseas Chinese living in Japan—or anywhere else, for that matter. Overseas Chinese like me, it seemed, were essentially foreigners. We were not "Chinese" in the sense that we were not born and raised in China and did not really possess a common cultural background or common experiences with the people there, such as the hardships of the Cultural Revolution. In my case, being half Japanese and educated in America further complicated the process of identity formation. In Japan, when people discovered that I am not a full-blooded Japanese, they tended to think of me as the opposite—as fully Chinese. It was the same in China: when people found out I was half Japanese, they referred to me as a Japanese. I always hated that, since there are more sides than that to my story. Fortunately, as some people came to know me better, they tended, in time, simply to consider me as an international person of indeterminate nationality.

Noticing my dissatisfaction with my experience in China, another overseas Chinese student from Japan told me something that I still remember vividly. He said that foreign students studying in China, whether ethnic Chinese or not, tend to fall into three categories. First, there are those who are charmed by the Chinese people and doctrine. Then, according to my friend, there are the majority, who tend to give less credit to the Chinese political system but love the Chinese people. And the third are those who end up developing feelings of disrespect for the Chinese people as well as for China's government. As I was about to leave Beijing University, he wished me luck and told me that he hoped I wouldn't fall into that third category. What he meant was that I should not hate the people that I'm supposed to be a part of. I assume my friend told me this because, in his eyes, I was already beginning to fall into that last, dangerous category. It was his wish and his warning that I should cool off once leaving China and always remember that it is the system, the circumstances, or the situation, and not the people, that should be blamed for the many frustrations I encountered while living in China. Even now, I still fall back on his advice.

That departure from China was one of my most memorable flights, since I was leaving with a brand-new identity—not as a Chinese whose home was China, but as an overseas Chinese who did not have to be so Chinese, and whose home was somewhere I still had to figure out. The valuable lesson I took with me from my experience at Beijing University was that, no matter how I present myself, depending on the preconception of the other party, I'll never be able to present myself as I perceive myself. Therefore, I should simply present myself in a natural way and disregard the perceptions of others.

In the end, it was this one-year study experience in China that helped lead me back to Japan. With the new understanding that I am not and do not necessarily have to be so Chinese, it seemed reasonable for me to take a look at Japan with a new attitude. My previous view had been that I didn't fit in here, that Japan wasn't my home; thus I had never even tried to understand the country. Now it seemed worthwhile to begin to do so. After all, I had spent my entire life in Japan until going to college, and I still felt some attachments to the country.

Over the years, I have built a life, and an academic career, in Japan. Many overseas Chinese here are involved in the business sector and have become relatively successful as a bridge between China and Japan. During the 1970s and 1980s, they contributed much to the building of trade ties between the two countries. As China began opening up to the outside world in the late 1970s and 1980s, I received offers, both in Japan and in the United States, to become involved in different sectors of the business world, particularly in import and export. With my father's name and my own connections, it would have been relatively easy for me put together business deals with China. But that possibility never interested or tempted me. For one thing, I did not want to live in my father's shadow. Even in the field of academics, I have stayed away from researching that period in China during which my father was prominent. Too many of the people mentioned in the research materials of that time were my father's good friends and colleagues. It would be impossible for me to read them objectively.

In Japan, there are barriers to foreigners becoming completely accepted in Japanese society. Overseas Chinese and Korean residents, even those who have been in Japan for generations, feel that they are looked down on and discriminated against. I did not encounter any mistreatment or hardships because of my nationality while growing up here. However, I was educated in the American school system, which was regarded as prestigious. But after returning to Japan to start a career, my turn came to experience such prejudice: I learned from personal experience that most Japanese corporations won't hire resident foreign nationals on a lifetime basis, as they will Japanese.

And so, by going to China I resolved one part of the puzzle of my identity, but by remaining in Japan, I have still to find the answer to that other question I often ask myself: "Where is home, and will I ever find a place where I will be comfortable enough to say, 'This is my home?'"

Coming Home

LILY WU

THE DEAN RARELY CALLED STUDENTS AT HOME, AND WITH ONLY
one term left until graduation, I was in no mood for surprises. I had
just spent three and a half years being in over my head at Caltech—
the venerable California Institute of Technology. It is a very small and
exclusive college, where the quiet of the olive-lined walks belie the often revolutionary discoveries that have been made on that campus by
some of the greatest scientists of this century. Keeping up with my classmates, some of whom had truly otherworldly intellectual capacities,
varied between being a struggle to being a trauma for me. I had enjoyed physics and computing in high school and had excelled among
my public schoolmates. However, after only one week at Caltech, I realized that real science was an art, and that understanding it was a gift
that I did not possess and for which I could not substitute hard work.

Despite this early realization, I stuck it out at Caltech—I appreciated being three thousand miles away from my parents, whose lives
were quietly falling apart. And perhaps even more important, a deeply
inbred sense of face and stubbornness compelled me forward, away from

*Lily Wu is the chief financial officer of a software company in Silicon Valley. After fourteen years
in Asia, Lily Wu now calls San Francisco her home.*

any notion of giving up or admitting defeat. Thus, my four years at Caltech were finally drawing to a successful close; I had downgraded my physics aspirations to a less rigorous engineering degree and padded my core curriculum course work with double the required dosage of humanities and social sciences classes, which I found much easier to handle—and even enjoyable. Little did I know then that the extra exposure to history and politics would come in handy so soon and that those classes would ultimately prove to be that part of my college course work of most direct value to me in my later years.

"So what are you planning to do after graduation? How are your job interviews coming along—you haven't applied for graduate school, right?" What, I wondered, could the dean possibly want? It was the spring of 1985, and I was quite close to accepting a job as an integrated circuit design engineer for a telecommunications company. Actually, I hadn't devoted that much time to planning my future, because my energy had been so singlemindedly focused on graduation. I wasn't about to relax until I had the diploma in my hand. Last-minute flame-outs were part of Caltech legend, and I couldn't afford to dream about my future before my present was even assured. Whatever I needed to figure out about my future was going to have to wait until the future had arrived.

But I have thus far been graced by the great fortune at a number of key points in my life of having my future find me. Although I was not to know it until much later, one of those moments came as I sat in the dean's office that day. As it turned out, Caltech was one of the colleges eligible to nominate candidates for Thomas Watson fellowships. Watson fellows were expected to spend a year pursuing long-held personal goals or exploring a hobby outside their major fields of study. The foundation paid for and lent legitimacy to the *Wanderjahre* of some fifty college graduates every year, in the interest of broadening horizons and opening eyes.[1] Applicants had to submit a set of essays and undergo an interview with the foundation's president. The dean urged me to apply.

An hour later, I was back sitting in my room staring blankly at the application wondering what to use as the theme of my year if I were to be chosen as a Watson fellow. Frankly, I didn't actually have any major interests outside my studies; I didn't even participate in sports. And the only major personal goals I seemed to have up to then was to get by the best I could at whatever grade or school I was in. Although an immediate idea did not come to mind, I decided to submit an application anyway.

To this day, I am not really conscious of where the thoughts or ideas came from. But late that evening, I completed my Watson essay stating that I wanted to go to China to seek my roots. At the time, it seemed an unexpected choice of themes. I was born in Taiwan but had grown up in the United States from the age of three (never in a Chinatown). After seventeen years in the States, I was thoroughly and totally American. I never had much understanding of or even interest in my racial background. I socialized and lived in typically American circles. I spoke Mandarin Chinese out of necessity, to communicate with my parents, but after four years away from home, my native language skills were rusty. I have no copy left of my Watson essay, and I am sure I would find it disappointingly shallow to read today. But that day, I needed a theme, and roots in China seemed like a ready-made one for me.

The last few weeks of my senior year passed in a blur. I accepted the job at the telecommunications company, and the final weeks of classes passed uneventfully. Then, right before commencement, I found out that, to my surprise, I had won a Watson fellowship! I was expected to pack my bags for China before the summer was out. Unprepared as I had been to choose a fellowship theme, I was even less prepared to actually carry it out. For a few days I even considered not accepting it.

I was swayed in large part by the reaction from others. The congratulations from faculty and friends was immediate and unstinting. Friends met my reservations with scorn: "You'll work every day and every year for the rest of your life, what's the hurry? What an opportunity to go out and see the world!"

My modern Chinese history professor, James Lee, volunteered to help provide the structure that I needed to make my year possible, and for this help I am forever grateful. Professor Lee explained that China, although officially "open" since 1979, still had many restrictions on travel and extended stays. I basically had to have a "permit" and a sponsor to remain there for more than a month. Having close ties to the history department at Beijing University, he offered to write me a referral so that I could be accepted as a student and therefore granted a student visa to stay in China legitimately for a year. From that base, I could then conveniently stay and travel in China for the whole year. I eagerly accepted his help, and the arrangements were thus made. My new employer, GTE Corporation, was equally accommodating; they assured me that my job would be held for a year until I returned. With no further excuses left, the decision was made, and I called the Watson Foundation to accept.

But there was still the matter of my parents. It may seem strange, and perhaps this is really the beginning of my story, but my parents were quite indifferent to the fact that I would soon be leaving to spend time in the country where they had been born and raised. They had other things to think about. I referred earlier to the fact that my parents' lives were unraveling during my Caltech years. By the time I received the Watson fellowship, they were separated and waiting for their divorce. My mother instigated it, and my father did not object. The divorce was a really long-awaited ending for them.

Both my parents were born in China, my father to an educated peasant family in 1921 in Anhui province, and my mother to an aristocratic Manchurian family in 1932 in Beijing. Through separate paths, as odd and serendipitous as the times themselves, they both landed in Taipei, Taiwan, in 1948, toward the end of China's civil war.[2] They met through mutual friends, and, after a courtship of only a few months, married in 1959.

I suspect that, even from the beginning, they were not very well suited for each other. Certainly, their backgrounds were entirely mismatched— the sexual politics were all wrong. China's inland provinces are notoriously male chauvinistic, and that would markedly be the case in my father's family of up-and-coming peasants. Manchurians, the northern peoples that conquered China to establish the Qing dynasty, China's last ruling dynasty, are, on the other hand, bordering on matriarchal.[3] My mother came from a family of strong and determined women. Her father's sisters had all received a college education in an era when most men even in the West had not, and this education included study abroad. As for my father's family, none of his sisters had even been educated beyond grade school. And to top it all off, both my parents were the coddled youngest in families of six siblings each and used to having their own way.

But the 1950s in struggling postwar Taiwan was not about love and match-making happiness. In my parent's circles, each person was a refugee, and life was about survival and building a new life. My father's engineering degree and serious attitude toward work surely appealed to my mother. And my father undoubtedly found comfort in the establishment nature (albeit fallen) of my mother's family. My father delivered where it counted the most in those days—his expertise, power plant civil engineering, netted us the greatly coveted visas to immigrate to America. And that is how I came to New York City in 1966, at the age of three.

My mother, as my father must have viewed it, did not fully deliver on her part. Sure, she cooked well and kept a tidy, frugal household. But she was headstrong in personality (weren't all the women in his village simply subservient?), a shade less than obedient, and perhaps worst of all, delivered three daughters and no sons. Not expressive to begin with, the combination of circumstances led him to withdraw emotionally from family life.

My mother did not react well to his stingy approach toward money and emotions and his lack of involvement in family affairs. As far back as I can consciously recall, we had a family atmosphere that was cold at best and actually hostile most of the time. My mother and father fought both openly and silently, since both felt great disappointment based on what their respective family upbringings had led them to expect from life and a spouse. They stopped sleeping together even before my younger sister was born. In better times, they fought furiously and physically, often using us as pawns. In the worst times, they simply ignored each other and would not trade words for months on end. There were many long evenings of silence in our house. It was a wonder that they maintained the same household for as long as they did. My father lacked the will and conviction to do anything about his family situation, and my mother lacked the financial resources and courage to strike out on her own and support us. This was the home from which

I sought distance and a chance to escape, three thousand miles away in Caltech, at the age of seventeen.

But if only that were all to my parents' story. Some time in my junior high school years, as I entered my teens, my sisters and I (and I suppose my father as well, though I'm not sure) noticed that my mother occasionally talked about incidents and events that seemed increasingly odd and unbelievable. In the beginning, this occurred only once in a while, and anyway, she was working by then for the U.S. Customs House as a bookkeeper and was mostly busy with her day-to-day schedule. However, as the years went by, the amount of time that her conversation was lucid dwindled.

We know now, in retrospect, that those symptoms marked the onset of her increasingly debilitating mental illness, most likely a form of paranoid schizophrenia. Clinically, her state is not that mysterious or even uncommon. Personally, however, I have always seen it as her way of dealing with the perceived disappointment of her life—hers was a family of great wealth, tradition, and heritage, but it was in the final stages of losing everything by the time she was born.

My mother did not enjoy her first peace-time year until she was sixteen, a refugee in Taiwan, forced to leave high school to work to support her mother and brother, who had contracted tuberculosis. Through family connections and their abilities, they rebuilt a good life in Taiwan, which she enjoyed till 1966. In 1966, she was to find herself stranded again, as a "refugee," in another new country, the United States, where she did not know the language, had no friends or relatives, and was dependent upon a man who was, as far as her sensibilities were concerned, a peasant, albeit a technically capable one.

After we were slightly older and going to grade school, she went to night school and got a high school equivalency diploma in New York, which led to her Customs House job. It was a job with secure benefits and minimal demands, but the work was mind-numbingly simple, and her colleagues were mostly uneducated and uninspired petty bureaucrats. The world that she fabricates to withdraw into provides telling insight into why she probably ended up there. In her world, she is someone very important, but her significance is not appreciated by those around her. She is constantly being hounded and watched by the few who do know of her "actual identity." And she has been unable to achieve her full potential as a result of the envy-inspired persecution to which she has been subjected. The conspiracies against her involve an incredible cast of characters from presidents and major corporations to childhood relatives, some long since dead. In what was probably her last sane action, my mother moved out into her own apartment and filed for a divorce from my father in 1984. By then, right or wrong, in her mind, he had become the cause and the symbol of all the disappointments in her life.

Neither of my parents had the interest in or presence of mind to attend my college commencement in June 1985, and, increasingly excited about the prospects of my Watson year, I also skipped the commencement ceremonies and went back to New York City to pack for China and inform my parents of my new plans. By then, my mother's mental state had deteriorated to the point where she denied that she was Chinese (technically she is not, since she is Manchurian) or that we had anything to do with China. So my plans really meant nothing to her.

My father seemed somewhat pleasantly surprised; however, he wasn't very focused on my trip. He had never been very involved or interested in his children's plans, and he was less so then, since my mother had just moved out. He had had no relationship to speak of with her for years, and her paranoid rantings must have been difficult to bear in the last years. But his level of indifference toward his surroundings is epic, and he had long since grown accustomed to shutting her out. What he was worrying about when I saw him that year was, Who would cook and clean for him? Who would do his shopping and the dishes? He had never done any household chores, and, in his older years, he would need help more than ever.

I was not interested then or now in how his house was being kept, but I was and am grateful for the one sign of concern he showed for my Watson year, and it turned out to be the critical one. Since I was going to Beijing, he gave me the contact telephone number of my mother's oldest brother who lived there with his wife and three of his four sons—my cousins. Oddly, although my fellowship was based on a theme of roots, I hadn't thought of relatives up to that moment, only of travel and a year abroad.

And so it was that, on August 27, 1985, I arrived in Beijing with a letter of introduction from Professor Lee to the history department at Beijing University, the telephone number of my maternal uncle in Beijing, a small suitcase of clothing, and a few notebooks. I pack more today for a weekend of golf than I did then for a year in China. It is ridiculous and almost funny when I think of how totally unprepared I was to be in China. I studied very little of relevance to provide background for what I was to see and experience. I had basically gone to hang out, travel, and enjoy the freedom that the Watson fellow funds bought for me. But I was to find that what I lacked in academic awareness I was to more than make up for on a very emotional and personal level.

At the end of the first day, I was established and settled in for the term at the foreign students' dormitory, Shao Yuan. The day was my first in what would be hundreds of lessons on the precious Communist commodity called power and connections *(guanxi)*. It was my first time ever in China, and my first time back in Asia since I had left it as a three-year-old child. I had never had any Chinese education and did not even know the characters for Beijing, much less for university. I barely knew how to write my name in Chinese, and that was it. It was my first language, and I spoke it fluently, but at an unsophisticated household level. I must have been the most illiterate and uneducated person in Chinese studies ever to be admitted to that most prestigious department of China's most prestigious university. I dread to imagine what the history department head thought that day when he met me. But I had *guanxi*. I had been recommended in a personal letter by Professor Lee, who was highly regarded by them, and that was sufficient to waive all formal entrance criteria, including the most basic level of literacy! My willingness and ability to pay a full year of tuition in hard currency must also have been a plus (tuition was about $2,000 for the year). However, tuition was only a secondary consideration—in those still decidedly planned-economy days, access always mattered more than money.

I had stumbled on to what turned out to be fascinating days indeed in China in 1985. Not only at Beijing University, but all throughout the country, China was taking its initial steps toward opening up to the outside world, dismantling the most burdensome aspects of its state apparatus, and warming to the idea that a new way of doing things would soon be in order.[4] That much is true even today about China. However, in 1985, the Communist system and lifestyle were still intact, and people's attitudes and nature were much as they had been in the 1970s. Wounds from the Cultural Revolution years were still open and sore in 1985, whereas now, it seems all but forgotten (oddly, though, it appears to be enjoying a chic revival among the young urban wealthy).[5] It was a precious time when the previous way of life was in the final days of being lived—ration tickets for staple foods, state-owned-and-operated everything, bicycles only, no foreign joint ventures, no foreign-built skyscrapers, no international five-star hotels—a time when instant coffee and a *Time* magazine were truly rare commodities.

I found myself in incredible company at Beijing University. The three hundred foreign students at Shao Yuan represented almost seventy countries. As at Caltech, I was well out of my depth. All my classmates there were serious Chinese studies majors, many pursuing advanced degrees, who had studied at great length some aspect of Chinese language, history, literature, arts, culture, or the legal or social tradition. Many of the students from developing nations or Soviet bloc countries were diplomats-in-training. Overall, the foreign community was small in 1985, with the foreign students and diplomats far outnumbering the business people. There was a strong sense of community among the foreigners. The greatest fascination was that, although I had grown up in multicultural America, I had never had a chance to meet people from the Soviet Union, New Zealand, East Germany, Belgium, Nigeria, Cuba, Sri Lanka, and from basically all over the world. Meals at the Shao Yuan cafeteria were a United Nations every day, and the funniest part was that we all shared one common language—Chinese!

The local Chinese student body was also remarkable. The merit-based exam system was reinstituted in the mid-1970s, so the level of intelligence among the students was high.[6] It was also before the great exodus of talent had begun to overseas or to language and M.B.A programs.[7] The students then were well conversant in classical studies and had an openness and curiosity that represented the leading edge of reform thought in China in 1985. China's intellectual society was not as cynical, or as single-mindedly commercial, as it is today. Both foreign and local students were there in quest of information and were intellectually hungry to make up for the time lost in China's three decades of self-imposed isolation.

Finally, there was an emotional rawness that was not often spoken of but was clearly felt in those days. I had studied and read about China's long and tortuous modern history: foreign siege, the end of the Qing dynasty, warlordism, Japanese occupation, World War II, civil war, the Communist victory, the Great Leap Forward, the Cultural Revolution, and the Gang of Four.[8] My mother had told us stories when we were young about some of her experiences during the occupation and World War II. But hearing such stories in the totally distant world of America had meant nothing to me growing up.

Intellectually, I was aware that China's modern history was tumultuous. Any one of the incidents listed above would have traumatized a nation for decades—that all of them had befallen one country in the space of less than one hundred years was incredible. By the 1970s the succession of events had left the country and its people almost numb. But China had finally reached the light at the end of its tunnel by 1979; Deng Xiaoping swept most of the Mao-era ideologues out of power and promised the emotionally exhausted Chinese that the period of pursuing nonsensical "-isms" was over, that he would put all his remaining years and energy into rebuilding the country. The worst travesties and injustices of the Cultural Revolution period were reviewed. Efforts were made to return property, and thousands of purge victims, mostly intellectuals, entrepreneurs, and former government officials, were released from prisons or returned from exile to their former positions. After a number of false starts in the early 1970s, the madness of the Mao era finally promised to be permanently behind them.[9]

Thus, the 1980s started as a time of new beginnings, a time to physically and emotionally re-collect. The university was filled with the recently rehabilitated victims of political purges. For many, it wasn't enough that they were allowed to return to society with their unjust verdicts reversed. Before they could finally move forward and get on with their lives, they needed to tell of what they had been through. And they needed to tell someone from the outside world who could validate how mad their experiences really had been, because, for them, the madness had become normal.

The stories were haunting. And the stories numbered in the millions. No amount of modern Chinese history lessons could have prepared me for the shock of the stories, which invariably spilled out in hushed, yet urgent, whispers. In those early autumn days in Beijing, all the concepts that I had been taught were self-evident about human rights and determination slowly started to slip away. Never again will I believe as I was taught in the States that the individual matters or that "where there's a will, there's a way." The fabric of our lives is mostly woven not by us, but by forces and fates greater than any individual, and we are all at their mercy.

I could go on for pages and days about the eye-opening world of Beijing in 1985. Also, inspired by the weight of the academic seriousness that surrounded me at Shao Yuan, I registered to audit a few classes, which was very interesting (my favorite was listening to American history, socialist style). I made many new friends at Beijing University, some of whom I remain close to even today. There were many carefree days spent bicycling through the alleyways and imperial gardens of Beijing with newfound friends making discoveries about China and about ourselves, and finding that some simple pleasures of life, like eating, are universal to all. Every day was an adventure.

It wasn't until the second month, when I had finally started to settle down a bit, that my uncle's phone number found its way to the top of my list of things to do. And even up to that time, that was how I viewed it—as a "to do" item. I was curious to meet my relatives, but also apprehensive. I had never known them and would not have recognized them if we were to meet by chance. My mother had four brothers; I did not know any of them well, but I had met and was aware of the ones who had fled China with my mother in 1949. They eventually settled in Melbourne, Australia (uncle no. two) and Palo Alto, California (uncle no. four). The two who stayed were total strangers to me—uncle no. one in Beijing, and uncle no. three in Guangzhou, in south China. I was apprehensive, because Chinese relatives are stereotypically meddling in unhelpful ways, and there were also stories of returning overseas Chinese being treated as Santa Clauses and presented with gift lists.

But most of all, I was apprehensive because of my mother's mental condition. At that time, I don't think it was clear even to her brothers in California and Australia that she was so far, and that she departed so often, from reality. All they knew then was that her correspondences had become much less frequent, and her phone manner more distant and unfriendly. If anything, whenever my uncle no. four saw me, he would try to pump me for information about what she was upset with him about. I'm not too sure why, but my sisters and I never told them point-blank that our mother was mentally deteriorating. I think for years, we ourselves were in a state of denial about her condition, and, also, it seemed somehow disloyal to her to reduce her to the label of mentally ill.

Therefore, there was no chance that her brothers in China, with its then very backward telephone system and restrictions on overseas travel, had any inkling of her condition. How was I to handle questions about her? How was I to explain that I carried no letter from her? I was the first in my generation born overseas to return to Beijing. If my mother were sane, she would have been enormously proud. The few stories that I remembered hearing her tell when I was a child indicated that, despite the hardships of war, she had loved Beijing and missed it through the years. The Manchurians are clannish people, and she came from a large clan that had a very well-defined sense of its heritage and its place in history. With a definite sense of trepidation, it was to this clan that I was about to return.

Uncle no. one's oldest son (my cousin, who I have always called Da Ge, meaning "big brother") was expecting my call. Uncle no. four in Palo Alto had sent them word that I was coming. He came to collect me from the university after work that day to take me home to meet his parents. My impressions of the first moments of that evening are not sharply etched in my mind. Looking back, I realize that that first meeting was more marked in what was not said than in what was. Only my uncle, his wife, and Da Ge were present that evening. My uncle's wife left the men to lead the conversation most of the time, but she smiled warmly at me and was clearly pleased that I had "come home." My uncle no. one shook my hand firmly and welcomed me. He and my Da Ge are tall, handsome men who stand straight and self-assuredly. What struck me most deeply on our first meeting was how much they looked like my mother. I had the mind-set that they were virtual strangers, but their physical likeness to her entirely dispelled that notion. Many questions were asked, but not in a prying manner. The first topic of conversation was how my mother and father were. I did not mention their imminent divorce or my mother's actual state of mind— instead, I made general noises about them being well. Uncle no. one responded with, "Hmm. So your mother did not send a letter? We have not heard from her in a while." I responded that she had been very busy but that she thought of them often. "Hmmm."

They spoke very little about themselves, and all our conversation centered around my sisters and me—what our life has been like, what we studied, what our hobbies and interests were, how I came to be in China, what my detailed plans were, and so on. Da Ge had many questions about the United States and the U.S. way of life and about my impressions of China. They had lost most of the old family pictures during the Cultural Revolution, but the few that remained were shown to me. It was the first time I had ever seen pictures of my mother's childhood. They were fascinating—old Beijing came through clearly in the photos as a way of life and a landscape that no longer exists. My mother grew up in a beautiful courtyard house with peach trees in the yard and many apartments on the four sides of the courtyard for the immediate clan. The house still existed and had been returned to them since 1979. My uncle's wife said that its condition is entirely different, and that many squatter families now live in it, but we could go to see it whenever I wanted.

It turned out to be a fascinating evening for me. Uncle no. one was a professor of traditional Chinese landscape architecture, and Da Ge followed in his footsteps as a traditional landscape architect at the Beijing Parks Design Institute. They lived in modern times, but embodied everything I imagined ancient Chinese scholars to be. Da Ge is a calligrapher and a painter in his spare time, and his favorite pastime is playing Chinese chess. My uncle's wife was addicted to Chinese opera. Our conversation ranged from politics to Chinese philosophy and history—our only major limitation was the breadth of my vocabulary in Chinese for those subjects.

All my apprehensions were dispelled as the evening wore on. My relatives couldn't have been less interested in things and wish lists. And they were not unpleasantly prying—my answers about my mother were clearly inadequate, but for that first evening, everyone was content to just let it go by. My uncle was, however, concerned that I knew so little about the history of the Manchus, and of our family. Of course, I made up for it greatly in some way simply by having come to Beijing for a whole year. I knew that evening that I wanted very much to see more of them and to learn about the Manchurian clans from which I am descended. My interest had moved quickly beyond intellectual curiosity for me that night and had become something very personal. Uncle's physical resemblance to my mother truly made me feel as if he were an extension of her. But it was also the idiosyncrasies and some obvious personality characteristics that reminded me of my mother. My mother has a proud manner and tends to hold herself slightly aloof—that was exactly the manner of uncle no. one and Da Ge. I also smiled broadly when early in the evening I noticed a barely perceptible tremble in Uncle's lower chin when he spoke, and a habit of outlining characters with his finger in the air on the side as he thought. My mother has the exact same tics.

Obviously, it is not revolutionary to discover similarities in siblings. However, for me, it was something special to see. These people lived in a different world from me and were effectively total strangers—but in those small things, I saw that we were the closest of relatives, and that even great distances and revolutions do not weaken the links. Having grown up as a new immigrant in the States, I also had no sense of being part of a larger family. Three of my grandparents had died before I was born, and my maternal grandmother, who died in Taiwan in the early 1970s, never got to visit us in New York. And so my parents existed independently in our world, as opposed to having come from somewhere or being a part of something. The realization started to dawn on me that night that although I may be a new stand-alone immigrant in America, I am also very much part of a huge clan with a rich tradition and history.

Because it was getting late and time for me to get back to the campus, my uncle's wife said that she supposed I'd want to see my aunt as soon as possible and that she could take me whenever I was free. I had been waiting for that topic to come up. My mother had not only four brothers, but also a sister who was the oldest of the siblings. My mother practically had two mothers while she was growing up—her own mother and her big sister, who was twelve years older and who adored her. My aunt was very smart—she excelled in school and passed the exams to enter Qinghua University, one of China's most prestigious universities, in 1945.[10] However, what happened thereafter broke everyone's heart, and perhaps most of all, my mother's.

By all accounts, my aunt was a sensitive child and had a definite soft spot for the underprivileged. Even in her late years, she would rail about how inequitable birth rights such as theirs were. The Communist movement appealed to her politically and emotionally, and she became the first in her family to join the Communist Party as they recruited students on campuses. There does not seem to be a clear accounting of what happened next. But we know that in 1947, she volunteered to join the front lines of the civil war and was assigned to the southern offensive in Guangxi province headed by General Lin Biao.[11] Despite her liberal leanings, she had led a very sheltered life, and it seems the hardships she witnessed in poor rural China and on the civil war front were mentally or emotionally upsetting to her. The actual situation that led her to a mental breakdown was dealing with the persistent, but unwanted, romantic or sexual attention of some of the male soldiers or officers. She suffered a mental collapse and started hearing tortuous voices in her head, which drove her to yell and scream through the nights and days.

They sent her back to Beijing, where the family still had the financial means to care for her at home with full-time help. In 1950, she recovered to a certain extent and went back to Qinghua to reclaim her student position to finish college. However, my aunt was turned away because her war participation record had ended on a dubious note. She attempted to commit suicide the very same day by jumping into Kunming Lake at the Summer Palace, which is next to the Qinghua campus.[12] She was saved by a passerby, but her mental condition deteriorated dramatically after that point. She was prone to fits of violence, screaming, and delusions, and was unable to attend to her own daily living needs or hygiene without full-time care. By 1957, however, our family circumstances in Beijing had deteriorated significantly. All property aside from the house they lived in was nationalized. In 1949, my mother's mother had left China for Taiwan with my mother, and uncles no. two and four. My mother's father passed away in 1951 in Beijing. Uncle no. one was then head of the household, but he and a number of other relatives came under attack during the antirightist movement of the late 1950s.[13] He was no longer in a position to even protect himself, much less provide full-time care at home for his sister. She was then committed to a mental hospital, where she lived until her death in 1996.

For my grandmother and my mother, it was not just the pain of knowing of her suffering, but also the guilt and frustration of having left China and not being able to go back to help in the very difficult times of need. Whenever my mother mentioned her sister and told us about how my aunt protected and cared for her growing up, there were tears in her eyes. We knew how bad mental institutions could be even in the States, and could only imagine what they were like in China. To make matters worse, the few letters that my mother received from my aunt over the years always included beseechments for help in leaving the mental institute. But there was nothing we could do from the United States. It was heartbreaking.

Of course, I told my uncle's wife, I definitely wanted to visit my aunt, and the sooner the better. They told me that in 1981, as soon as their family circumstances were better, they had brought my aunt home. Although all went well in the first few weeks, the situation rapidly degenerated thereafter. Without a daily regimen such as was enforced in the institute, my aunt became increasingly uncooperative, belligerent, and reclusive. She still could not handle basic shopping and cooking chores and paid no attention to personal hygiene. She eventually had to be recommitted. They tried again in 1984, but with the same end result. Her physical health was good considering the circumstances and her age, and her mental state was stable and reasonably coherent, but everyone knew that she could not last very long outside the institute.

A few days later, my uncle's wife and I took a taxi to an outer suburb called Heilongguan. It is more than one hour north of Beijing in
the direction of the ancient Ming Tombs. We hardly talked on the way
out—I was a bit nervous and unsure of what to expect. Finally, we turned
off the main road onto a dusty one-lane path, and fifteen minutes later,
we came to a large arch gateway that proclaimed the An Ding Mental
Hospital. There were a number of single-story courtyard wards and
offices built in the standard nondescript gray cement bricks commonly
used throughout China. Out there, the environs were quite deserted
and dusty. We had passed only one other work unit on the small road,
and it seemed more like a truck junkyard than like the repair and manufacturing company it proclaimed to be.

We stood at the hospital gate where the taxi left us, and I shivered.
The landscape was flat and gray, with nothing to block the chilly autumn winds from the north. Clutching our plastic bags filled with cookies, preserved meats, chocolates, apples, and oranges for my aunt, my
uncle's wife led me to the my aunt's ward. The reception area was a
sparse room with a wooden bench and table for visitors, and it had the
typical Chinese hospital sense of clean that somehow still always seems
dirty to my American senses. My uncle's wife told the disinterested nurse
that we'd come to see the patient Jin Zhuangju. After both ignoring
and scrutinizing us for a few beats, she brusquely told us to sit and wait
while she shuffled off. The next ten minutes seemed like an eternity
to me.

The nurse returned, and following her was my aunt—my mother's
oldest and only sister, who had spent thirty years in mental institutes
in China. She was shorter than my mother, about five foot two. She
slouched slightly with age and had a round belly, but stick-thin arms
and legs. Her hair was cut short in a bob and streaked with white and
gray. It was slightly unkempt, having a slept-on look, and she wore a
large pajama overcoat with a bold blue prison stripe pattern. I noticed
later that all the patients were dressed that way so they could be easily
identified if they were to wander off, away from the hospital yard. She
walked slowly, but steadily. There was a slight hint of a glaze in her
gaze, which was to worsen in her last years as her mind focused increasingly in imaginary worlds beyond. But that day, her eyes met ours,

and I could see her trying to place who I was. What struck me most in that first moment was that she looked exactly like my mother—just an older, more worn, version.

My aunt greeted her sister-in-law (my uncle's wife), who sat her down and pointed to me. "This is Zhuangmei's second daughter. Your niece. This is her first time to Beijing; she has come to see us from America and will stay in Beijing for one year." My aunt nodded her head slightly and continued to scrutinize me as I smiled timidly. After a few seconds, which seemed like minutes to me, she said, "You must look like your father." And it is true; I look much more like my father than my mother. Before I could answer, however, my uncle's wife presented her with our gifts. The pretty packages immediately distracted my aunt as she greedily fingered one package, then another. The preserved meat got pushed back to us, because she said her teeth were not good enough to eat them, but she immediately ripped open and started in on a package of cookies. Through a mouthful, she asked for a pen, which my uncle's wife produced. My aunt then proceeded to carefully write her name in large characters on each of the packages she was keeping. She said in a hushed voice that the other patients or the nurses were likely to take her food if she didn't label them carefully and guard them.

I was speechless, and I could feel a lump rise up in my throat. I was overwhelmed by her resemblance to my mother, but also by the indignity of her appearance and circumstances. I tried to control my rising emotions as I watched her absorbed in labeling her food in a shaky hand. I addressed her formally, "Elder aunt, I am so happy to meet you. I have heard about you all my life from my mother. My mother is well in the United States, and she sends you her best wishes. She thinks of you often and hopes you are well."

The bitterness of the irony of telling that lie hit me hard, but with it, we started our tentative conversation. She asked me about whether my mother was still working, how old my sisters were, and what they were working at or studying. Although she asked the questions, I noticed that she did not really focus on the answers. I asked about her health, and about her daily routine. There, too, her answers were fairly short and without much elaboration. In fact, we occasionally lapsed into silences, at which point my uncle's wife would interject news about how relatives were in Beijing.

Her conversation was basically lucid; however, there was a distracted quality to it. And she was also comfortable to just sit and stare and not say anything at times. After I asked about her health, my uncle's wife asked her directly how her mental condition was. My aunt answered calmly that it wasn't very good and that she still heard them. "Who's them?" I asked. My aunt said it was all the people in her head—they can get so noisy sometimes that she gets really tired. I tried asking who "they" were and what "they" said, but got vague answers that were increasingly disinterested.

It was a really sad meeting. The nurses were slightly rude and condescending towards my aunt. Intermittently, they even sat on the sidelines of our conversation as if we were a soap opera, since it was more interesting than their chores. Their attitude toward her infuriated me, and I wanted to shoo them away for privacy, but my uncle's wife placed a restraining hand on my arm and told me that we had to be nice to them, otherwise they wouldn't be nice to my aunt after we left.

Hearing my aunt's matter-of-fact description of her lack of proper medical care and the wasted way in which she spent her days left me deeply upset. Psychiatry is entirely undeveloped as a science in China, and with basically only three psychiatrists for the over one thousand patients at An Ding, no proper attention could be paid to any of them. My aunt was visited by one of those doctors not more than once a month, for only a few minutes each time. Every day, she was given pills to take, and she couldn't even tell me what exactly they were. My uncle's wife said that they were mostly nutritional supplements and sedatives. Whatever they were, my aunt got almost a whole bowl of them a day! There was a small yard where the patients have recess for an hour a day, three fixed meal times, and a TV hour each day. My aunt couldn't really tell me what else she did all day long—in any case, there was no privacy, since she had only one bed and a small bedstand in a room with ten other women. There were no desks or libraries. I asked her if she had any friends there, and she said not really. Then my aunt leaned over and said conspiratorially to us, "You know, most of the people here are crazy."

Even if I didn't originally hear voices in my head, I would if I had to spend even one day at An Ding, much less a lifetime. And An Ding is a good mental hospital by Chinese standards.

I continually had to blink back tears all through the hour, and I spoke less and less for fear of losing control of my emotions. Finally, as we were supposed to leave, since the time for the patients' nap period was approaching, I asked what she wanted and if there was anything she needed that I could do. My aunt said that she didn't want anything, but that she hoped to leave the hospital some day for good and that she wanted to see my mother again because she hadn't seen her in over fifty years. "Do you think your mother will come see me?"

I had to walk outside at that point and, in the cold afternoon, I stood against the wall and cried openly and with an anguish deeper than I had ever known. For weeks in China, I heard about the wasted years, the lost lives, and the incredible tragedies. And though the stories shocked me, it wasn't until I had come to An Ding that the weight of all the losses touched me personally and emotionally.

My aunt was clearly not so insane or sedated that she didn't know how little she had to live for there. But how could I tell them that their beloved little sister, my mother, was also so schizophrenic that she didn't even understand that she was Chinese, and that there was no chance that she'd ever come to China and see them? In fact, the sister they had known and grown up with had disappeared a long time ago. And I knew that my aunt would never leave the hospital. I cried bitterly at my utter sense of helplessness and the unfairness of the situation. For all that she had gone through, to want to see her little sister once more did not seem to be asking too much, yet it was impossible.

I cried with a feeling of loss so deep that it hurt me physically. I cried for my lovely aunt's entire lost life and lost mind, which might have been salvaged if she'd only lived in a different time or in a different country. I cried for all the lost years forfeited by all my uncles and cousins in China to the whimsical madness of a movement that still nobody fully understands. But most of all, I cried for my mother and for my-self. My mother, in losing touch with her foundations and support net-work, had lost her mind slowly in the emotional isolation of America with no rapport with her husband, and children too small to be of comfort or to be her friends when she needed them most. And I cried for the first time in my life for the thirteen-year-old girl who was me, slowly watching my mother's mind ebb away, when I most needed and counted on her to be there as I grew up. All my pent-up anger and bitterness that my mother had to be the one stricken came welling up that day. And the incredible feeling of frustration and helplessness that I felt about my mother's deterioration came storming back at me as I sat with my aunt, listening to and taking in her circumstances.

One does things sometimes without consciously knowing why—that's how I was back in the States when I was writing a Watson essay about coming to China. My reaction to seeing my aunt and uncles was so visceral that it shocked me into the gradual realization that year of how emotionally needy I was and of how much I had yearned to find a surrogate mother or family base. I did not know or realize it until much later, but I had, in fact, not come to China in search of my roots. I had come in search of my mother and a deep need to resurrect her being or to get closer to her in any way that I could. I needed to understand why she had left us for her own world. And in fact, I too, had whispered my aunt's prayer and wish to see her again millions of times before. And the answer was no, we none of us, would ever be able to see the woman who was my only sense of family and support as a child. Although her physical being is still here, her person had long ago retreated forever, as had the essence of the young woman my aunt was—both victims and the product of our family's heritage and history.

A week later, I met my Da Ge for a day visit to the Summer Palace. Touring the sprawling palace grounds with him was a treat, since he is an expert on its history, architecture, and landscaping. The palace was the subject of his graduate thesis; it is the most common subject of his watercolors, and, professionally, he has led the design team at his institute in restoration and restructuring projects for sections of the Summer Palace on numerous occasions. The palace also held a personal meaning—as a latter generation Manchurian clansman, he had a great pride and interest in the legacy of the Qing dynasty.

But we hardly focused on palace particulars that day. As we reached the magnificent Kunming Lake at the foot of Longevity Hill, Da Ge said, "This is where your aunt tried to kill herself." I knew it sounded inappropriate, but I told him that I wished she hadn't been saved that day. He nodded. We both knew firsthand how anguishing it was for the mentally ill and their relatives to linger for years.

Da Ge told me that his mother and father were touched by my reaction to my aunt. I hadn't said anything on the ride back from An Ding that day, but the tears streamed down my face endlessly. It meant a lot to my uncle; it meant that despite the generation away from Beijing, despite our decades of lost correspondence and despite my having grown up in the safe comfort and distance from tragedy in America, the family ties persisted and were strong, and that our past was not forgotten. I had come to China and met my relatives as a stranger, but I recognized them from my heart and instinctively as their niece, and I was as emotionally involved as if I had lived with them all my life.

My emotions that year were numerous and tumultuous. It was a time of incredible personal discovery and coming to terms. I ended up becoming closer than I ever imagined I would to my uncle and his wife in Beijing. I think we fulfilled mutual emotional needs—theirs that they not be forgotten, and mine for a sense of family and belonging. They became almost surrogate parents for me, and the polite reservations that had existed during our first dinner together were to fall away entirely. My uncle's wife raised four sons, and, in her last years, I became the daughter she had always wanted. In 1991, on her first trip to the States to visit her fourth son, she contracted pneumonia. I sat vigil with her son by her bedside in her last week and brought her belongings back to Beijing to her mourning family after she passed away. My uncle died of cancer in Beijing a year later.

In the years before my aunt and uncle passed away, Beijing had become my home both physically and emotionally. I returned to the United States after my Watson year ended, but I couldn't concentrate on work in Silicon Valley. I quit after only one year and returned to Beijing to work for a German electrical equipment manufacturing company. Despite the rigors of doing business in China, those were very happy and contented years for me. I, of course, never found my mother in China, but in many ways, I found myself and the foundation that I needed to moved forward with strength. Emotionally, I needed the love and acceptance that my uncle and his wife gave me, and the interest they took in my life and in my cultural education filled the vacuum that my disinterested father and mentally ill mother had left. Just facing up to the fact that I needed those things was an important discovery for me. I had convinced myself over the years that I was a strong and smart person and that I didn't need anybody's help to get by in the world. In fact, it wasn't true at all, and I'd only convinced myself of that because it couldn't be otherwise.

A few of my cousins in China became my closest friends, since we naturally share a great deal in common in our personalities and interests. We have all marveled at how great our similarities are despite the incredible differences in our life experiences. Last year, when I got married in Hawaii, my Da Ge came from Beijing to give me away, and another cousin from Beijing was there to watch. Neither of my parents were at my wedding, but it did not matter to me as it had in 1985, when they showed no interest in my college graduation commencement. That my cousins came meant a lot to me. Da Ge was as nervous as any proud father could have been, and his sense of responsibility as the head of our clan now is deep. But most of all, I thought on my wedding day about how happy and thrilled my uncle's wife would have been if she were alive to see me. And how she would have fussed over my dress and my hair. . . .

My aunt finally passed away in April 1996. She died in An Ding Hospital, alone, and strapped to a bed to prevent her from pulling out the intravenous tubes that sustained her because she was convinced that "they" were trying to poison her. We all visited her often, and I arranged a number of outings for her during my years in Beijing. My conversations with my aunt never changed over the years. The vacant gaze became more pronounced, but she always came back to the same thing. Even in our last meeting, four months before she passed away, she told me as earnestly as ever that she had nothing to live for but to see her little sister again. My mother never went to China to see any of them, and she never will, though I guess it doesn't matter anymore.

My time in China was not only emotionally important to me, but it also opened new dimensions for me on an intellectual level. Before my trip to China, being "Chinese" meant almost nothing to me, and even being "American" was something that I had simply taken for granted. Ironically, both levels of awareness sharpened at the same time. Even as I gained an appreciation of my personal and cultural heritage, the realities of modern-day China also deepened my appreciation for, and understanding of, being an American. Fourteen years after my first arrival in China, I finally moved back to the States, and, in the truest sense of the word, I did so as a Chinese-American.

During that first year in China, and since, I have met countless young overseas Chinese like me. It is surprising how many were distanced from their parents for various reasons and had grown up in relative cultural isolation somewhere in the world. And I hope that they have found even a part of what I did that year and have been able to move on.

Epilogue

JOSEPHINE M. T. KHU

THIS BOOK IS A COLLECTION OF THIRTEEN PERSONAL ACCOUNTS written by ethnic Chinese—including those of mixed ethnicity—who were born or raised outside China about their encounter with the country of their ancestors. In each story, the participants, who together count at least nine different countries in their backgrounds, address the question of how they have assessed or reassessed their identities after that encounter.

The search for identity is a personal task, but both in the reasons prompting such a search and in its results are entwined larger questions involving the nature of a society. "One thinks of identity whenever one is not sure of where one belongs," one scholar has written. "Identity is a name given to the escape sought from that uncertainty."[1] The questions of why one may come to wonder why one does not belong and of where one thinks one belongs have become the subject of innumerable studies not simply because of the importance of the personal task but because of the link between the personal and the political. The concept of identity and concepts of race, ethnicity, gender, class, nationality, and the nation are interlocking and have become increasingly complex in a world ever more characterized by transnational and global exchanges.

Scholars of the Chinese diaspora have noted that most of the large numbers of emigrants from China in the late nineteenth and through the first half of the twentieth centuries initially regarded themselves as sojourners and not as permanent settlers in the countries to which they had journeyed in search of better opportunities. The migrants thus tended to identify themselves less with their country of residence than with their place of origin. Identification with place of origin initially often focused on a hometown or home province and revolved around shared kinship, language, cultural, and religious practices rather than on the Chinese nation as a whole—"nation" and "nationalism" being relatively new and unfamiliar concepts in China at the time.[2]

Without necessarily diluting earlier local Chinese identities, various developments led to the fostering of a new Chinese national identity among ethnic Chinese communities abroad. Foremost among these was the threat to China's sovereignty posed by foreign imperial powers. The resulting sense of national and cultural crisis that swept through China from the late nineteenth century onward also manifested itself in émigré Chinese communities. A new Chinese republic actively sought the support of the overseas Chinese, who had come to be regarded by Chinese authorities as a valuable resource in the modernization of a backward and threatened country. Most of all, perhaps, the overseas Chinese were courted for the financial and political support they could bring in bolstering the legitimacy of factions in China struggling for supremacy. Valued as never before by China's national authorities, the overseas Chinese were, at the same time, subjected to restrictive citizenship and immigration policies in many countries where Chinese populations were found. The creation, by various colonial authorities of the countries where overseas Chinese resided, of legal or occupational distinctions based on race were further obstacles to the integration and identification of the ethnic Chinese with their countries of residence and further encouraged their leanings toward China.[3]

Post–World War II studies on overseas Chinese identities have addressed three developments. The first arose from the isolation of mainland China from much of the outside world from 1949 to 1978, along with immigration restrictions in the newly independent states of Southeast Asia, a traditional area of Chinese emigration. These restrictions resulted in the locally born ethnic Chinese population there outnumbering the China born. Meanwhile, in 1957, the government of mainland China relinquished its policy of regarding all ethnic Chinese overseas as citizens of China, regardless of citizenship, place of birth, or residence.[4] Scholars began to study how and to what extent the overseas Chinese managed to adapt themselves to the new political and social conditions in their host countries—particularly the degree to which they were able to maintain their Chinese practices and identity.[5]

The second development is that since the latter half of the twentieth century, emigration from China has increasingly shed its sojourning character. In the last two decades in particular, the majority of people emigrating from China have done so with the express intention of making permanent homes and lives for themselves abroad. At the same time, many of these new émigrés retained an interest in and concern for China as well as a desire to maintain some degree of Chinese culture and identity. Far better educated as a whole than the Chinese immigrants of the pre–World War II period, they began to ponder how they could retain a Chinese identity in the face of their consciously made decisions to live away from China and take up the citizenship of another country.[6] The third development was the fact that the ethnic Chinese were actively involved in the rapid rate of economic growth that occurred in East and Southeast Asia in the past two decades. As a prominent scholar of the Chinese diaspora noted: "The question began to be asked whether the role of Chinese enterprise in the rapid economic development in Southeast Asia had any connection with, or more specifically, any effect on, Chinese identity."[7]

These developments have led to an emerging debate over the meaning of "being Chinese." At the risk of oversimplifying matters, this debate may be divided into two basic camps. One approaches the subject of "Chineseness" in essentially cultural terms. A leading proponent of this camp, Tu Wei-ming, sees "Chineseness" as something shaped through continuous interaction and debate among three groups or "symbolic universes" that together constitute a "cultural China." The first group consists of the countries and regions largely made up of Chinese populations such as mainland China, Taiwan, Hong Kong, and Singapore. The second group is the diaspora Chinese, while the third comprises intellectuals, businessmen, and writers, ethnic Chinese or not, who try to understand China and share their conceptions of it with others.[8]

Another conception, proposed by Aihwa Ong and Donald Nonini, among others, sees Chinese identities in diaspora as transnationalist in nature, that is, as "increasingly independent of place, self-consciously postmodern," in which identity is "formed out of the strategies for the accumulation of economic, social, cultural, and educational capital as diasporic Chinese travel, settle down, invest in local spaces, and evade state disciplining in multiple sites throughout the Asia Pacific."[9] To Ong and Nonini, a shared Chinese identity consists of a pattern marking a common condition that peoples separated by space perceive themselves as sharing, such as "multi-plex and varied connections of family ties, kinship, commerce, sentiments and values about native place in China, shared memberships in transnational organizations" and that they reconstitute and replicate in the different countries in which they may settle.[10]

Somewhat lost in this debate over diaspora and Chinese identities are the viewpoints of those of Chinese ethnicity who were born or raised outside mainland China or in countries and regions settled by a majority Chinese population. Such people are not necessarily the transmigrants of the Ong/Nonini conception, that is, conscious of sharing similar conditions with other ethnic Chinese in other countries. Indeed, they may not even be familiar with such patterns and practices. Nor would they necessarily regard themselves as participants in a "cultural China." To many ethnic Chinese, China is a foreign country, the Chinese language is a foreign language, and the issue of Chinese identity is not something they consider relevant to their everyday lives.

Indeed, it is questionable whether the terms *diaspora* or even *Chinese* are meaningfully used in relation to people of Chinese ethnicity who have to a large degree assimilated to other cultures and do not think, or wish to think, of themselves as Chinese except by ethnicity—and even that identity might be only reluctantly acknowledged. The above conceptions, which involve cultural or self-conscious definitions of "Chineseness," would certainly not be applicable to this group, and thus, neither would the term *diaspora*, which, almost by definition, involves people who regard themselves as part of dispersed communities in relation to a lost or idealized homeland.[11]

That being said, a number of studies, as well as several of the stories in this book, cast light on why "diaspora Chinese" is not an entirely inappropriate term to describe such a group. For regardless of the personal identification of an ethnic Chinese individual, one fact is not always easily avoided or ignored by others: that of one's race and appearance.[12] As one contributor of mixed Chinese ethnicity, Milan Lin-Rodrigo, from Sri Lanka, wrote: "I was Chinese only in appearance; neither my sister nor I spoke a word of Chinese, and we did not cook or eat Chinese food or wear Chinese clothes. Moreover, I always got straight As in Sinhala, the local language, and in Sinhala literature in school. Yet whenever somebody picked a fight with me, they would call me a 'damn Chinese.'" Identifying a person as Chinese based on that individual's ethnicity is not confined to non-Chinese people, of course, but is also just as common if not more common among ethnic Chinese and can result in certain expectations. As Nancy Work put it, "I've had Chinese come up to me and ask me if I was Chinese and when I said yes, start talking to me in Chinese. When I looked stupefied, they would be incredulous that someone Chinese couldn't speak her mother tongue."

Appearance enforced an identity on people that they did not necessarily feel, even when no unkindness was meant—on the contrary, even when special, favorable attention was intended:

> At school, there was one teacher who kept us all in constant dread simply with his unpredictability: one moment he would be calm and kind, the next he would go into a boiling fury, raging at us, cuffing us with the flat of his hand, shriveling us with sarcasm. I still occasionally have nightmares about him, but actually he seemed to have a soft spot for me. He had served in the army overseas, and he had some knowledge of Chinese history and culture. He would allude to ancient Chinese legends and quote Chinese proverbs and invite me to confirm the truth of what he had said. I would do so meekly, and afterward, when my schoolmates questioned me further, I would have to admit that I had had no idea what he was talking about. I was glad to be exempt

from the effects of his temper, but I was embarrassed at being singled out and treated as different from the rest of the class. (Graham Chan)

As Ien Ang expressed it: "[T]he ethnicization of subjects in diaspora signals the impossibility of their complete nationalization within the dominant culture of the adopted new country. The 'ethnic' subject highlights the fact that s/he does not (quite) belong to the 'host country'— or at least, s/he is positioned as such. The very name with which the 'ethnic' is referred to—in this case, 'Chinese'—already transposes her or him to, and conjures up the received memory of, another site of symbolic belonging, a site which is not 'here.'"[13] Not everyone would completely subscribe to such sentiments. One of the contributors to this book, Maria Tham, who was born and raised in Pakistan, avers: "In daily conversation, people would call us Chinese, but that was only a term to refer to us. Nobody questioned the 'Pakistaniness' of our 'Chineseness,' or vice versa." She explains: "Everybody lives in small communities, and everyone knows all the locals, if not by name, then by sight. . . . So even though we Chinese were a minority in a South Asian Islamic country, because we were born and brought up in the neighborhood, we were considered locals." It is significant, however, that most of the contributors to this volume mentioned the impact of an identity forced on them because of their appearance as a major motivating factor in making the trip to China. Meilin Ching says,

And so it was my Chinese appearance that would get the most attention, but ironically it was my lack of feeling for whatever it meant to be Chinese that eventually led me to Asia. I was searching for the one aspect of my background that I knew so little about. My brother and sister and I were always being asked if we could speak or read Chinese. Had we ever visited China? To these questions I sensed disappointment and puzzlement upon my usual answer of no. I knew absolutely no Chinese and very little about China. It was my responsibility to find out. I speculated about what it would be like to live in a place where not so much focus was placed on my appearance—a land where I would naturally blend in with the majority, a place where I believed I would feel more at home. I thought it would have to be some-where in Asia.

China, then, is not without some significance even in the minds of many people of Chinese ethnicity who may know virtually nothing of China or of Chinese culture. Some link the country with the idea of home or think of it as some undefined and strangely undeniable part of their being:

> [Dad] never tried to push Chineseness onto me. He realized it made me uncomfortable and that it was more important that I succeed in the white, British world. But when the invitation arrived for me to go to Hong Kong to work as a consultant on a short-term computing assignment, I knew that both he and Mum would be deeply disappointed if I turned it down. Even though we no longer had any friends or relatives there, even though I had been there only once before, when I was an infant too young to remember anything about it, even though Mum and Dad had never been back since then either—in some indefinable way Hong Kong was still home, and I felt that to say no would be to slam the door forever on my Chinese identity. No matter what my fears were, I could not bring myself to do that. (Graham Chan)

To others, curiosity, more about family or other matters than about "Chineseness," was a main consideration for wishing to visit China:

> [J]ust as great an impetus was the opportunity to connect with my grandfather by learning about him and becoming acquainted with him. I knew just enough about him to find him intriguing, and what I didn't know tantalized me. Also, I began to understand then how events beyond anyone's control had worked to divide Chinese families like mine, even when its members could finally be together again. The resulting sense of loss was not confined to members of those generations with immediate experience of those events. (Carolyn Koo)

> Reflecting now on my trip to China, I still cannot pinpoint any one reason or goal for having made that journey to meet my relatives.

Mostly it was probably just to satisfy my curiosity about my father's relatives and his home country. I suppose that I wanted to visually witness that they existed and find out more about them. I also felt that I had a duty to visit them at least once; since my father could not return to China, I thought that I owed his family this visit. (Milan Lin-Rodrigo)

As more people asked me about my background, I began to truly question myself for the first time, and that is why I decided I needed to research my roots. The impetus for doing so was not that I felt being See Yip made me more or less Chinese. I never believed that one's clan, roots, or heritage makes one superior or inferior to anyone else. I believe that all human beings are alike, regardless of race or ethnicity; being different only adds to the diversity and richness of humankind. I had simply become curious about my See Yip heritage and wanted to add to my knowledge. Another factor in my search for my roots was my desire to meet some relatives. We did not have any relatives in Pakistan or in the United States, so while growing up, I often wondered what it would be like to have grandparents, uncles, aunts, and cousins. While I will never know what it is like to have grandparents, I realized that I still had the chance to meet some aunts and cousins. (Maria Tham)

It is curious that so few studies on the topic of diasporic encounters with the ancestral country exist, despite the fact that such encounters, whether in the form of travel, study, work, or self-exploration are a development of our transnational world in which global travels, movements, and exchanges of various kinds have become easier and more common.[14] In China's case, the country had been politically isolated from much of the world for several decades since the founding of the communist-led People's Republic of China in 1949. Internal political turmoil during such campaigns as the antirightist movement of the late 1950s and the Cultural Revolution of 1966–76, during which any Chinese person with foreign relatives or connections was the target of persecution, also discouraged communication between the Chinese in China and their relatives abroad.[15] But China's decades of isolation from the world ended in the late 1970s with diplomatic recognition from most countries and China's adoption of economic and political reforms and an "open-door policy," making the country once again accessible to visitors.[16]

One purpose of this volume of personal accounts, therefore, is to address this gap in the literature on immigration and ethnic history by presenting for study and discussion the experiences of thirteen members of the Chinese diaspora who have journeyed to the country of their ancestors and assessed its influence on their lives. Above all, the aim of this volume is to convey, through the intimacy and emotional immediacy of the personal writings of various individuals on the subject of their Chinese identity, something of the complexity of identity in a world increasingly transnational in nature.

As noted in this book's preface, this volume is itself one product of the technology that characterizes a transnational world. I recruited about half the participants in this project over the Internet, to which nearly all have access, and the remaining half through personal acquaintance or by word of mouth. Benedict Anderson has pointed out the intimate links among identity, nationalism, and technology, identifying the emergence of "print capitalism, which made it possible for rapidly growing numbers of people to think about themselves, and to relate themselves to others, in profoundly new ways" as the ultimate source of the rise of nationalism.[17] One might profitably reflect, therefore, on the implications for both identity and nationalism arising from the spread and commercialization of the Internet and the now widespread use of English as the chief international language. For this book, it was the Internet more than anything else that made it possible for me to bring together people from various parts of the world, who had no previous connection to or knowledge of one another, to contribute their reflections on an issue that was meaningful to all of them. Technology, then, can lead to the creation of global communities of a sort, connected by particular issues of common concern. Whether these new communities might result in the further encouragement of identities less rooted in geography and culture—a development already observed by some scholars of transnationalism such as Ong and Nonini—is, at present, difficult to say.

The contributors to this book range in age from late twenties to early seventies. Some left mainland China, Taiwan, or Hong Kong in early childhood; others are the children of emigrants. For yet others, China is the country from which grandparents or more remote ancestors originated. The writers were born or raised in Australia and New Zealand, Colombia, Denmark and Italy, England, Indonesia, Japan, Pakistan, the Philippines, Sri Lanka, and the United States. Many now live in, and are citizens of, the United States. Reflecting traditional patterns of emigration from China, the contributors' search for their Chinese roots largely involved the coastal regions of China as well as the city of Beijing. Despite the diversity of their backgrounds, the participants share these traits: the resources to make a trip to China and the ability to write in English, although for some, English is the second, third, or even fourth language.

With their unusually high level of education, English literacy, and means for traveling overseas, the participants in this volume clearly belong to a privileged stratum of global society, although not all were born or raised in affluent circumstances. Several of the contributors have multiple backgrounds: they are Chinese-Pakistani-American, Chinese-Filipino-American, Chinese-Italian-Danish, Chinese-Colombian-American, and so on. Before their encounter with China, therefore, some already identified themselves with more than one nationality and had familiarity with more than one culture. Thus, while the visit to China may represent the opportunities of an increasingly transnational world, the cosmopolitan background of individual participants reflects the fact that global exchanges, while they may not have been as easy or as frequent as they are today, were also not uncommon before the last two decades or so when transnationalism began to gain popularity as a concept.[18]

Nevertheless, the stories in this book show some of the new opportunities made available by the development of the global economy in recent years. One contributor visited China when he was invited to act as a consultant in Hong Kong, while several other participants found employment in mainland China or Hong Kong and were therefore able to prolong their stays or even to establish homes in those places. For others, academic exchanges or scholarship programs were what allowed them even to contemplate making such a trip. And for most of the remaining participants, tourist travel, once a luxury but now an activity within the reach of the middle classes of many countries, brought about the first encounter with the ancestral country.

Without a doubt, the accounts in this book provide evidence for that view of identity that emphasizes its relational character—that is, the assertion that identity is shaped by a multitude of factors such as particular local and historical conditions, race and ethnicity, class, gender, transnational developments and opportunities, and so on and that, therefore, identity is more fruitfully understood as multiple rather than singular in nature—and subject to reassessment rather than fixed.[19] It is no exaggeration to say that while the stories collected here are unique, the numerous issues interwoven in them are not just those common to members of the Chinese diaspora but are to be found in the stories of diasporic peoples of other ethnicities as well.

These issues include one of central concern to many scholars of the Chinese diaspora: the meaning of "Chineseness." Although immigrants or the descendants of immigrants of other diasporas might not relate to the specific issue of "Chineseness," it would not be difficult for them to understand the remarks made by several of the contributors indicating that to them, "Chineseness" seems somewhat remote from abstractions such as a "cultural China" or "a product of the multiple and contradictory effects of ultramodernist attitudes, transnational subjectivities, and the nostalgic imaginaries marketed by late capitalism and its culture industries."[20] Rather, the contributors often conceived of their "Chineseness" in highly personal terms, at least during some stages of their lives. One participant wrote of her "rebellious feelings towards [her] father, and therefore anything Chinese" (Graziella Hsu). Henry Chan wrote: "My feelings of alienation from, and my rejection of, my Chineseness was most of all linked with, and intensified by, the growing rift with my father." The sentiment is perhaps expressed most clearly by Meilin Ching: "To me, everything Chinese was represented by my father; he was, after all, the Chinese parent. But paralleling my ignorance of the Chinese culture was the strangeness of never ever really being able to understand him. . . . My quest to find out what it means to be Chinese has also been a search to learn more about the man from whom I am descended and to understand what his life in China was like."

Before their encounter with China, the contributors were influenced in their ideas about what constituted "Chineseness" by what their parents had specifically pointed out to them.

> He was constantly pointing out as examples the students who had come from China to study at Harvard and M.I.T., how plainly they dressed, but how intelligent and pure they were. I had an image of all Chinese as scholastically brilliant and moral. My father was quick to point out how bad Americans were: they drank too much alcohol, didn't study, and quickly drifted from their families. Later, when I first went to China, I remember feeling shocked at the sight of Chinese playing drinking games and getting very drunk on beer; I had grown up believing that Chinese didn't do this. More recently, such undesirable vices as prostitution, corruption, and theft, which have been emerging along with China's booming economy, have further added to my disillusionment with my father's impossible ideals. (Meilin Ching)

In part, what were presented as Chinese traits by parents or by the local Chinese community arose out their idealization of the qualities best suited for immigrant or minority survival in their part of the world.[21] Contributor Richard Chu writes that: "Through the rags-to-riches stories that my mother told me about Chinese-Filipinos, I also came to connect working hard and being disciplined with being Chinese." Richard Chu suggests that, perhaps also as part of minority survival strategies, the perceived ways and values of the local majority population were unfavorably contrasted with traits idealized as being specifically Chinese:

> Filipinos, on the other hand, were supposed to possess entirely different characteristics. When I wanted to buy something expensive, my mother would sometimes reprimand me for being extravagant like the *hoan-nas* [a derogatory term for foreigners in general, here referring to Filipinos]. I have sometimes also heard parents

blaming the failure of their children in their studies on the influence of Filipino culture. . . . My mother was only acting like any other good Chinese mother. Her desire for me to avoid the ways of the *hoan-na* and to retain or follow the ways of the *lan-lang* [a term referring to the Chinese] came from her belief that it is by way of the latter that I would succeed later in life.

On occasion, the values and myths of Chineseness cultivated as part of immigrant strategies for survival as a community appeared to contradict one another. Richard Chu describes his puzzlement at his mother's reception of choice of the relatively poorly paid profession of academics instead of becoming a businessman:

Initially, I thought my mother would be proud of my desire to be a scholar, for wasn't Confucius, whom we call the "Great Teacher," a role model for many Chinese? Didn't they teach us in school about China's long history of selfless and courageous Confucian scholar-officials? However, the Chinese community in the Philippines is predominantly mercantile and entrepreneurial. Many parents, therefore, including my own, want and expect their children, especially their sons, to follow in their footsteps— that is, to take over the family business, or at least to start their own business.

Some participants drew their ideas about being Chinese from the realities of diaspora Chinese life as it was lived around them. Thus, contributor Graham Chan described his mother as being an atypical Chinese wife in that she did not work alongside his father in the family business. He added: "We have never been the typical Chinese family: we have never lived above the shop, and it was only on rare occasions, when Dad was absolutely desperate, that we children were summoned to help out in the chip shop or the restaurant." In addition, the geographical origins of the Chinese that the contributors encountered around them also exercised a strong influence on their concept of what it meant to be Chinese: "[I]n those days, apart from a few relatives on our mother's side, every Chinese person we met also seemed to come from Hong Kong. Even now it is unusual to hear Chinese people in Britain speaking anything other than Cantonese, the version of Chinese spoken in Hong Kong. We children therefore tended to equate being Chinese in Britain with coming from Hong Kong" (Graham Chan).

A number of the stories in this volume discuss the issue of citizenship and identity. Contributor William Shang's Chinese citizenship was a tangible link to a country he had never set foot in until adulthood. He wrote of his shock when, on visiting China, he discovered that many people there seemed to take their citizenship lightly:

> Even the Chinese immigration officials could not understand why I was still legally a Chinese citizen. I was always asked the same question: "How come you haven't changed your nationality? Living overseas in either the United States or Japan, it would be easier to use an American or Japanese passport." What really bothered me was that China's propaganda machine was always calling for patriotism, love, and construction of the motherland, yet no one there could even see the point of being a citizen of China if the opportunity arose to become a citizen of someplace else.

The connection between citizenship and national identification is addressed by both Myra Sidharta and Richard Chu in their description of the situations faced by the ethnic Chinese of Indonesia and the Philippines during colonial rule. The Chinese Exclusion Act in force in the United States was also extended to the Philippines when the latter became an American colony: "This prevented many Chinese without Filipino citizenship from entering the country. Only people born in the Philippines could be considered citizens. . . . Furthermore, many Chinese already in the Philippines who wanted to apply for Filipino citizenship were discouraged by the exorbitant fees or were refused by the courts" (Richard Chu). The Dutch policy of classifying the Chinese in the Netherlands Indies (now Indonesia) as "alien Orientals" and denying them local citizenship put the Chinese there in an even more difficult position: "At that time, we considered ourselves marginal people. Officially, we were Dutch subjects, but we were Chinese by blood, by citizenship, and to some extent by language and culture. At the same time, Indonesia was our home; yet before the establishment of Indonesia as a nation, we had no claim to Indonesian nationality" (Myra Sidharta). Meanwhile, during this period when ethnic Chinese in Southeast Asia and elsewhere faced difficulties with obtaining citizenship in the countries where they resided, the Chinese government not only claimed all ethnic Chinese overseas as citizens of China, but it also sought their support. As Myra Sidharta noted: "It is not surprising, therefore, that Grandfather never stopped looking to China as his real home, even though he had become so well established in Indonesia." Together, the above three stories suggest that the possession of a country's citizenship is indeed an important, if not always a sufficient, condition for identification with that country.[22]

Education as a major force in the shaping of identity is discussed in several of the stories, but perhaps most interestingly in William Shang's account of growing up as a Chinese citizen in Tokyo while attending an American school there. He observed: "Attending the American School had a greater effect on me, linguistically and culturally, than perhaps any other influence in my life." On leaving Japan for the first time in his life to attend college in the United States, he found himself feeling more at home in the United States than in Japan: "In fact, I had a feeling of being liberated. I had finally reached the place where I felt most comfortable, in terms of language and culture. Some people thought I had grown up in Hawaii, while others assumed that I was raised in the Los Angeles area. I never tried to act like a local student, but after attending an American school, my thought processes seemed to be similar to those of the rest of the students."

Yet the stories also show that the link between an education in a given language and culture and national identification with the country concerned is far from clear, particularly when other factors, such as foreign citizenship, are considered. Whereas Richard Chu, as a citizen of the Philippines, wrote of how his first conscious identification as a Filipino came from attending a school that exposed him to the history and larger society of the Philippines, William Shang mused, "I wonder sometimes whether I would ever have left the land where my education had groomed me to feel most comfortable if I had known that, in leaving, circumstances would take me in other directions and that I would never again return to America to live. Placed in that predicament again, I would probably do the same. I had to search out my roots and come to terms with my Asian background—with my Chinese citizenship and with the Japanese culture I had grown accustomed to over the years." The limitations of education in shaping national identity were expressed more forcefully by Myra Sidharta, who attended a Dutch-language school when Indonesia was under colonial rule: "[Grandfather] said that he knew that we had been taught Dutch patriotic songs in school and was worried that we would abandon our Chinese identity. I assured him that going to Dutch school was only a means to advance in life, and that we had no intention of becoming Dutch."

As earlier noted, an identity forced on participants because of their racial appearance was what first put the thought of China into the minds of several of the contributors. On visiting China, many initially experienced a feeling of relief, even of liberation, because their appearance did not attract attention there. For some, the experience of not standing out physically was in itself an affirmation of, or at least constituted a link with, their Chinese identity.

> I fell in love with China on arrival. It seemed as if here was a place where I could fit in, where I could easily belong. Without opening my mouth, I could venture through tucked-away neighborhoods, not even receiving a second glance. I could bicycle through the crowded avenues and not be noticed. Although I was really a stranger, I felt a peacefulness within me that seemed so right. (Meilin Ching)

> [W]hen I'm around my Chinese friends, or even among the masses in China's streets and countryside, a profound sense of comfort washes over me. I'm uncertain why. Perhaps it's all those faces or all that black hair—and the fact that I can blend in and be at home, although the country is not my birthplace. (Brad Wong)

> It was such a relief not to be different, to be able to blend anonymously into the crowd, not to be immediately marked out for special treatment or abuse. . . . It made me almost giddy to realize

that here I had a perfect right to go anywhere I liked—it was the whites who were the strangers. This was my country, not theirs. (Graham Chan)

Although not standing out physically contributed to their sense of closeness and bonding with China and the Chinese, the contributors nevertheless all discovered that race or appearance, sufficient factors in themselves to create difference and alienation in the countries in which they grew up, were only two elements of the complexity that is ethnic identity and were of limited effect in any search for a greater degree of ethnic belonging: "In China, I thought I would easily blend in with the crowd because I looked Chinese, but I was wrong, because my thinking, attitudes, reactions, body language, and behavior stood out" (Nancy Work).

Some of the participants' inability to speak Chinese proved to be an obstacle to communication, and some felt that the key to unlocking their Chinese identity lay in being able to speak Chinese fluently:

> It was the key to joining the fold, without which I could never hope to belong. (Graham Chan)

> I greatly regretted not having been able to learn Chinese as a child. One's ethnic identity is truly measured by one's language skills, more than by anything else, I thought. (Milan Lin-Rodrigo)

Being able to communicate verbally in Chinese, even in a limited fashion, was certainly meaningful: "When locals instinctively address me in Chinese, whether it be a bank teller or someone asking for directions, I am reminded of my Asian appearance. Accepting the invitation to speak, I answer in disjointed Chinese, and a conversation usually arises. I gain a small amount of satisfaction for the bond achieved through such communication. At such times, I feel as Chinese as I could ever feel" (Meilin Ching). For others, the ability to speak Chinese brought a kind of personal confidence that had been lacking previously, although this confidence did not necessarily translate into enhanced feelings of Chineseness. This was the case for Nancy Work, who noted:

"Before my China days, I generally avoided Chinese-looking people, partly because I was embarrassed and ashamed that I couldn't speak Chinese. . . . Now I am comfortable and sure of myself. I can hold my head up when I am approached." Yet she also affirmed that "living in China showed me how American I was in most of my ideas and principles."

In fact, those who learned to speak Chinese fluently during their stay in China and, significantly, some of those who already spoke it perfectly before going there felt that valuable though linguistic ability might be, true communion with the Chinese in China could not be achieved solely through the possession of a common verbal language. Richard Chu expressed this idea most succinctly:

> Our worldviews and beliefs, our memories and experiences, our upbringing and education—all that constitutes the deepest core of our identities—had been shaped by very different socio-historical and political forces in the last few decades, making it difficult for us to find common ground. I felt much more at home with my Filipino classmates and friends who were studying at Xiamen University than with the local Chinese friends I made there. Although I may look and speak Chinese, the gap that existed between my Chinese friends and me was too wide to be bridged by physical and linguistic similarities.

This perception, he noted, also appeared to be shared by the local Chinese who had dealings with ethnic Chinese from overseas: "Once I happened to overhear the conversation of the service personnel at our foreign students' dormitory. They were clearly talking to one another about the foreign students, including me and the other Chinese-Filipinos in the dormitory, and one of them referred to us as *hoan-na* [lit. 'foreign barbarian']." He concluded: "Although the Chinese government, and some local Chinese, might constantly call the overseas Chinese 'compatriots' or 'brothers,' despite our shared Chinese blood and language I realized that we were foreigners to them, as they were to us."

A number of the stories in this volume bring up the important issue of how the question of "Chineseness" is complicated by the existence of localized Chinese identities, connected particularly with speaking specific local dialects. The mutual incomprehensibility of some of these dialects can be understood by reading Maria Tham's account of how the members of the small Chinese community in Karachi, Pakistan, were obliged to communicate with one another in English, Urdu, or even by hand signals because of the difficulty of making themselves understood to speakers of different Chinese dialects. Such a situation often led to social differentiation and exclusion based on specific place of origin. Growing up in an Auckland suburb, contributor Henry Chan was not only discouraged by his father from playing with non-Chinese children, but he was also told not to play with the children of the only two other Chinese families living nearby, because, apart from being business rivals, these families did not come from the same county in China as his parents had. Maria Tham explained the origins of her particular interest in her localized heritage:

> One may wonder why I put so much emphasis on See Yip heritage as opposed to just my Chinese heritage. It is because whenever I asked about my heritage, my mother always told me that I was See Yip Chinese, not Hubei or Hakka Chinese. . . . People tended to stick to their own group: Hubeis with Hubeis, Hakkas with Hakkas. My family tended to be left out. Each group settled into its own profession: Hubeis in dentistry and Hakkas in restaurant management. The members of each group also tended to live close together in certain parts of town. Most of them also were related through marriage or blood. In general, even though the Chinese have lived in Pakistan for generations, most still preferred to marry their own kind. Ideally, one married someone from one's own group. The next best was to marry someone Chinese from another group.

As Maria Tham observed, holding a strong localized Chinese identity did not necessarily conflict with one's perception of oneself, or of other ethnic Chinese individuals, as fully Chinese:

> [M]ost of us Chinese [in Karachi] simply accepted the fact that we were all Chinese, and that we were See Yip, Hubei, and Hakka

respectively. . . . I personally thought that the people from the Chinese embassy were different from us, because the embassy staff spoke to us in Mandarin, which most of us local Chinese did not understand. As far as I could tell, they did not speak English. I accepted that they were Chinese, but just as we considered ourselves a subset of the Chinese race, I considered them China Chinese.

Indeed, this was precisely the lesson that some drew from their encounter with China: that there did not exist one single way or definition of being Chinese. For Richard Chu, visiting China, besides showing him that a shared language and race did not equate to a shared identity, opened his eyes to the link between ethnic identity and other issues, such as class:

> Before going to China, I had never seen Chinese people working in the "lowly" occupations that only the *hoan-nas* take in the Philippines. Back then I associated being Chinese with being a businessman or with being part of the higher economic stratum of society. This class identity may be true of the majority of the Chinese living in Southeast Asia, but as I found out in China, being Chinese does not have to be linked to a particular class or profession. . . . The impact, therefore, of my visit to China was to make me realize that my search for the identity of a *lan-lang* did not begin or end there. I had thought that by going to China I would discover the true meaning of being Chinese, and that maybe I could learn to become more Chinese. For wasn't China the place where we, the *lan-langs* in the Philippines, could trace our true selves? Weren't her people and her culture the standards by which we should measure our *lan-lang*-ness? Instead, I learned that there is no one true *lan-lang*.

Likewise, Milan Lin-Rodrigo, who already understood that "racial and ethnic identity is not entirely independent of one's social position," observed that the trip to China had helped to free her from her "previous obsession with attempting to define myself in any one particular way."

As with Richard Chu, William Shang concluded from his encounter with China that being Chinese meant more than looking Chinese and being able to speak the language and that a common Chinese identity required shared experiences: "After some months in Beijing, I began to realize the complexity of Chinese identity, especially the gap between mainland Chinese and overseas Chinese living in Japan—or anywhere else, for that matter. Overseas Chinese like me, it seemed, were essentially foreigners. We were not 'Chinese' in the sense that we were not born and raised in China and did not really possess a common cultural background or common experiences with the people there, such as the hardships of the Cultural Revolution." In the face of the obvious impossibility of someone like him, born and raised overseas, sharing the same experiences as those who had grown up amid the turbulence of modern China, William Shang decided that, even though his Chinese citizenship made him legally Chinese, he was "an overseas Chinese who did not have to be so Chinese." Unlike Richard Chu, therefore, William Shang concluded not that there were different kinds of Chinese but rather that Chineseness is largely a product of the ways and experiences that had shaped the people of mainland China, or at least of places in which Chinese people and culture predominate.

Graham Chan, who visited Hong Kong when it was still a British colony, and admired what he saw there as a successful synthesis of "a culture somewhere in between East and West, ancient and modern," came to believe both that there is not one form of Chineseness and that a hybrid culture is, in itself, just as valid as any conception of "Chineseness":

> The standard complaint about Hong Kong is that the people
> there never think of anything but money. They are superficial,
> have no culture, and have somehow ceased to be Chinese without
> acquiring any of the nobler features of Western civilization. This
> attitude is one aspect of the snobby view of mainland China as
> the only true repository of Chineseness, or at least those parts
> of it that have not yet inconveniently turned themselves into
> replicas of Hong Kong. It is the same complaint that is leveled
> against us, the overseas Chinese everywhere—the attitude that
> would have us all learning Mandarin and tai chi.[23]

After his stay in Hong Kong, Graham Chan eventually came to this conclusion: "I no longer need to define myself, to choose between Chinese or British. I see now that we can have our own culture combining both, as valid and valuable as anyone else's." This view was echoed by Henry Chan: "I have finally become at ease with my cultural hybridity, and that is the important thing."

Brad Wong, Meilin Ching, Carolyn Koo, and Graziella Hsu all felt that their awareness of the "Chinese" part of their bicultural or multicultural identities was raised by their encounter with mainland China or Hong Kong. As Graziella Hsu put it: "Before, I used to say, 'My father is Chinese'; now I say, 'I am half Chinese.' And I say it with pride, with a sense of belonging to a great culture which—although I may not always agree with it—I have come to love and admire." Both Carolyn Koo and Graziella Hsu further commented on how this stronger sense of Chinese identity also coexisted with their tendencies toward already perceiving themselves "citizen[s] of the world."

Lily Wu, on the other hand, felt that her experience in China awakened a consciousness of both parts of her bicultural identity that had not existed before: "Before my trip to China, being 'Chinese' meant almost nothing to me, and even being 'American' was something that I had simply taken for granted. Ironically, both levels of awareness sharpened at the same time. Even as I gained an appreciation of my personal and cultural heritage, the realities of modern-day China also deepened my appreciation for, and understanding of, being an American. Fourteen years after my first arrival in China, I finally moved back to the States, and in the truest sense of the word, I did so as a Chinese-American." In contrast, Nancy Work felt that her stay in China had brought to her the unexpected understanding of how non-Chinese she was: "Living in China showed me how American I was in most of my ideas and principles," while Myra Sidharta's visit to China confirmed a decision that she had made decades earlier when forced to choose between Chinese and Indonesian citizenship: "My world, the present-day Indonesia, has its problems and controversies, but that is the place where I work and feel most needed."

For Maria Tham, who had always believed that there were different types of Chinese and that "no matter what differences there may be, a Chinese was always a Chinese," the trip to her parents' villages in China brought her a feeling of liberation connected with having finally satisfied a lifelong curiosity about her roots, thereby attaining "a deeper and more personal understanding of [her] parents and of Chinese emigration in general."

In fact, to Maria Tham, as to many of the contributors to this book, perhaps the most important thing about the journey to China was not the insights gained into ethnic identity, however valued those were. Rather, it was the achievement of personal or familial goals, while the attainment of a greater understanding of one's identity was, to some, something of a by-product:

> Back from China, I decided to study Chinese full-time and
> enrolled at the university. Growing more and more involved, I
> had no choice but to let go of my previous life. I was submerged in
> the study of my father's culture, finally surrendering to the heritage
> I had been rejecting for so long. The more I learned and under-
> stood, the more I could "read" my father. I had finally found
> the key to genuine communication between us. (Graziella Hsu)

> I took my trip to China to prepare myself linguistically to commu-
> nicate with my mother. I did succeed in finding her, two years after
> I'd first arrived in China. However, I found that the difficulty wasn't
> in communicating with her in Chinese after all. Rather, the prob-
> lems were with having different expectations and ideas, being
> separated since childhood, and with leading such different lives. . . .
> I feel fulfilled in having attained my lifelong dream of reuniting
> with her, even though the ending was not the fairy-tale one that
> I had hoped it would be. (Nancy Work)

> I, of course, never found my mother in China, but in many ways,
> I found myself and the foundation that I needed to move forward
> with strength. Emotionally, I needed the love and acceptance that
> my uncle and his wife gave me, and the interest they took in my
> life and in my cultural education filled the vacuum that my disin-
> terested father and mentally ill mother had left. Just facing up to
> the fact that I needed those things was an important discovery for

me. I had convinced myself over the years that I was a strong and smart person and that I didn't need anybody's help to get by in the world. In fact, it wasn't true at all, and I'd only convinced myself of that because it couldn't be otherwise. (Lily Wu)

More important to me [than clarifying details of my grandfather's past] is the knowledge that he appreciated my visits and perhaps grew to love me. After all, I was his granddaughter and the first member of his family to return to China and visit him. I know I never replaced my second cousins, who grew up with him, in his heart, and it was folly to think I could have, given the short amount of time we spent together. But I'm confident that Gna-gong cared about me. . . . I felt I'd achieved that goal of connecting with him as his grandchild. (Carolyn Koo)

The initial act of migration from China had an impact on an emigrant's descendants far beyond the important one of offering them better economic opportunities. In many cases, succeeding generations had also to face the effects of the separation of families, cultural isolation, or cultural confusion. The thirteen contributors to this volume brought to their encounter with China a diversity of personal, social, and cultural backgrounds and experiences, all of which influenced how they reacted to China, how people in China reacted to them, and ultimately what they derived from their visits to their ancestral country. For all of them, however, that visit to China, although often intended as no more than a matter of a few weeks of travel or a year or two of language study, was a defining event in their lives. Almost without exception, visiting their ancestral country helped the contributors deal with the impact of that long-ago act of migration—the repercussions of which, prior to their visit, some had not even realized existed.

Reading this collection of accounts also surely leaves one with a deep impression of that sentiment so admirably expressed by contributor Richard Chu: "Identity is not simply a matter of race, language, or nationality; it means different things to people of different ages, sexes, classes, ideologies, places, and times. Thus one's identity is capable of being constructed, invented, or manipulated." And thus, identity is in a constant state of flux, as its myriad components and their relations to one another shift and are reassessed and redefined. The journey to the ancestral country, therefore, however major a role it may have played in an individual's life, in light of the complex nature of identity, is still only one segment of that never-ending journey toward personal understanding, personal fulfillment, and self-definition.

NOTES

With the exception of the notes to Henry Chan's story, "Ears Attuned to Two Cultures," Richard Chu's story, "Guilt Trip to China," and some of the notes in Graham Chan's story, "Through a Window," all the notes to the stories in this collection were added by the editor.

FULL CIRCLE

1. Mandarin, or Putonghua, as it is also called, is the official language of China.
2. People who had owned land before the Communist takeover in 1949, and those with relatives overseas, were particular targets during the Cultural Revolution. See Thurston, *Enemies of the People*.
3. As part of the modernization program begun in the late 1970s, the Chinese government promulgated a number of economic incentives designed to encourage ethnic Chinese overseas to invest in China. Among these was the policy that those with titles or certificates to property or ancestral homes in China could reclaim them.

THROUGH A WINDOW

1. Weihjau is almost certainly the city of Huizhou, located east of Guangzhou, the capital of Guangdong province. Doongwoon is the town of Dongguan, also located east of Guangzhou, and is now one of the favored destinations of Hong Kong and Taiwanese businessmen establishing factories in south China. Sekloong is Shilong, which is adjacent to Dongguan. Tintong-weih is the village of Tiantangwei, located in the southeast corner of greater Dongguan.

2. A railway line still runs past the village of Tiantangwei, although today the nearest stop on the line is called Hanwu; *China Reconstructs* is a monthly magazine published in Beijing since 1952. In 1990, its title was changed to *China Today.*

3. See "Chinese Seamen," *Brushstrokes* 4 (Nov. 1996): 4.

4. Wong, *Chinese Liverpudlians,* 3–8.

5. Watson, "The Chinese," 181–213.

6. See Chan and Chan, "The Chinese in Britain," 123–31, and Parker, *Through Different Eyes,* 51–82.

7. Large-scale Chinese emigration to Russia took place at various times during the early part of the twentieth century, and the Trans-Siberian Railway, which at its European end terminated in Paris, was a main route by which Chinese migrants arrived in France. See Benton and Pieke, eds., *The Chinese in Europe,* 97–99 and 281–300. However, it is not known if our grandmother's group was motivated by any knowledge of opportunities in Russia or if they ever intended to travel as far as they did.

8. *The Secret Seven* is by the popular children's author Enid Blyton and was first published by Brockhampton Press in 1949. *Swallows and Amazons* was written by Arthur Ransome and published by Jonathan Cape in 1930.

9. The Monkey King is the principal character in an ancient Chinese folktale, "Journey to the West." He is born from stone, and the story recounts his adventures in search of the Sutra, the Buddhist holy book. It is as well known to Chinese people as "Sleeping Beauty" or "Little Red Riding Hood" are to Westerners. See Wu, *Monkey/Folk Novel of China.*

10. China exploded its first atomic device in October 1964. Regarding the damming of the Yangzi River, the Three Gorges Project currently underway is the largest hydroelectric project ever undertaken. It has provoked vehement opposition from environmentalists and others; see, for example, Dai, *Yangtze! Yangtze!* On Hong Kong's return to Chinese sovereignty, see the epilogue, note 23.

11. The British National (Overseas) passport, for example, is a travel document allowing the holder the right to enter Britain but not to live there.

12. Cantopop is a form of popular music emanating primarily from Hong Kong and characteristically sung in Cantonese, although all the major performers also perform and record in Mandarin and even include a few songs in English in their repertoires. There is evidence that Cantopop constitutes a significant segment of the cultural identity of young British Chinese people. See Parker, *Through Different Eyes,* 151–55. Sally Yip is one of Cantopop's biggest female stars.

TRAVELS AFAR

1. The Chinese community in India, including a discussion of its history, is the subject of Oxfeld's *Blood, Sweat, and Mahjong.* See also her entry on the Chinese in India in Pan's *The Encyclopedia of the Chinese Overseas,* 344–46.

2. For studies on Pakistan-China relations, see Vertzberger, *The Enduring Entente;* Bhola, *Pakistan-China Relations;* and Syed, *China & Pakistan.*
3. The Scholastic Aptitude Test is an examination required for undergraduate admission to many American colleges and universities.
4. This is the Durfee Foundation's American/Chinese Adventure Capital Program. The Durfee Foundation, based in Santa Monica, California, was established in 1960 by Dorothy Durfee Avery and her husband, R. Stanton Avery.

IN SEARCH OF LIN JIA ZHUANG

1. With somewhat less than 20 percent of the population, Tamils form the second largest ethnic group in Sri Lanka after the Sinhalese, who make up about three-quarters of the population.
2. The majority of Tamils in Sri Lanka are Hindu, while the majority of Sinhalese are Buddhists.
3. In 1972, the name of the country was changed to Sri Lanka.
4. On the Japanese invasions of China beginning in the 1930s, see Duus, Myers, and Peattie, *The Japanese Wartime Empire;* Li, *The Japanese Army in North China;* and Hsiung and Levine, eds., *China's Bitter Victory.*
5. The Portuguese ruled Sri Lanka from 1505 until they lost control of the island to the Dutch East India Company in 1658.
6. A wall extending about six thousand kilometers across north China, intended as a military barrier. See Waldron, *The Great Wall of China.*
7. The Summer Palace was constructed in the 1880s during the final decades of China's last dynasty, the Qing (1644–1911), and is located in the outskirts of northwest Beijing.

NO ROOTS, OLD ROOTS

1. On the Japanese invasions of China, see "In Search of Lin Jia Zhuang," note 4.
2. For a discussion of the Chinese in Italy, including an overview of the history of Chinese immigration and immigrants in Italy, see Carchedi and Ferri, "The Chinese Presence in Italy," 261–77. Some references to the history of the Chinese in Italy can also be found in Pan's *The Encyclopedia of the Chinese Overseas,* 319–21.
3. An account of the history and present situation of the Chinese in Denmark is found in Thunø's "Chinese in Denmark," 168–91, and in her "Chinese Immigrants in Denmark after 1949," 141–66.
4. A famous British ballet film of 1948, one of the first created directly for cinematography. It was written, produced, and directed by Michael Powell and Emeric Pressburger. The choreography was by Robert Helpmann (who was English) and Léonide Massine (who was Russian), and the leading role was danced and played by the English ballerina Moira Shearer.

5. On the evening of June 3, 1989, soldiers of the Chinese military fired on protesters and bystanders in Beijing along the approaches leading to Tiananmen Square and on the square itself. Numerous books and articles have been written on the incident. For a work containing thoughts of both Chinese and American scholars, see Des Forges, Luo, and Wu, eds., *Chinese Democracy and the Crisis of 1989*.

6. During the Qingming festival, graves are swept and sacrifices of food are offered to the dead. The festival usually falls in early April. See Eberhard, *Chinese Festivals*, 113–27.

7. On the tightening of Danish immigration restrictions in 1983 and in 1992, see Thunø, "Chinese Immigrants in Denmark," 151.

MY FATHER'S LAND

1. This dialect is spoken in and around the town and county of Taishan, in southern Guangdong province.

2. Chinese New Year is celebrated on the first day of the year according to the lunar calendar. The Mid-Autumn Festival, celebrated on the fifteenth day of the eighth lunar month (usually around September), is a festival held to celebrate the autumn harvest and the full moon. See Eberhard, *Chinese Festivals*, 97–112.

3. This was due to immigration restrictions in the United States, targeted against the Chinese. See the epilogue, note 22, for selected works on the Chinese Exclusion Act of 1882 to 1943.

4. The writer cannot confirm the Chinese characters for these surnames.

5. The Immigration Act of 1965 ended the United States' racially discriminatory immigration policies and put into place a system of immigration based on country quotas. For a brief discussion of how this affected Chinese immigration to the States, see Pan's *The Encyclopedia of the Chinese Overseas*, 266–73.

6. The Chinese characters for this name could not be confirmed by the writer.

EARS ATTUNED TO TWO CULTURES

1. For information on the history of Chinese migration to Australia, see the following: Choi, *Chinese Migration and Settlement in Australia*, and Yong, *The New Gold Mountain*. A popular account intended for the general reader is provided by Rolls in *Sojourners* and in *Citizens*. For a history of the Chinese in Sydney, see Fitzgerald, *Red Tape, Gold Scissors*.

2. For Chinese migration to New Zealand, see the two studies by Ip: *Dragons on the Long White Cloud* and *Home Away from Home*, and Ng, *Windows on a Chinese Past*. On New Zealand's restrictions on Asian immigration, see McKinnon, *Immigrants and Citizens*.

3. The two villages, consisting of Chans in Sun-gai and Wongs in Gua-lang, were the source of many migrants to New Zealand since the New Zealand gold rushes

in the second half of the nineteenth century. A booklet of the history of the Sun-gai Chans in New Zealand has been produced; see Chan, comp. and ed., "Sun-Gai Village and the New Zealand Connection."

4. The store was a major supplier for shipping lines from the 1930s to the 1950s. Its company name was C. W. Wah Jang & Co. Ltd., with C. W. Wah Jang standing for Chan and Wong United Warehouse. For some details, see Chan, "Sun-Gai Village," 27–28.

5. Discussions about the Chinese and their search for identity in contemporary Australia are provided by Giese, *Astronauts, Lost Souls and Dragons*.

6. See "Full Circle," note 3.

7. See, for example, Rosen, *Red Guard Factionalism and the Cultural Revolution in Guangzhou*.

8. A reference to the age of sixty. A partial quotation of passage 2:4 of the *Analects* of Confucius. For a recent translation of the *Analects*, see Leys, trans., *The Analects of Confucius*.

GUILT TRIP TO CHINA

1. Hokkien is Fujian in Mandarin, and, as used in this context, refers to the language popularly spoken by many people in the coastal regions of southern Fujian province.

2. For studies on this war, see "In Search of Lin Jia Zhuang," note 4.

3. As in many other countries in Southeast Asia with overseas Chinese communities, Chinese schools were set up in major urban centers of the Philippines. During the first half of the twentieth century, more than fifty Chinese schools were established around the country. Their curricula and textbooks followed closely those prescribed by the Education Ministry in China. After a Communist government assumed power in China in 1949, most of these schools, which by the 1960s had increased to a total of 168, with some fifty thousand students, continued to follow directives from the education ministry of the Nationalist government that had relocated to Taiwan. See Tan, *The Chinese in the Philippines*, 154–75, and Purcell, *The Chinese in Southeast Asia*, 563.

4. For an overview of China's foreign relations during the first half of the twentieth century, see Spence, *The Search for Modern China*.

5. See Tan, *The Chinese in the Philippines*, 95–108. For references to two recent works on the Chinese Exclusion Act, see the epilogue, note 22.

6. See Willmot, *The National Status of the Chinese in Indonesia*, 12.

7. Escolta is the name of a street in Binondo, otherwise known as the Chinatown of Manila. The street was once the commercial hub of Binondo.

8. Also known as P.D. 176, this decree in effect implemented the 1973 constitutional provision on the Filipinization of all "alien schools." Along with the Letter of Instruction 270, which paved the way for the mass naturalization of Chinese residents in the Philippines, it was promulgated to strengthen the political

allegiance of the Chinese to the Philippines. See See, "The Chinese in the Philippines," 107–9.

9. Jackie Chan is a Hong Kong martial arts movie actor. Lin Ch'ing-hsia is a Taiwanese dramatic actress who was popular in the 1970s and 1980s; on the Mid-Autumn Festival, see "My Father's Land," note 2.

10. In 1985, President Ferdinand E. Marcos, after years of protests and demonstrations following the assassination of opposition leader Benigno Aquino, called for snap elections. These elections pitted his party against the opposition party, whose candidate was Corazon Aquino, widow of the slain opposition leader. For more information on the participation of the Chinese community in Manila in this political event, see Baviera, *Contemporary Attitudes and Behavior of the Chinese in Metro Manila.*

11. Kaisa was founded in 1987, in Manila.

12. The majority of Chinese in the Philippines trace their origins to southern Fujian, of which Jinjiang county is an important and large region. See Wickberg, *The Chinese in Philippine Life,* 171–72.

13. See "Full Circle," note 3.

IN SEARCH OF MY ANCESTRAL HOME

1. A highly regarded work on the history of the Hakkas is Leong, *Migration and Ethnicity in Chinese History.*

2. For a study of Chinese settlement in the Indonesian islands and the employment of Chinese in the mines, see Somers Heidhues, *Banka Tin and Mentok Pepper.*

3. See Franke, *The Reform and Abolition of the Traditional Chinese Examination System.*

4. In 1854, a law was passed dividing the people of the Netherlands Indies into three categories: the Dutch; the "alien Orientals," such as the Chinese, the Arabs, Javanese, and the Indians; and the natives. The three categories of peoples were subject to different laws and regulations. Williams, *Overseas Chinese Nationalism,* 27–33.

5. Ba Jin (1905–); Lu Xun (1881–1936).

6. China was then going through a civil war. See the following studies: Pepper, *Civil War in China;* Eastman, *Seeds of Destruction;* and Levine, *Anvil of Victory.*

7. Although Indonesian leaders had declared the country independent in 1945, it was not until 1949 that Indonesia's independence was internationally recognized.

8. Sukarno was president of Indonesia from independence until 1967. The decree, known as the PP 10 in Indonesia, was enforced in May 1959 and was an attempt to break ethnic Chinese dominance of the retail trade sector in favor of businessmen of indigenous race. See Somers Heidhues, *Southeast Asia's Chinese Minorities,* 23–25.

9. See Coppel, "The Indonesian Chinese in the Sixties." Also see Suryadinata, *Pribumi Indonesians,* and Coppel, *Indonesian Chinese in Crisis.*
10. On the Great Wall, see "In Search of Lin Jia Zhuang," note 6. The Forbidden City refers to the former Imperial Palace in Beijing.
11. On the Cultural Revolution, see the epilogue, note 15.
12. Deng Xiaoping (1904–97). Works on Deng Xiaoping include Yang, *Deng;* Evans, *Deng Xiaoping and the Making of Modern China;* and Goodman, *Deng Xiaoping and the Chinese Revolution.* On Deng's reforms, see also the epilogue, note 16.
13. An instant chocolate milk drink manufactured by Nestlé.
14. On the one-child policy, see Croll, Davin, and Kane, eds., *China's One-Child Family Policy,* and Becker, "A Failure to Control the Population," 17.

A YELLOW AMERICAN IN CHINA

1. See the epilogue, note 22, on the Chinese Exclusion Act.
2. Angel Island in San Francisco Bay was a point of entry to the United States for many immigrants from 1910 to 1940. Here they underwent questioning and processing by U.S. immigration officials, after which the immigrants were detained for further questioning, allowed into the United States, or, more often, deported.
3. See "In Search of My Ancestral Home," note 14.
4. This is the Qingming Festival. See "No Roots, Old Roots," note 6.
5. This is a reference to China. "Middle Kingdom" is the literal translation of the Chinese name for China.

ONE FAMILY, TWO FATES

1. Shanghainese belongs to the Wu dialect family. The Wu dialect group is the second-largest speech community in China, after Mandarin, with some fifty million speakers. See Sherard, "Shanghai Phonology."
2. Du Yuesheng was Shanghai's most notorious gangster in the pre–1949 period and an ally of Chiang Kai-shek. Chiang Kai-shek (1887–1975) was president of the Republic of China. The wealthy and powerful Soong family played a pivotal role in the politics of modern China. For an overview of the backgrounds and careers of the above figures, see the appropriate entries in Boorman, ed., *Biographical Dictionary of Republican China.*
3. For sources on China's war with Japan, see "In Search of Lin Jia Zhuang," note 4. For studies of life in Shanghai during the Japanese occupation, see Wakeman, *The Shanghai Badlands;* Fu, *Passivity, Resistance, and Collaboration;* and Yeh, ed., *Wartime Shanghai.* On China's civil war, see "In Search of My Ancestral Home," note 6.
4. Prime minister of Australia from 1983 to 1991.

1. A sketch of the career of Shang Zhen is found in Boorman, *Biographical Dictionary of Republican China,* vol. 3, 89–90.
2. On Deng Xiaoping, see "In Search of My Ancestral Home," note 12.
3. Zhou Enlai (1898–1976). On the life and career of Zhou Enlai, see Wilson, *Chou,* and Han, *Eldest Son.* Fu Zuoyi (1894–1974). For an overview of the career of Fu Zuoyi, see Bartke, ed., *Who Was Who in the People's Republic of China,* vol. 1, 106, 107.
4. Qinghua University, located in northwest Beijing, is often referred to as the "M.I.T. of China."
5. For sources on the Cultural Revolution, see the epilogue, note 15.

COMING HOME

1. The Thomas J. Watson Fellowship Program was established in 1968. The program is administered by the Thomas J. Watson Foundation, which was founded in 1961 by Mrs. Thomas Watson, Sr., and is based in Providence, Rhode Island.
2. For sources on China's civil war, see "In Search of My Ancestral Home," note 6.
3. On the Manchus, and the dynasty they founded, see Wakeman, *The Great Enterprise,* and Crossley, *Orphan Warriors.*
4. On China's political and economic reforms during this period, see the epilogue, note 16.
5. 1966 to 1976. For sources on the Cultural Revolution, see the epilogue, note 15.
6. See Du, *China's Higher Education,* and Pepper, *China's Education Reform in the 1980s.*
7. See Zweig and Chen, *China's Brain Drain to the United States.*
8. For a survey discussion of the pivotal events in China's recent history, see Spence, *The Search for Modern China.*
9. For sources on Deng Xiaoping's economic and political reforms, see the epilogue, note 16.
10. See "In My Father's Shadow," note 4.
11. For sources on China's civil war, see "In Search of My Ancestral Home," note 6. For an overview of Lin Biao's (1907–71) career, see Bartke, *Who Was Who in the People's Republic of China,* vol. 1, 265–66.
12. On the Summer Palace, see "In Search of Lin Jia Zhuang," note 7.
13. For references on the antirightist movement, see the epilogue, note 15.

EPILOGUE

1. Bauman, "From Pilgrim to Tourist—Or a Short History of Identity," 19.
2. For a succinct account of the subject of changing overseas Chinese identities, including the subject of localized identities, see Wang Gungwu, "The Study of

Chinese Identities in Southeast Asia," 1–21; and Cohen, "Being Chinese: The Peripheralization of Traditional Identity," 88–108.

3. For a study focusing on the early role of the overseas Chinese in the modernization of China, see Godley, *The Mandarin-Capitalists from Nanyang.* Some works discussing Chinese nationalism among overseas Chinese during this period, including the role played by exclusion policies and citizenship restrictions, are Wang, "Nationalism among the Overseas Chinese," 103–5; Williams, *Overseas Chinese Nationalism;* Purcell, *The Chinese in Southeast Asia;* Ma, *Revolutionaries, Monarchists, and Chinatowns;* Wang, "Upgrading the Migrant: Neither *Huaqiao* nor *Huaren,*" 15–33; Chan, *Entry Denied;* and Tan, *The Chinese in the Philippines, 1898–1935,* 95–108.

4. See Fitzgerald, *China and the Overseas Chinese,* 102–55. This move thus effectively brought to an end the 1909 law enacted by the Manchu government that "claimed as a Chinese citizen every legal or extra-legal child of a Chinese father or mother, regardless of birthplace." See Willmot, *The National Status of the Chinese in Indonesia.*

5. See, for example, Purcell, *The Chinese in Southeast Asia;* Cushman and Wang, *Changing Identities;* Suryadinata, *Ethnic Chinese as Southeast Asians;* and Wong and Chan, eds., *Claiming America.*

6. This is the concern of the majority of the essays contained in *The Living Tree,* ed. Tu Wei-ming.

7. Wang, "The Study of Chinese Identities in Southeast Asia," 8. Some recent works on the subject include Haley, *New Asian Emperors,* and Hodder, *Merchant Princes of the East.*

8. Tu, "Cultural China," 1–34.

9. Nonini and Ong, "Chinese Transnationalism as an Alternative Modernity," 26. Ong and Nonini, "Toward a Cultural Politics of Diaspora and Transnationalism," 327.

10. Nonini and Ong, "Chinese Transnationalism as an Alternative Modernity," 18.

11. Ang, "On Not Speaking Chinese," 5.

12. See, for example, Ang, "On Not Speaking Chinese," 8–11, and Li, "Living Among Three Walls?" 167–83.

13. Ang, "On Not Speaking Chinese," 17.

14. Three works that focus on diaspora Chinese encounters with China are Louie, "Renegotiating and Rerooting Chinese Identities in the Diaspora"; Ang, "On Not Speaking Chinese"; and Eng, *Rebuilding the Ancestral Village: Singaporeans in China.* The following article discusses African-American tourists in Ghana: Bruner, "Tourism in Ghana."

15. For material on the antirightist movement, see MacFarquhar, *The Hundred Flowers Campaign and the Chinese Intellectuals,* and Das's *China's Hundred Weeds.* Numerous works on the Cultural Revolution exist. Two dealing with the human impact of the violence of the movement are Thurston, *Enemies of the People,*

and Luo, *A Generation Lost.* The following study examines the organizational causes of the violence: White, *Politics of Chaos.*

16. For an overview of these reforms in historical perspective, see Tsou's *The Cultural Revolution and Post-Mao Reforms.* For studies on the reforms, see Chang, *China under Deng Xiaoping;* Kau and March, eds., *China in the Era of Deng Xiaoping;* and Baum, *Burying Mao.*

17. Anderson, *Imagined Communities,* 44–45. Anderson theorizes that the foundations for national consciousness were laid down by print languages in three ways: "First and foremost, they created unified fields of exchange and communication below Latin and above the spoken vernaculars. . . . Second, print-capitalism gave a new fixity to language, which in the long run helped to build that image of antiquity so central to the subjective idea of the nation. . . . Third, print-capitalism created languages-of-power of a kind different from the older administrative vernaculars. Certain dialects inevitably were 'close' to each print-language and dominated their final forms."

18. Nonini and Ong discuss global trade and travel for various purposes by Chinese during the late nineteenth and early twentieth centuries and earlier, calling such practices "precursors to modern Chinese transnationalism." See Nonini and Ong, "Chinese Transnationalism as an Alternative Modernity," 17–18.

19. See Hall, "Cultural Identity and Diaspora," 222–37.

20. Ong and Nonini, "Toward a Cultural Politics of Diaspora and Transnationalism," 327.

21. An illuminating discussion of such qualities and survival strategies, and a persuasive explanation of the relationship that minorities such as the Chinese in Southeast Asia, the Jews in Europe, and the Indians in East Africa often have with local populations, is found in Bonacich's "A Theory of Middleman Minorities," 583–94.

22. The Chinese Exclusion Act of 1882 to 1943 barred laborers, but not teachers, students, merchants, travelers, and government officials, from entering the United States. In addition to Chan's *Entry Denied,* see also Gyory, *Closing the Gate.* For sources on restrictions on immigration and citizenship in the Philippines and in the Netherlands Indies (Indonesia), see note 3.

23. Hong Kong reverted to Chinese sovereignty on July 1, 1997.

GLOSSARY

TRANSLITERATED TERMS APPEARING IN TEXT	CHINESE CHARACTERS	PINYIN
An Ding	安定	Anding
Anhui	安徽	Anhui
Babaoshan	八寶山	Babaoshan
Ba Jin	巴金	Ba Jin
Baoding	保定	Baoding
Bart It Tui	八一村	Bayicun
Beijing	北京	Beijing
bok choy	白菜	baicai
Canton	廣州	Guangzhou
Chan	陳	Chen
Chang'an	長安	Chang'an
Changyi	昌邑	Changyi
Charp harn lei there farn hong sarng.	執行李啦，返唐山。	Zhi xingli la, fan Tangshan.
Chiang Kai-shek	蔣介石	Jiang Jieshi
Chung Ah Kee	鐘亞記	Zhong Yaji
Chu Ongco	朱汪哥	Zhu Wangge

Da Ge	大哥	da ge
Deng Xiaoping	鄧小平	Deng Xiaoping
Doongwoon	東莞	Dongguan
Du Yuesheng	杜月笙	Du Yuesheng
fen	分	fen
Fujian	福建	Fujian
Fuxin	福芯	Fuxin
Fu Zuoyi	傅作義	Fu Zuoyi
Gansu	甘肅	Gansu
Gna-Boo	外婆	waipo
Gna-gong	外公	waigong
gong	戇	gang
Gua dio kong langlang ue.	我得講咱人話。	Wo dei jiang zanren hua.
Guaizitu	乖子土	Guaizitu
Gua-lang	瓜陵	Gualing
Guangdong	廣東	Guangdong
Guangxi	廣西	Guangxi
Guangzhou	廣州	Guangzhou
guanxi	關係	guanxi
Hakka	客家	Kejia
Hanwu	韓屋	Hanwu
Heilongguan	黑龍關	Heilongguan
hoan-na	番仔	fanzai
hoan-na gong	番仔戇	fanzai gang
Hoi Ping	開平	Kaiping
Hokkien	福建	Fujian
Hong Kong	香港	Xianggang
Huang	黃	Huang
Hubei	湖北	Hubei
Hu Then Lei	河清里	Heqingli
Jackie Chan	成龍	Chenglong
Jiangsu	江蘇	Jiangsu
Jing An Si	靜安寺	Jing An Si
Jinjiang	晉江	Jinjiang

Jintian bu yong gei gou chi, ta chi le.	今天不用給狗吃，它吃了。	Jintian bu yong gei gou chi, ta chi le.
Jinxin	進芯	Jinxin
Jin Zhuangju	金莊菊	Jin Zhuangju
Kai Tak	啓德	Qide
Keren	科任	Keren
Khui Mei	橋尾	Qiaowei
Kowloon	九龍	Jiulong
Kunming	昆明	Kunming
lai see	利是	lishi
Lan Kwai Fong	蘭桂坊	Languifang
lan-lang	咱人	zanren
Lanzhou	蘭州	Lanzhou
Lee	李	Li
Li Gwan Mei	李冠美	Li Guanmei
Lin	蘭	Lin
Lin Biao	林彪	Lin Biao
Lin Ch'ing-hsia	林青霞	Lin Qingxia
Lin Jia Zhuang	蘭家莊	Lin jia zhuang
Long An	龍安	Long'an
longan	龍眼	longyan
Lu Xun	魯迅	Lu Xun
lychee	荔枝	lizhi
mahjong	麻將	majiang
Maijishan	麥積山	Maijishan
Man	滿	Man
Mao	毛	Mao
Mao Zedong	毛澤東	Mao Zedong
Meixian	梅縣	Meixian
Meizhou	梅州	Meizhou
Ming	明	Ming
mu	畝	mu
Nanjing	南京	Nanjing
Ngo Tingseng	吳秉陞	Wu Bingsheng
Ni hao	你好	Ni hao

Ou Sheng	杜澄	Ducheng
Ou-yang	歐陽	Ouyang
Panyu	番禺	Panyu
Peking	北京	Beijing
Putonghua	普通話	Putonghua
Qing	清	Qing
Qinghai	青海	Qinghai
Qinghua	清華	Qinghua
Qingming	清明	Qingming
Sally Yip	葉倩文	Ye Qianwen
Sam Wei	新會	Xinhui
See Yip	四邑	Siyi
Sekloong	石龍	Shilong
Sen Sheng	新昌	Xinchang
Shandong	山東	Shandong
Shang Chen	商震	Shang Zhen
Shanghai	上海	Shanghai
Shang Zhen	商震	Shang Zhen
Shao Yuan	勺園	Shaoyuan
Shi Di	士迪	Shidi
Sichuan	四川	Sichuan
Soong	宋	Song
Sun-gai	新街	Xinjie
Sze Yup	四邑	Siyi
Taibei	台北	Taibei
tai chi	太極	taiji
Taishan	台山	Taishan
Taiwan	台灣	Taiwan
Taixing	泰興	Taixing
Tham	譚	Tan
Tiananmen	天安門	Tiananmen
Tian Hua	天華	Tianhua
Tianjin	天津	Tianjin
Tintong-weih	天堂圍	Tiantangwei

Toisan	台山	Taishan
Wah Jang	合棧	Hezhan
Wang	王	Wang
Weihjau	惠州	Huizhou
Wenzhou	溫州	Wenzhou
Wong	黃	Huang
wonton	餛飩	huntun
Wu	吳	Wu
Xiamen	廈門	Xiamen
Xi-an	西安	Xi'an
Xingfu	幸福	Xingfu
Xintong	新塘	Xintang
Xiu	秀	Xiu
Yangzi	揚子	Yangzi
Yin Ping	恩平	Enping
Yixin	奕芯	Yixin
yuan	圓	yuan
Yuyuan	愚圓	Yuyuan
Zengcheng	增城	Zengcheng
Zengkeng	增坑	Zengkeng
Zhou Enlai	周恩來	Zhou Enlai
Zhuangmei	莊梅	Zhuangmei

REFERENCES

Anderson, Benedict. *Imagined Communities: Reflections on the Origin and Spread of Nationalism,* rev. ed. London and New York: Verso, 1991.

Ang, Ien. "On Not Speaking Chinese: Postmodern Ethnicity and the Politics of Diaspora." *New Formations* 24 (Winter 1994): 1–18.

Bartke, Wolfgang, ed. *Who Was Who in the People's Republic of China,* 2 vols. Munich: K. G. Saur, 1997.

Baum, Richard. *Burying Mao: Chinese Politics in the Age of Deng Xiaoping.* Princeton: Princeton University Press, 1994.

Bauman, Zygmunt. "From Pilgrim to Tourist—Or a Short History of Identity." In *Questions of Cultural Identity,* eds. Stuart Hall and Paul du Gay, 18–36. London: Sage, 1996.

Baviera, Aileen. *Contemporary Attitudes and Behavior of the Chinese in Metro Manila.* Quezon City: Philippine-China Development Resource Center, 1994.

Becker, Jasper. "A Failure to Control the Population." *South China Morning Post,* 19 April, 1999, 17.

Benton, Gregor, and Frank N. Pieke. *The Chinese in Europe.* London and New York: Macmillan and St. Martin's Press, 1998.

Bhola, P. L. *Pakistan-China Relations: Search for Politico-Strategic Relationship.* Jaipur, Raj.: R. B. S. A. Publishers, 1986.

Bonacich, Edna. "A Theory of Middleman Minorities." *American Sociological Review* 38.5 (Oct. 1973): 583–94.

Boorman, Howard Lyon, ed. *Biographical Dictionary of Republican China,* 3 vols. New York: Columbia University Press, 1967–79.

Bruner, Edward M. "Tourism in Ghana: The Representations of Slavery and the Return of the Black Diaspora." *American Anthropologist* 98.2 (June 1996): 290–304.

Carchedi, Francesco, and Marica Ferri. "The Chinese Presence in Italy: Dimensions and Structural Characteristics." In *The Chinese in Europe,* eds. Gregor Benton and Frank N. Pieke, 261–77. London and New York: Macmillan and St. Martin's Press, 1998.

Chan, Raymond, comp. and ed. "Sun-Gai Village and the New Zealand Connection." Auckland: Sun-Gai Chan Gathering Organising Committee, 1999.

Chan, Sucheng. *Entry Denied: Exclusion and the Chinese Community in America, 1882–1943.* Philadelphia: Temple University Press, 1991.

Chan, Yiu Man, and Christine Chan. "The Chinese in Britain." *New Community* 23.1 (Jan. 1997): 123–31.

Chang, David Wen-Wei. *China under Deng Xiaoping: Political and Economic Reform.* Basingstoke: Macmillan; New York: St. Martin's Press, 1988.

"Chinese Seamen." *Brushstrokes* 4 (Nov. 1996): 4.

Choi, C. Y. *Chinese Migration and Settlement in Australia.* Sydney: Sydney University Press, 1975.

Cohen, Myron. "Being Chinese: The Peripheralization of Traditional Identity." In *The Living Tree: The Changing Meaning of Being Chinese Today,* ed. Tu Wei-ming, 88–108. Stanford: Stanford University Press, 1994.

Coppel, Charles A. *Indonesian Chinese in Crisis.* Kuala Lumpur: Oxford University Press, 1983.

————. "The Indonesian Chinese in the Sixties: A Study of an Ethnic Minority in a Period of Turbulent Political Change." Ph.D. diss., Monash University, 1975.

Croll, Elisabeth, Delia Davin, and Penny Kane, eds. *China's One-Child Family Policy.* London: Macmillan, 1985.

Crossley, Pamela. *Orphan Warriors: Three Manchu Generations and the End of the Qing World.* Princeton: Princeton University Press, 1990.

Cushman, Jennifer, and Wang Gungwu, eds. *Changing Identities of the Southeast Asian Chinese Since World War II.* Hong Kong: Hong Kong University Press, 1988.

Dai, Qing. *Yangtze! Yangtze!* Edited by Patricia Adams and John Thibodeau. Translated by Nancy Liu et al. London: Earthscan, 1994.

Das, Naranarayan. *China's Hundred Weeds: A Study of the Anti-Rightist Campaign in China (1957–1958).* Calcutta: K. P. Bagchi, 1979.

Des Forges, Roger V., Luo Ning, and Wu Yen-bo, eds. *Chinese Democracy and the Crisis of 1989: Chinese and American Reflections.* Albany: State University of New York Press, 1993.

Du, Ruiqing, *China's Higher Education: A Decade of Reform and Development (1978–1988).* New York: St. Martin's Press, 1992.

Duus, Peter, Ramon H. Myers, and Mark R. Peattie. *The Japanese Wartime Empire, 1931–1945.* Princeton: Princeton University Press, 1996.

Eastman, Lloyd E. *Seeds of Destruction: Nationalist China in War and Revolution, 1937–1949.* Stanford: Stanford University Press, 1984.

Eberhard, Wolfram. *Chinese Festivals.* New York: Henry Schumann, 1952.

Eng, Kuah Khun. *Rebuilding the Ancestral Village: Singaporeans in China.* Aldershot, England: Ashgate, 2000.

Evans, Richard. *Deng Xiaoping and the Making of Modern China.* New York: Viking, 1994.

Fitzgerald, Shirley. *Red Tape, Gold Scissors: The Story of Sydney's Chinese.* Sydney: State Library of New South Wales Press, 1997.

Fitzgerald, Stephen. *China and the Overseas Chinese: A Study of Peking's Changing Policy, 1949–1970.* Cambridge: Cambridge University Press, 1972.

Franke, Wolfgang. *The Reform and Abolition of the Traditional Chinese Examination System.* Cambridge: Center for East Asian Studies, Harvard University, 1960.

Fu, Poshek. *Passivity, Resistance, and Collaboration: Intellectual Choices in Occupied Shanghai, 1937–1945.* Stanford: Stanford University Press, 1993.

Giese, Diana. *Astronauts, Lost Souls and Dragons: Conversations with Chinese Australians.* St. Lucia: University of Queensland Press, 1997.

Godley, Michael R. *The Mandarin-Capitalists from Nanyang: Overseas Chinese Enterprise in the Modernization of China, 1893–1911.* Cambridge: Cambridge University Press, 1981.

Goodman, David S. G. *Deng Xiaoping and the Chinese Revolution: A Political Biography.* London: Routledge, 1994.

Gyory, Andrew. *Closing the Gate: Race, Politics, and the Chinese Exclusion Act.* Chapel Hill: University of North Carolina Press, 1998.

Haley, George T. *New Asian Emperors: The Overseas Chinese, Their Strategies and Competitive Advantages.* Oxford: Butterworth Heinemann, 1998.

Hall, Stuart. "Cultural Identity and Diaspora." In *Identity: Community, Culture, Difference,* ed. Jonathan Rutherford, 222–37. London: Lawrence & Wishart, 1990.

Han, Suyin. *Eldest Son: Zhou Enlai and the Making of Modern China.* New York: Hill and Wang, 1994.

Hodder, Rupert. *Merchant Princes of the East: Cultural Delusions, Economic Success, and the Overseas Chinese in Southeast Asia.* Chichester, N.Y.: Wiley, 1996.

Hsiung, James C., and Steven I. Levine, eds. *China's Bitter Victory: The War with Japan, 1937–1945.* Armonk, N.Y.: East Gate Books/M. E. Sharpe, 1992.

Ip, Manying. *Dragons on the Long White Cloud: The Making of Chinese New Zealanders.* North Shore, New Zealand: Tandem Press, 1996.

———. *Home Away from Home: Life Stories of Chinese Women in New Zealand.* Auckland: New Women's Press, 1990.

Kau, Michael Ying-Mao, and Susan H. March, eds. *China in the Era of Deng Xiaoping: A Decade of Reform.* Armonk, N.Y.: M. E. Sharpe, 1993.

Leong, Sow-Theng. *Migration and Ethnicity in Chinese History: Hakkas, Pengmin, and Their Neighbors.* Stanford: Stanford University Press, 1997.

Levine, Steven I. *Anvil of Victory: The Communist Revolution in Manchuria, 1945–1948.* New York: Columbia University Press, 1987.

Leys, Simon, trans. *The Analects of Confucius.* New York and London: Norton, 1997.

Li, Lincoln. *The Japanese Army in North China, 1937–1941: Problems of Political and Economic Control.* Tokyo: Oxford University Press, 1975.

Li, Minghuan. "Living Among Three Walls? The Peranakan Chinese in the Netherlands." In *The Last Half Century of Chinese Overseas,* ed. Elizabeth Sinn, 167–83. Hong Kong: Hong Kong University Press, 1998.

Louie, Andrea. "Renegotiating and Rerooting Chinese Identities in the Diaspora." Ph.D. diss., University of California at Berkeley, 1996.

Luo, Zi-ping. *A Generation Lost: China Under the Cultural Revolution.* New York: Henry Holt, 1990.

Ma, L. Eve Arementrout. *Revolutionaries, Monarchists, and Chinatowns: Chinese Politics in the Americas and the 1911 Revolution.* Honolulu: University of Hawaii Press, 1990.

MacFarquhar, Roderick. *The Hundred Flowers Campaign and the Chinese Intellectuals.* New York: Praeger, 1960.

McKinnon, Malcolm. *Immigrants and Citizens: New Zealanders and Asian Immigration in Historical Context.* Wellington: Institute of Policy Studies, Victoria University, 1996.

Ng, James. *Windows on a Chinese Past,* 3 vols. Dunedin: Otago Heritage Books, 1993.

Nonini, Donald M., and Aihwa Ong. "Chinese Transnationalism as an Alternative Modernity." In *Ungrounded Empires: The Cultural Politics of Modern Chinese Transnationalism,* eds. Aihwa Ong and Donald M. Nonini, 3–33. New York and London: Routledge, 1997.

Ong, Aihwa, and Donald M. Nonini. "Toward a Cultural Politics of Diaspora and Transnationalism." In *Ungrounded Empires: The Cultural Politics of Modern Chinese Transnationalism,* eds. Aihwa Ong and Donald M. Nonini, 323–31. New York and London: Routledge, 1997.

————, eds. *Ungrounded Empires: The Cultural Politics of Modern Chinese Transnationalism.* New York and London: Routledge, 1997.

Oxfeld, Ellen. *Blood, Sweat, and Mahjong: Family and Enterprise in an Overseas Chinese Community.* Ithaca: Cornell University Press, 1993.

Pan, Lynn, ed. *The Encyclopedia of the Chinese Overseas.* Richmond, Surrey: Curzon Press, 1999.

Parker, David. *Through Different Eyes: The Cultural Identities of Young Chinese People in Britain.* Aldershot: Avebury, 1995.

Pepper, Suzanne. *China's Education Reform in the 1980s: Policies, Issues, and Historical Perspectives.* Berkeley: Institute of East Asian Studies, University of California at Berkeley, Center for Chinese Studies, 1990.

————. *Civil War in China: The Political Struggle, 1945–1949.* Berkeley: University of California Press, 1978.

Purcell, Victor. *The Chinese in Southeast Asia,* 2nd ed. London: Oxford University Press, 1965.

Rolls, Eric C. *Citizens: Continuing the Epic Story of China's Centuries-old Relationship with Australia.* St. Lucia: University of Queensland Press, 1996.

———. *Sojourners: The Epic Story of China's Centuries-old Relationship with Australia*. St. Lucia: University of Queensland Press, 1992.

Rosen, Stanley. *Red Guard Factionalism and the Cultural Revolution in Guangzhou (Canton)*. Boulder, Colo.: Westview Press, 1982.

See, Teresita Ang. "The Chinese in the Philippines: Assets or Liabilities?" In *Chinese in the Philippines: Problems and Perspectives,* ed. Teresita Ang See, 107–19. Manila: Kaisa Para Sa Kaunlaran, 1990.

———, ed. *Chinese in the Philippines: Problems and Perspectives*. Manila: Kaisa Para Sa Kaunlaran, 1990.

Sherard, Michael. "Shanghai Phonology." Ph.D. diss., Cornell University, 1972.

Sinn, Elizabeth, ed. *The Last Half Century of Chinese Overseas*. Hong Kong: Hong Kong University Press, 1998.

Somers Heidhues, Mary F. *Banka Tin and Mentok Pepper: Chinese Settlement on an Indonesian Island*. Singapore: Institute of Southeast Asian Studies, 1992.

———. *Southeast Asia's Chinese Minorities*. Melbourne: Longman, 1974.

Spence, Jonathan. *The Search for Modern China*. New York and London: Norton, 1990.

Suryadinata, Leo. *Ethnic Chinese as Southeast Asians*. Singapore: Institute of Southeast Asian Studies, 1997.

———. *Pribumi Indonesians, the Chinese Minority, and China: A Study of Perceptions and Policies,* 2nd ed. Singapore: Heinemann, 1986.

Syed, Anwar Hussain. *China & Pakistan: Diplomacy of an Entente Cordiale*. Amherst: University of Massachusetts Press, 1974.

Tan, Antonio. *The Chinese in the Philippines, 1898–1935: A Study of Their National Awakening*. Quezon City: Garcia Publishing, 1972.

Thunø, Mette. "Chinese Immigrants in Denmark after 1949: Immigration Patterns and Development." In *The Last Half Century of Chinese Overseas,* ed. Elizabeth Sinn, 141–66. Hong Kong: Hong Kong University Press, 1998.

———. "Chinese in Denmark." In *The Chinese in Europe,* ed. Gregor Benton and Frank N. Pieke, 168–91. London and New York: Macmillan and St. Martin's Press, 1998.

Thurston, Ann F. *Enemies of the People*. New York: Knopf, 1987.

Tsou, Tang. *The Cultural Revolution and Post-Mao Reforms: A Historical Perspective*. Chicago: University of Chicago Press, 1986.

Tu, Wei-ming. "Cultural China: The Periphery as the Center. " In *The Living Tree: The Changing Meaning of Being Chinese Today,* ed. Tu Wei-ming, 1–34. Stanford: Stanford University Press, 1994.

———, ed. *The Living Tree: The Changing Meaning of Being Chinese Today*. Stanford: Stanford University Press, 1994.

Vertzberger, Yaacov. *The Enduring Entente: Sino-Pakistani Relations, 1960–1980*. Washington, D.C.: Center for Strategic and International Studies, Georgetown University; New York: Praeger, 1983.

Wakeman, Frederic E. *The Great Enterprise: The Manchu Reconstruction of the Im-*

perial Order in Seventeenth-Century China. Berkeley: University of California Press, 1985.

———. *The Shanghai Badlands: Wartime Terrorism and Urban Crime, 1937–1941.* Cambridge and New York: Cambridge University Press, 1996.

Waldron, Arthur. *The Great Wall of China: From History to Myth.* Cambridge: Cambridge University Press, 1990.

Wang, Gungwu. "Nationalism among the Overseas Chinese." In *The Encyclopedia of the Chinese Overseas,* ed. Lynn Pan, 103–5. Surrey: Curzon Press, 1999.

———. "The Study of Chinese Identities in Southeast Asia." In *Changing Identities of the Southeast Asian Chinese Since World War II,* eds. Jennifer Cushman and Wang Gungwu, 1–21. Hong Kong: Hong Kong University Press, 1988.

———. "Upgrading the Migrant: Neither *Huaqiao* nor *Huaren.*" In *The Last Half Century of Chinese Overseas,* ed. Elizabeth Sinn, 15–33. Hong Kong: Hong Kong University Press, 1998.

Watson, James L. "The Chinese: Hong Kong Villagers in the British Catering Trade." In *Between Two Cultures: Migrants and Minorities in Britain,* ed. James L. Watson, 181–213. Oxford: Basil Blackwell, 1977.

White, Lynn T. *Politics of Chaos: The Organizational Causes of Violence in China's Cultural Revolution.* Princeton: Princeton University Press, 1989.

Wickberg, Edgar Bernard. *The Chinese in Philippine Life, 1850–1898.* New Haven: Yale University Press, 1965.

Williams, Lea E. *Overseas Chinese Nationalism: The Genesis of the Pan-Chinese Movement in Indonesia, 1900–1916.* Glencoe, Ill.: Free Press, 1960.

Willmot, Donald E. *The National Status of the Chinese in Indonesia.* Ithaca: Cornell University Southeast Asia Program, 1956.

Wilson, Dick. *Chou: The Story of Zhou Enlai, 1898–1976.* London: Hutchinson, 1984.

Wong, K. Scott, and Sucheng Chan, eds. *Claiming America: Constructing Chinese American Identities During the Exclusion Era.* Philadelphia: Temple University Press, 1998.

Wong, Maria Lin. *Chinese Liverpudlians: A History of the Chinese Community in Liverpool.* Liverpool: Liver Press, 1989.

Wu, Ch'eng-en. *Monkey/Folk Novel of China.* Trans. Arthur Waley. New York: Grove Press, 1994.

Yang, Benjamin. *Deng: A Political Biography.* Armonk, N.Y., and London: M. E. Sharpe, 1998.

Yeh, Wen-Hsin, ed. *Wartime Shanghai.* London and New York: Routledge, 1998.

Yong, Ching Fatt. *The New Gold Mountain.* Adelaide: Raphael Arts, 1977.

Zweig, David, and Chen Changgui. *China's Brain Drain to the United States: Views of Overseas Chinese Students and Scholars in the 1990's.* Berkeley: Institute of East Asian Studies, University of California, China Research Monographs, no. 47, 1995.

Text: 12/14.5 Adobe Garamond
Display: Perpetua and Adobe Garamond
Designer: Nola Burger
Compositor: Integrated Composition Systems
Printer and binder: Sheridan Books, Inc.